THE ELEMENTS OF LANGUAGE CURRICULUM

A Systematic Approach to
Program Development

THE ELEMENTS OF LANGUAGE CURRICULUM

A Systematic Approach to Program Development

James Dean Brown

University of Hawaii at Manoa

HEINLE
CENGAGE Learning

Australia • Brazil • Japan • Korea • Mexico • Singapore • Spain • United Kingdom • United States

The Elements of Language Curriculum: A Systematic Approach to Program Development
James Dean Brown

Editorial Director:
David C. Lee

Production Editor:
Martha M. Leibs

Market Development
Director: John F. McHugh

Publisher: Stanley J. Galek

Editorial Production
Manager: Elizabeth
Holthaus

Assistant Editor: Kenneth
Mattsson

Production Assistant:
Maryellen Eschmann

Manufacturing Coordinator:
Mary Beth Hennebury

Interior Designer: Gabrielle
McDonald

Cover Illustrator:
Susan Schön

Cover Designer: Kimberly
Wedlake

For product information and
technology assistance, contact us at **Cengage Learning Customer & Sales Support, 1-800-354-9706**

For permission to use material from this text or product, submit all requests online at **www.cengage.com/permissions**
Further permissions questions can be emailed to **permissionrequest@cengage.com**

ISBN-13: 978-0-8384-5810-5

ISBN-10: 0-8384-5810-6

Heinle
20 Channel Center Street
Boston, MA 02210
USA

Cengage Learning is a leading provider of customized learning solutions with office locations around the globe, including Singapore, the United Kingdom, Australia, Mexico, Brazil, and Japan. Locate your local office at **www.cengage.com/global**

Cengage Learning products are represented in Canada by Nelson Education, Ltd.

Visit Heinle online at **elt.heinle.com**

Visit our corporate website at **www.cengage.com**

Printed in the United States of America
14 15 16 17 18   19 18 17 16 15

TABLE OF CONTENTS

ACKNOWLEDGEMENTS

I would like to thank the hundreds of graduate students who suffered patiently through manuscript versions of this book, making comments and suggestions along the way. I would also like to thank my colleagues in both Guangzhou and Honolulu, who made curriculum development and numerous curriculum revisions possible. Without the inspiration that these colleagues provided as well as their comments, criticisms, and questions, this book would not exist.

PREFACE

The field of language teaching has undergone profound changes during the last 30 to 40 years. The expanded scope of language teaching programs around the world has led to a need for new technology in language teaching. Increasingly, successful language programs depend upon the use of approaches drawn from other domains of educational planning. This often involves the adoption of what has come to be known as the systematic development of language curriculum, that is, a curriculum development approach that views language teaching and language program development as a dynamic system of interrelated elements. The systematic approach focuses on the planning, development, implementation, and evaluation phases of language teaching, and has been widely adopted in many areas of educational planning. Aspects of this approach are seen in the work of Munby and others, but *The Elements of Language Curriculum* is the first book that examines language teaching in detail from a systematic curriculum development perspective. This book presents a comprehensive, but practical, overview of the different phases and activities involved in developing and implementing a sound, rational, and effective language program.

Each of the seven chapters contains a discussion of the theoretical and practical parameters involved, as well as summary checklists where appropriate. In addition, numerous practical examples are drawn from the author's curriculum development experiences as an ESL/EFL teacher and program administrator. Every chapter also includes a summary, a list of key terms, discussion questions, and application exercises. The book is organized as follows:

Chapter One: Introduction. Chapter One describes a system whereby all language teaching activities can be classified into approaches, syllabuses, techniques, exercises, or packaged pedagogies. These categories are discussed in relation to the systematic design of curriculum, which involves a number of separate elements: needs assessment, goals and objectives, testing, materials, teaching, and program evaluation. Each of the subsequent chapters covers one of these components in depth.

Chapter Two: Needs Analysis. Chapter Two includes a detailed description of needs analysis. This survey of the different approaches to needs assessment will suggest how best to prepare, gather, and use information within the context of a specific language program to meet the individual and group needs of the particular students enrolled at the time.

Chapter Three: Goals and Objectives. Chapter Three examines effective techniques for developing program goals and objectives from the information gathered during the needs analysis phase. Criteria are also given for formulating instructional objectives in clear and unambiguous terms. A variety of different types of objectives are included in the discussion, including everything from behavioral to experiential objectives.

Chapter Four: Testing.   Chapter Four begins with an explanation of the role of testing in language teaching. Different kinds of tests are explained in terms of their use in decision making and curriculum development. These include both criterion-referenced and norm-referenced instruments designed for proficiency, placement, achievement, and diagnostic decisions. Guidelines are provided for putting decent tests in place and for setting up a sound testing program.

Chapter Five: Materials.   Using needs analysis data, instructional objectives, and testing information, the materials can then be adopted, developed, or adapted to fit the particular language program involved. Chapter Five provides strategies for accomplishing these tasks so that materials become a resource that teachers can draw on, rather than a straitjacket hindering their classroom efforts.

Chapter Six: Teaching.   With a fairly complete curriculum in place, full attention can be focused on supporting the teachers in every way possible. Chapter Six argues that such support can take many forms, but focuses on logistical, curricular, and administrative support. The purpose of such support is to free teachers from extra burdens so that they can do what they do best: teach.

Chapter Seven: Evaluation.   The final chapter pulls together all of the information contained in the preceding ones to explain various approaches to program evaluation in language teaching. Essentially, all the information and knowledge gained in preparing each of the elements of the program can be used to appropriately maintain and modify each of the other elements. This process can result in a program that has the flexibility to continually fine tune itself, adapt to new conditions, and improve in a never–ending system.

The book was designed as a text to be used in teacher training courses at the graduate level, but it can also serve as a useful, and much needed, curriculum development handbook for language teachers, course designers, and program administrators throughout the world.

Chapter 1
Overview of Curriculum

INTRODUCTION

Language teachers have long been faced with a plethora of "methods" from which to choose. Each "method" has tended to claim for itself authority concerning what students need to learn, the best way to match the students' learning styles, or in some cases the truth about how to present or practice language. Most teachers will recognize all, or at least a majority, of the "methods" named in Table 1.1. One aspect of this table of "methods" (indeed, one aspect of the way the term "method" is generally used) that should be readily apparent is that these "methods" do not all represent the same type of activities.

Anthony (1965, p. 93) argues that this bewildering variety of labels has evolved because, "over the years, teachers of language have adopted, adapted, invented, and developed a bewildering variety of terms which describe the activities in which they engage and the beliefs that they hold." Fortunately, three authors have attempted to sort out and make sense of this confusion: Anthony (1965), Richards and Rogers (1982), and McKay (1978).

Table 1.1: Methods		
Audiolingual	Eclecticism	Situational
Classical Approach	Communicative	
Pair Work		Functional
Dictocomp	Task	
Natural Way	Suggestopedia	Direct
Method Dictation	Silent Way	Counseling-Learning
Structural Approach		Dartmouth Method
Grammar-Translation	Speed Writing	
Topical		
Drama		Total Physical Response
The Army Method	Skills	Cloze
	Notional	Jazz Chants
Problem Solving		

Anthony (1965) provides a framework for comparing and understanding the relationships among the various different language teaching activities that he identified even at that early date. His framework includes three categories into which all such activities can be classified: approach, method, and technique.

For Anthony, the term *approach* encompasses all points of view on the nature of language and the nature of language teaching and learning. Anthony uses as his example the aural-oral approach, which he illustrates in terms of a set of linguistic assumptions and attendant corollaries about the nature of language learning. Anthony uses the term *method* to describe different plans for presenting language to students in an orderly manner. Anthony's examples of methods include mim-mem (mimic-memorize) and pattern practice, which he further describes as two ways of presenting the material within the single aural-oral approach. Finally, he employs the term *technique* to define what actually happens in the classroom: "It is a particular trick, stratagem, or contrivance used to accomplish an immediate objective" (p. 96). The example he gives is based on the stereotypical problem of teaching the pronunciation of /l/ and /r/ to "oriental students." According to Anthony, different techniques would be appropriate in different situations. Simple imitation might suffice, or the teacher might use "a pencil in the mouth to prevent the student's tongue from touching the alveolar ridge" (p. 96), or drawings of the vocal apparatus might help. Such teaching activities would be classified as techniques.

Since the publication of Anthony's article, the list of activities available to language teachers has grown exponentially. Richards and Rodgers (1982) provide a more recent response to the need for understanding the distinctions in the growing list of terms associated with existing language teaching activities, summarized in Figure 1.1. Using Anthony's terms as a jumping-off point, Richards and Rodgers adopted his definition of an *approach* as a theory of the nature of language and of language learning. Instead of adopting Anthony's second term, *method,* Richards and Rodgers substituted the term *design,* which they delineate as the specification of content, as well as specification of the roles of learners, teachers, and materials. Finally, Richards and Rodgers broadened Anthony's notion of *technique* into what they call *procedure,* which includes all of the tactics, practice exercises, and activities in an instructional system. Their model provided a useful step in the direction of understanding and clarifying the distinctions and similarities among the various terms used to describe the activities available to language teachers. Note that Richards and Rodgers avoided using the term "methods" (which has caused so much confusion) except as a general cover term for all these activities taken together.

Also attempting to find patterns in the confusion that is language teaching methodology, McKay (1978) describes the types of syllabuses that have been used in language teaching. She offers a different, somewhat narrower perspective than those taken in the other two articles. She focuses on syllabuses, which she defines as different ways of organizing and planning language teaching and learning. She points to three ways of organization that have appeared during the

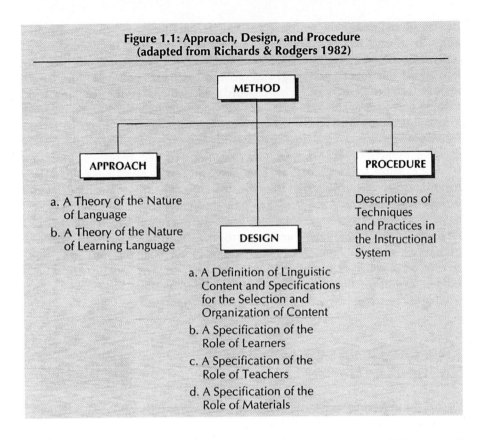

Figure 1.1: Approach, Design, and Procedure
(adapted from Richards & Rodgers 1982)

METHOD

APPROACH

a. A Theory of the Nature of Language
b. A Theory of the Nature of Learning Language

DESIGN

a. A Definition of Linguistic Content and Specifications for the Selection and Organization of Content
b. A Specification of the Role of Learners
c. A Specification of the Role of Teachers
d. A Specification of the Role of Materials

PROCEDURE

Descriptions of Techniques and Practices in the Instructional System

history of language teaching: structural syllabuses, situational syllabuses, and notional syllabuses. Then she describes these three categories in an attempt to help teachers understand the nature of at least one aspect of teaching languages, in this case, ways of organizing their teaching.

McKay's article led me to search for some systematic way to combine the most useful aspects of the three articles I have just discussed into one set of categories that would classify all, or at least most, language teaching activities into a clear and useful pattern—one that would help language teachers to understand the options available to them, to choose from these options, and to adapt their choices when necessary to meet the needs of their own students.

Both the Anthony and the Richards and Rodgers articles created categories that were sequential and perhaps static steps in the logical development of sound teaching: first, teachers start with a set of assumptions about, or a theory of, the nature of language and language learning; second, they make an overall plan and design specifications for their curriculum; and third, they present the instruction using some set of rational techniques or procedures.

The experiences of many language teachers are less sequential than the steps listed above. Few teachers systematically decide on a theory of language learning, define and design the course according to that theory, and then rationally adopt the correct techniques and procedures to deliver their instruction. The experience for most language teachers is much more holistic (or even chaotic), with all the theoretical, planning, and technical activities going on simultaneously in a frenzy of activity. In other words, all elements of the teaching and learning processes might seem to be happening simultaneously, with each component interacting with all the others. Theory, planning, and technique often become integrated—each changing constantly and each influencing the others. Thus the distinctions between approach, design, and procedure become blurred.

For example, good teachers are continuously learning new things about the theory of language and language learning, and changing the design and delivery of their instruction as a result of this new information. Or, while delivering instruction, some theoretical issue may arise, the pursuit of which will change the teacher's plans completely, and so forth. Is such an adaptable approach to teaching so unusual? Numerous observations of language teachers in action have led me to conclude that good language teachers must be very flexible, especially in light of the heavy demands that are placed on them and the isolation (from other language teachers) that they so often experience.

FOUR CATEGORIES OF LANGUAGE TEACHING ACTIVITIES

For me, the sequential and static nature of the categories proposed by Anthony and those modifications suggested by Richards and Rodgers seem inadequate. I suggest that we consider the various language *teaching activities* in terms closer to what language teachers and their students actually do, that is, that we divide them into categories that describe ways of doing things in the language teaching situation.

Table 1.2 presents four different categories into which language teaching activities can be divided: (1) ways of defining what the students need to learn, (2) ways of organizing the instruction to meet those needs, (3) ways of actually presenting the lessons, and (4) ways of practicing what has been taught. If, as I argued above, all four types of activities are going on simultaneously, changing any one of them may affect the other three.

□ WAYS OF DEFINING NEEDS: APPROACHES

Every teacher enters the classroom with some idea of what the students need to learn. Untrained teachers will attempt to re-create the activities used when they were taught a language or mimic what they think language teaching should be. Most trained language teachers will have a more theoretically motivated idea of what their students need to learn. In either case, teachers begin with precon-

Table 1.2: Four Language Types of Teaching Activities

CATEGORIES	DEFINITION
Approaches	Ways of defining what and how the students need to learn
Syllabuses	Ways of organizing the course and materials
Techniques	Ways of presenting the materials and teaching
Exercises	Ways of practicing what has been presented

ceptions that often change after they enter the classroom and begin to work with their students. These preconceptions, assumptions, and theoretical underpinnings for what happens in the classroom will be lumped together here under the term *approach*. Over the years, language teachers have drawn on many disciplines in formulating their views of what students need. Linguistics, psychology, and education have been the most influential source disciplines. Examples of approaches, or ways of defining what students need to learn, are shown in Table 1.3.

Let's first consider the view held over many centuries by teachers in the *classical approach*. Based on notions of Latin usage and belief in the humanistic tradition, teachers felt that what students needed in education as a whole was to read the "classics." In a world in which Europeans could actually hope to read all the major works of Western thought, this made a good deal of sense. Since the purpose of learning languages was to gain access to these great works, the teachers of the time felt that students needed to read, translate, and memorize various bits and pieces of text in the target language. This tradition, like all of the other approaches discussed here, no doubt survives and flourishes today in classrooms all over the globe.

Table 1.3: Approaches

APPROACHES	WAYS OF DEFINING WHAT THE STUDENTS NEED TO LEARN
Classical approach	Humanism: students need to read the classics
Grammar-translation approach	Students need to learn with economy of time and effort
Direct approach	Students need to learn communication so they should use only second language in class
Audiolingual approach	Students need operant conditioning and behavioral modification to learn language
Communicative approach	Students must be able to express their intentions, that is, they must learn the meanings that are important to them

Another strain of thought on what students needed to learn surfaced around the time of World War I. Based on notions of prescriptive grammar and what constituted proper usage, the *grammar-translation approach* advocated economy of time through deductive teaching of language involving reading and translation, but also the emergence of writing and speaking as ultimate goals.

The *direct approach* was another view based on prescriptive grammar. Drawing on the work of Gouin and on gestalt psychology, language teachers believed that students needed to learn inductively by using only the target language in the classroom and learning the oral skills (listening and speaking) before the written ones (reading and writing). Notable figures in this movement were Diller, Lenard, and de Sauze.

Owing its genesis during World War II to the *army approach,* the *audiolingual approach* drew on new ideas from descriptive linguistics and upon the notions of behavioral psychology, especially the ideas of operant conditioning and behavioral modification. The view of what students needed consisted of inductive learning, primarily of listening and speaking, through habit formation based on stimulus-response exercises like pattern and transformation drills. Notable figures in this approach were Fries and Lado.

Increasingly important since the 1970s is the view that students need to learn to communicate their own personal intentions. The *communicative approach* focuses on the need for students to express meanings that are important to them and their lives. This approach assumes that language teaching can utilize both inductive and deductive learning, based on what is known from analysis of natural discourse about semantics and pragmatics, to meet the particular needs of the target learners. What students need may be reading, writing, listening, or speaking skills, each of which can be approached from a communicative perspective.

The approaches mentioned here are not meant to be a definitive list. Other major movements defining what students need to learn have been overlooked (for instance, I did not mention the cognitive code approach). Moreover, language teaching is a dynamic field that no doubt will continue to produce new and exciting ways of defining what students need. Perhaps content-based instruction (see Mohan 1986; Brinton, Snow, & Wesche 1989) will emerge as the dominant approach or perhaps the comprehension approach will do so (see Winitz 1981). The approaches, or ways of defining needs, listed in Table 1.3 have been deliberately limited to those around which considerable consensus developed in the field of language teaching at one time or another. The important thing to remember is that an approach is a way of defining what students need to learn.

□ WAYS OF ORGANIZING: SYLLABUSES

Each belief system about what students need to learn in the language classroom depends on organizing a global order of presentation. In other words, regardless of the approach a teacher adopts, she or he must plan and organize, and make decisions about what should be taught first, second, third, and so on. McKay (1978, p. 11) uses the term *syllabus* in a special way that seems to apply here: "A syllabus provides a focus for what should be studied, along with a rationale for how that content should be selected and ordered. Currently, the literature reflects three major types of syllabuses: structural, situational, and notional."

The following discussion will present my modified views of the three syllabuses covered by McKay, plus explanations of four other types of syllabuses that I have come across in my ESL/EFL teaching and materials. These seven syllabuses are shown in Table 1.4.

Structural Syllabuses

According to McKay, *structural syllabuses* focus on grammatical forms. Over the years, a large number of textbooks and classroom materials have been organized

Table 1.4 Syllabuses	
SYLLABUSES	**WAYS OF ORGANIZING COURSES AND MATERIALS**
Structural	Grammatical and phonological structures are the organizing principles—sequenced from easy to difficult or frequent to less frequent
Situational	Situations (such as at the bank, at the supermarket, at a restaurant, and so forth) form the organizing principle—sequenced by the likelihood students will encounter them (structural sequence may be in background)
Topical	Topics or themes (such as health, food, clothing, and so forth) form the organizing principle—sequenced by the likelihood that students will encounter them (structural sequence may be in background)
Functional	Functions (such as identifying, reporting, correcting, describing, and so forth) are the organizing principle—sequenced by some sense of chronology or usefulness of each function (structural and situational sequences may be in background)
Notional	Conceptual categories called notions (such as duration, quantity, location, and so forth) are the basis of organization—sequenced by some sense of chronology or usefulness of each notion (structural and situational sequences may be in background)
Skills	Skills (such as listening for gist, listening for main ideas, listening for inferences, scanning a reading passage for specific information, and so forth) serve as the basis for organization sequenced by some sense of chronology or usefulness for each skill (structural and situational sequences may be in background)
Task	Task or activity-based categories (such as drawing maps, following directions, following instructions, and so forth) serve as the basis for organization—sequenced by some sense of chronology or usefulness of notions (structural and situational sequences may be in background)

in terms of phonological and grammatical structures. As Table 1.4 indicates, the structures that are selected for such a syllabus are usually those the author regards as important in the language (although such decisions are far from scientific). The sequencing of structures is typically based on the idea of starting with easy structures and gradually progressing to more difficult ones. In some cases the sequencing starts with the most frequently occurring structures and gradually moves to the less frequently occurring ones. Following the easy-to-difficult rationale for tenses, for example, a textbook might begin with the present tense, move on to the future tense, then introduce the past tense forms, the past perfect, and so on. If an author follows the frequency rationale, his or her textbook might begin with the high frequency parts of speech, for example, articles, prepositions, and pronouns, and gradually progress to the less frequent verb tenses. Still other materials may simply be grouped around different parts of speech or structures, with little regard for sequencing. In most cases, such sequencing—whether by degree of difficulty or frequency—has typically been fairly intuitive.

Materials based on a structural syllabus are easy to identify because the table of contents is organized around grammar points. For instance, the following sample of headings from the table of contents of Azar (1989) is obviously organized around structures:

Chapter 1 Verb tenses
1–1 The simple tenses
1–2 The progressive tenses
1–3 The perfect tenses
1–4 The perfect progressive tenses
1–5 Summary chart of verb tenses
1–6 Spelling of *–ing* and *–ed* forms
Chapter 2 Modal auxiliaries and similar expressions
. . . . . .
Chapter 3 The passive
. . . . . .
Chapter 4 Gerunds and infinitives
. . . . . .

Situational Syllabuses

According to McKay, *situational syllabuses* are based on the idea that language is found in different contexts, or situations. Consequently, the organization in a situational syllabus will be based on common situations like the following: *at a party, at the beach, in a tourist shop, at the airport, at a theater, in a taxi, at a hotel, in a restaurant,* and the like. The selection of situations is usually based on some feeling for the likelihood that the students will encounter such situations. The sequencing usually moves from situation to situation based, perhaps, on chronology or based on the relative likelihood that students will encounter the situations in question. For instance, based on a mixture of chronology and likelihood, the situations listed above would probably make more sense in the following sequence: *at the airport, in a taxi, at a hotel, in a restaurant, at the beach, in a tourist shop, at a theater,* and *at a party.*

A selection of main headings from the table of contents of Brinton and Neuman (1982) reveals an overall organizational structure that is basically situational:

Introductions
Getting acquainted
At the housing office
Deciding to live together
Let's have coffee
Looking for an apartment
At the pier
. . . . . .

Topical Syllabuses

A number of language texts are organized on the basis of what might be called *topical syllabuses.* McKay does not discuss this category, but I will. Topical syllabuses are similar to situational syllabuses. However, they are organized by topics or themes, rather than situations. Typically, the topics are selected by the textbook author on the basis of his or her sense of the importance of the topics or themes to the lives of the students for whom the text is designed. For reasons unclear to me, such syllabuses often include such happy topics as *divorce, single parents, abortion, crime, terrorism, nuclear disasters,* and so on. The topics are often sequenced on the basis of their perceived importance or on the basis of the relative difficulty of the reading passages involved.

Some of the main headings from the table of contents of Smith and Mare (1990) will illustrate a topical syllabus:

Unit I   Trends in Living
   1   A Cultural Difference: Being on Time
   2   Working Hard or Hardly Working
   3   Changing Life–Styles and New Eating Habits
Unit II   Issues in Society
   4   Loneliness
   5   Can Stress Make You Sick?
   6   Care of the Elderly: A Family Matter

Functional Syllabuses

McKay also identified a category of syllabuses that she called "notional syllabuses," which focus on "semantic uses." I will call such syllabuses *functional
syllabuses* because this label more correctly designates the principle around
which such materials are typically organized: semantic uses, or meaning packets,
called functions (after van Ek & Alexander 1980). For instance, an English
course in an adult school in Utrecht, Holland, might be designed to teach general–purpose social English, and be organized around language functions like
*seeking information, interrupting, changing a topic, saying good-bye, giving infor-
mation, introducing someone, greeting people,* and the like.

Authors select functions on the basis of their perceived usefulness to the
students and then sequence them on the basis of some idea of chronology, frequency, or hierarchy of usefulness of the functions. For instance, a more logical
sequence for the functions listed above might be *greeting people, introducing
someone, seeking information, giving information, interrupting, changing topics,*
and *saying good-bye.*

A few of the headings from the table of contents of Jones and Baeyer (1983)
will exemplify a typical functional syllabus:

1. Talking about yourself, starting a conversation, making a date
2. Asking for information: question techniques, answering techniques,
   getting more information
3. Getting people to do things: requesting, attracting attention, agree-
   ing and refusing
4. Talking about past events: remembering, describing experiences,
   imagining *What if . . .*
5. Conversation techniques: hesitating, preventing interruptions and
   interrupting politely, bringing people together

Notional Syllabuses

A related class of syllabuses, not mentioned by McKay, that could best be
labeled *notional syllabuses* is organized around abstract conceptual categories
called general notions (again, after van Ek & Alexander 1980). General notions
include concepts like *distance, duration, quantity, quality, location, size,* and so
on. This type of materials organization is related to functional organization and
on occasion serves as a general set of categories within which functions form
subcategories. The author selects general notions based on their perceived utility, and then sequences them according to chronology, frequency, or the utility
of the notions involved.

A sample of the unit headings from the table of contents of Hall & Bowyer (1980) suggests what a notional syllabus looks like:

Unit 1	Properties and Shapes
Unit 2	Location
Unit 3	Structure
Unit 4	Measurement 1 [of solid figures]
Unit 5	Process 1 Function and Ability
Unit 6	Actions in Sequence

. . . . . .

Note that using the phrase *notional syllabuses* in this way breaks with the common perception that notional syllabuses, functional syllabuses, and notional-functional syllabuses are all the same thing. The phrases *notional syllabuses* and *functional syllabuses* are being used separately here to represent two distinct, though related, types of syllabuses: one organized around general notions and the other organized around language functions.

Skills-Based Syllabuses

A number of different *skills-based syllabuses* have also emerged over the years. An author who uses a skills-based syllabus organizes materials around the language or academic skills that he or she thinks the students will most need in order to use and continue to learn the language. For instance, a reading course might include such skills as *skimming a reading for the general idea, scanning a reading for specific information, guessing vocabulary from context, using prefixes, suffixes, and roots, finding main ideas,* and the like. The selection of skills is based on the author's perception of their usefulness, while their sequencing is usually based on some sense of the chronology, frequency, or relative usefulness of the skills.

Some of the main headings from the table of contents of Barr, Clegg, and Wallace (1983) will provide an example of a skills-based syllabus:

Scanning
Key Words
Topic Sentences
Reference Words
Connectors

. . . . . .

Task-Based Syllabuses

Recently, *task-based syllabuses* have begun to appear. Authors who favor task-based syllabuses organize materials around different types of tasks that the students might be required to perform in the language. Such tasks might include *reading job ads, making appointments, writing a résumé, filling out a job application, being interviewed, solving a problem,* and so on. An author's selection of the tasks to be included in a task-based syllabus is typically based on their perceived usefulness to the students.

A sample of the main headings from the table of contents of Jolly (1984) provides an example of a task-based syllabus:

1   Writing notes and memos
2   Writing personal letters
3   Writing telegrams, personal ads, and instructions
4   Writing descriptions
5   Reporting experiences
6   Writing to companies and officials

Mixed or Layered Syllabuses

Readers need only look at the tables of contents of some of the language textbooks on their bookshelves to verify the existence of the seven types of syllabuses I have just discussed. But in the process of reviewing these tables of contents, they may notice that some materials appear to diverge from the seven patterns described here. Such divergences will usually occur in one of two ways: sometimes two or more types of syllabuses may be mixed together into what appears to be a different type of syllabus, and other times there may be secondary or tertiary syllabuses operating in layers underneath the primary syllabus.

Mixed syllabuses occur when authors choose to mix two or more types of syllabuses together into what looks like a different type of syllabus—at least in the table of contents. Consider, for example, a mixture of situational and topical syllabuses that is drawn from my old Spanish textbook (Turk & Espinosa 1970). This syllabus was basically situational in design (for instance, *en un restaurante español, en un hotel mexicano, la casa y la familia de María*), but also had topics mixed in on a regular basis (for example, *fiestas, los deportes, exploradores y misioneros*). In the process of developing the materials, the authors clearly used situations and topics as separate organizational principles: situations were used to organize the individual lessons, and topics were used to organize the regular readings sprinkled throughout the book. The point I wish to make is that the organization of some materials may involve interspersing elements from two or more types of syllabuses. Such syllabuses can be best labeled with mixed descriptions like a *situational-topical syllabus,* or *predominantly a situational syllabus mixed with a topical syllabus.*

Other authors may choose to use *layered syllabuses,* secondary or tertiary syllabuses in layers that operate underneath the primary syllabus. Indeed, most materials have some sort of structural syllabus buried somewhere below the primary syllabus. For instance, closer examination of the subheadings from the example of a situational syllabus I used (Brinton & Neuman 1982) will reveal that underneath the overall situational syllabus (Introductions, Getting acquainted, At the housing office, and so on) is a structural syllabus used to organize the material within and between lessons. Consider the subheadings for the first chapter.

Introductions
    Nouns
    Cardinal Numbers
    The Present Tense of the Verb Be: statement form
    Subject Pronouns
    Contractions with Be
    Article Usage: An Introduction
    Basic Writing Rules, Part I

Other syllabuses that are primarily functional, notional, task-based, or skills-based may have underlying topical or situational syllabuses. For instance, the subheadings from the example I used for a skills-based syllabus (Barr, Clegg, & Wallace, 1983) indicate that underneath the overall skills-based syllabus (scanning, key words, topic sentences, and so on) is a secondary topical syllabus used to organize the material within the units:

Scanning
    Unit One   A Place of Your Own
        Section 1   Leaving Home
        Section 2   A Roof Over Your Head
        Section 3   An Englishman's Home
        Section 4   No Place Like Home
Key Words
    Unit Two   People Who Matter
        Section 1   Falling in Love
        Section 2   Problem Page
        Section 3   For Better, For Worse
        Part A   —Marriage
        Part B   —Divorce
        Section 4   A Death in the Family

Notice that the secondary topical syllabus is itself layered into three levels: broad categories of topics for Units One and Two, topics for the individual sections, and subtopics as shown in Parts A and B.

The point I wish to make is that some materials may be organized into layered syllabuses, which should be labeled with more complex descriptive labels. Perhaps the Brinton and Neuman (1982) example would most accurately be referred to as a *situational-structural syllabus,* while the Barr, Clegg, and Wallace

(1983) example would best be labeled as *predominantly a skills-based syllabus with a topical subsyllabus.*

There is nothing wrong with the complexity that results from mixing or layering syllabuses. Certainly, the fact that such syllabuses exist does not invalidate the other seven, purer forms of syllabuses I discussed. In fact, the mixing or layering of syllabuses underscores the fact that the seven types outlined here do exist, and that knowing about them can help in disentangling and understanding any syllabuses that we encounter—whether they involve simple or complex organizational patterns.

All of the syllabuses discussed here are being used in today's language teaching, a truth demonstrated by the fact that all of the example texts (except Turk & Espinoza, 1970) were published in the 1980s or 1990s. However, my list of syllabuses is not meant to be the final or definitive set of categories. Language teaching is a dynamic field, and new ways of organizing our materials and teaching will undoubtedly surface in the future. In addition, the organizing principles presented here may ebb and flow in importance within the field. Perhaps tasks will eventually replace functions as the most typical way of organizing language teaching. Or perhaps topics will once again gain importance if content-based teaching increases in significance. Regardless of how many or which kinds of syllabuses are currently in fashion, the term *syllabuses* will always be used in this book to refer to ways of organizing courses and materials.

□ WAYS OF PRESENTING: TECHNIQUES

Techniques, simply put, are ways of presenting the language to the students. Techniques form a category of teaching activities that seems relatively independent from approaches and syllabuses. For instance, a variety of techniques might be used to present a structural syllabus based on the direct approach. Of course, the approach used to define learners' needs and the syllabus selected for organizing the materials will affect which techniques are chosen by individual language teachers for presenting the language to the students.

Typically, techniques are chosen because they represent ways of presenting language material which the teacher feels are going to do the most good for the largest number of students—that is, teachers usually want to maximize efficiency in learning. There is considerable disagreement about how to go about maximizing this complex process, which explains why a number of different techniques have surfaced over the years.

Table 1.5 offers a list of some of the techniques that are found in Rivers and Temperley (1981). These techniques are only meant to serve as examples. There are many other ways to go about presenting language to students. Perhaps a teacher will choose to use jazz chants (Graham 1978) to begin each class, then shift to lecturing about language, do a dictocomp for listening and writing fluency, and carry on with a term project involving drama. Jazz chants, lecturing,

Table 1.5: Techniques
TECHNIQUES: WAYS OF PRESENTING THE LANGUAGE

Bridging activities	Directed dialogue
Discussion	Grammar demonstration dialogue
Idea frame	Lecture on rules of language
Object-centered lesson	Verb-centered lesson

dictocomp, and drama are all ways of presenting langauge. Many more teaching activities exist that could be labeled techniques, all of which are ways of presenting language material to the students.

□ WAYS OF PRACTICING THE LANGUAGE: EXERCISES

The line between techniques and exercises, that is, between ways of presenting and ways of practicing language, is sometimes a fine one. In good teaching, presentation and practice may be indistinguishable, at least to the students involved, as the teacher presents the language to them and the students play with it or practice it, and hopefully learn or acquire something new in the process. Nevertheless, we are in the language teaching business and can therefore profit from thinking about classroom activities in terms of these two distinct categories in order to better match the ways that we present language with the ways we have our students practice it.

Perhaps the best way to separate the two types of activities is to think of *exercises* as those types of activities that could probably be used to test or assess the students after the lesson or unit is finished, while techniques would probably not be usable in assessment. However, there will be times when exercises will be used in presenting and in practicing language as with a cloze procedure used to demonstrate predictability as a reading strategy and then used to practice that strategy. The fact that techniques and exercises are not 100 percent discrete categories does not lessen the value of looking at them as two different types of activities.

The different ways of practicing language are even more numerous and diverse than the ways of presenting it. Table 1.6 lists some types of exercises discussed in Rivers and Temperley (1981). Such exercises might equally well include other activities like dictation, pair work, group work, problem solving, doing tasks, and the like.

□ "PACKAGED" PEDAGOGIES

A group of teaching activities that are sometimes labeled "innovative approaches" does not fit neatly into any of my four categories. I will refer to

Table 1.6: Exercises

EXERCISES: WAYS OF PRACTICING WHAT HAS BEEN TAUGHT

Autonomous interaction	Chain dialogue
Cloze procedure	Conversion
Copying	Expansion
Fill-in	Matching
Multiple-choice	Pattern drill
Proofreading	Replacement
Response drill	Restatement
Rosetta procedure	Sentence combining
Sentence modification	Speed writing
Substitution drill	Transformation drill
Translation	True-false

these activities as "packaged pedagogies." As Table 1.7 shows, packaged pedagogies include Counseling-Learning, the Dartmouth Pedagogy, the Natural Way, the Silent Way, Suggestopedia, and Total Physical Response. The label "packaged pedagogy" will be used here instead of "innovative approaches" for four reasons. First, since the term "approach" is being used in this book in a restricted way, using the phrase "innovative approaches" would create confusion. Second, most of these techniques could no longer be considered truly innovative since they have all been around for some time. Third, they are "packaged" in that, in most cases, we can contact enthusiasts of each and buy packaged materials that follow the particular pedagogy in question. Fourth, each pedagogy is complete in a sense, including its own approach and some form of syllabus, as well as its own types of techniques and exercises.

Table 1.7: Packaged Pedagogies

PACKAGED PEDAGOGIES	AUTHOR
Counseling-Learning	Curran
Dartmouth Pedagogy	Rassias
Natural Way	Krashen
Silent Way	Gattegno
Suggestopedia	Lozanov
Total Physical Response	Asher

Despite their packaged nature, however, packaged pedagogies are often most closely associated in our minds with the idea of techniques, as defined above. This is so because the central focus of each pedagogy is on ways of presenting language material to students in order to maximize learning. Though wrapped up in elaborate rationales, and though sometimes backed up by research, the central argument in all cases is that presenting language "in such and such a way" will help the students to learn more effectively, easily, or enjoyably. Counseling-Learning (Curran 1972, 1976) requires the students to be comfortably seated in a group, while the teacher remains outside of the group as a facilitator—helping with language only when requested to do so. Suggestopedia (Lozanov 1978) uses breathing and relaxation exercises and slow baroque music in presenting language. Total Physical Response (Asher 1983) uses a command-based approach for presenting language to students. The Silent Way (Gattegno 1972), the Natural Way (Krashen & Terrell 1983), and the Dartmouth Pedagogy (Rassias 1968, 1972) likewise require special equipment, seating, or types of input in the presentation of language to the students. My aim is not to provide an in-depth review of these packaged pedagogies, such reviews exist elsewhere (Blair 1982; Oller & Richard-Amato 1983; Larsen-Freeman 1986). Rather, my aim is to indicate how these packaged pedagogies are essentially perceived by members of the language teaching profession as techniques, or ways of presenting language to students.

However, packaged pedagogies differ from the other techniques discussed above in a number of ways: (1) packaged pedagogies are available as elaborate packages including built-in approaches, syllabuses, techniques, and exercises; (2) packaged pedagogies are usually identified with a single personality (Counseling-Learning with Curran, the Dartmouth Pedagogy with Rassias, the Natural Way with Krashen, the Silent Way with Gattegno, Suggestopedia with Lozanov, and Total Physical Response with Asher); and, (3) packaged pedagogies generally have a central point for distribution of the package in the form of information and materials.

□ PUTTING IT ALL TOGETHER

Ultimately, if we accept the notion that approaches, syllabuses, techniques, and exercises are all happening simultaneously in any given language program and that such activities all interact with each other and affect one another, we must always remain flexible and leave options open. This kind of informed picking and choosing from among the options available to the teacher has sometimes been labeled *eclecticism*, which will be fairly narrowly defined here as the practice of (or belief in) making informed choices among the available approaches, syllabuses, techniques, and exercises in order to adapt to a particular group of students in a particular situation for the purposes of most effectively and efficiently helping them to learn language. Because in some circles eclecticism has a bad name (that is, it has become a label for disorganized teaching composed of an irrational hodgepodge of activities), I wish to emphasize my belief that true eclecticism involves informed and rational choices based on knowledge and experience. Putting all of the individual choices of approach, syllabus, techniques, and exercises together at a given time almost inevitably makes the teacher eclectic. In some cases, of course, the teacher may abdicate responsibility by accepting a packaged pedagogy or by simply letting the textbook make all the choices.

Another aspect of language teaching that we must recognize is that making such choices from the extensive menu of all possible teaching activities is a form of political action. Our power and prestige as teachers is brought to bear on students, sometimes regardless of their views, to help them learn. If our way of defining what students need to learn is communicative, we will probably (though not necessarily) use the functional way of organizing our course and materials. The techniques that we choose may include a variety from those available or we may use only a few (for example, a lecture, a video presentation, and a pair-work demonstration). In addition, the means that we choose for having the students practice the language may include many different types of exercises, or we may prefer to use just problem solving and pair work. The point is that we make decisions about all of the activities that go on in language teaching: approaches to defining the needs of the students, syllabuses for organizing the course and materials, techniques for presenting the language to the students, and exercises to help the students practice the language.

These decisions are necessarily political because they involve the use of our positions as teachers to make the students do what we think they should do. Yet our task is a very complex one; we must fit all of these different types of activities (approaches, syllabuses, techniques, and exercises) into a framework that will maximize the efficiency and quality of learning among students who may differ from one another to a staggering degree, both cognitively and affectively (see Brown 1988 for a discussion of how students may vary from each other). Perhaps the very complexity of these tasks is justification enough for considering language teaching a profession, one that deserves considerable respect.

The remainder of this book will be dedicated to providing a framework for curriculum activities that will be more or less independent of the four language teaching activities described above. In other words, the framework provided here can be used to focus curriculum activities regardless of the choices made about approaches, syllabuses, techniques, and exercises. From my point of view, these four categories are entirely the responsibility of the language teaching professionals in charge of a given program. After all, the teachers and administrators in a particular program are much more likely than anyone else to understand the specific students and situations involved. The framework, as the reader will see, can help teachers and administrators make choices and implement those choices in a viable and flexible curriculum that will assist teachers in doing what they do best: teaching.

OVERVIEW OF CURRICULUM COMPONENTS

Given the political nature of what individual teachers do, consider how much more political curriculum development must be since almost inevitably more than one teacher is involved. The view that I wish to promote is that curriculum development is a series of activities that contribute to the growth of consensus among the staff, faculty, administration, and students. This series of *curriculum activities* will provide a framework that helps teachers to accomplish whatever combination of teaching activities is most suitable in their professional judgment for a given situation, that is, a framework that helps the students to learn as efficiently and effectively as possible in the given situation. In a sense, the *curriculum design* process could be viewed as being made up of the people and the paper-moving operations that make the doing of teaching and learning possible.

Historically, models of language curriculum design have undergone considerable evolution, an evolution reflected in the models and flow charts proposed by various authors to represent different curriculum design processes over the last 30 years. While discussion of these models is beyond the scope of this book, the influence of certain authors must be acknowledged because of their impact on the model I am proposing here. Readers interested in the development of curriculum design models would profit by referring to the models and associated text in the following: Halliday, McIntosh, and Strevens (1964, p. 222), Corder (1973, p. 155), Howatt (1974, p. 5), Perry (1976, p. 80), Strevens (1977, p. 35), Munby (1978, p. 28), Candlin, Kirkwood, and Moore (1978, p. 191), Mackay (1981, p. 137), and Richards and Rodgers (1982, p. 165).

The model shown in Figure 1.2 (adapted from Brown 1989a) not only draws on the language teaching literature listed above but also fits the more general models used to describe long established systems approaches to curriculum design. This model is meant to be applicable to language programs, yet complete and consistent with the widely accepted systems approach used in educational technology and curriculum design circles, particularly that of Dick and Carey (1985). As shall become evident, the model provides both a set of stages for logical program development and a set of components for the improvement and maintenance of an already existing language program. The model is also meant to provide for a continuing process of curriculum development and maintenance while accounting for possible interactions among the various components of the design.

The model, the explanation of the model, and the examples I give here should help in developing consensus among teachers about the essential elements of curriculum and how those components interact in particular teaching situations. To that end, let's next turn to a brief explanation of each of the components of the model so that the relationships among them will be clear. Note, however, that these components also form the titles for the next six chapters of the book. Consequently, only brief overviews are presented here, that is, only those issues are included that explain why each component is a crucial element in the development and maintenance of a sound language curriculum.

Figure 1.2: Systematic Approach to Designing and Maintaining Language Curriculum (adapted from Brown 1989a)

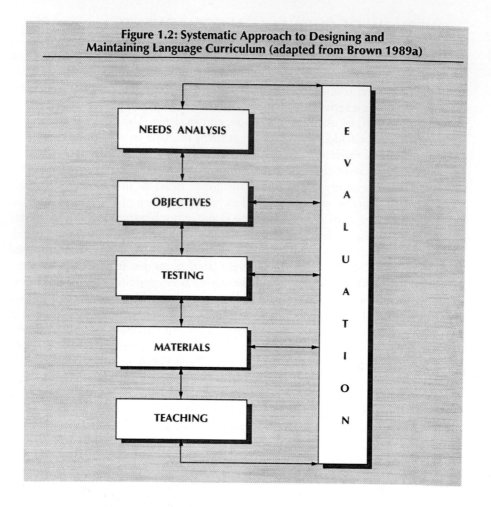

□ NEEDS ANALYSIS

Needs analysis in language programs is often viewed simply as identification of the language forms that the students will likely need to use in the target language when they are required to actually understand and produce the language. The analytical focus is on the learners, and their needs are viewed in linguistic terms. In truth, it *is* logical to make the learners the focus of any sound needs analysis. Learners are, in a sense, clients and their needs should be served. But at the same time, teachers, administrators, employers, institutions, societies, and even whole nations have needs that may also have a bearing on the language teaching and learning situation. The view I take in this book is that the learner should be the focus of a needs analysis but, as I shall argue in Chapter Two on needs analysis, many other sources and types of information must be considered in doing a sound assessment of their needs.

The same principle applies to the language focus of many needs analyses. Students have needs and concerns other than linguistic ones. Thus the learners' human needs must also be acknowledged alongside their purely language-related ones. This in turn means that the definition of needs analysis should be broadened to include this wider view of needs. *Needs analysis* will be defined tentatively as the systematic collection and analysis of all relevant information necessary to satisfy the language learning requirements of the students within the context of the particular institutions involved in the learning situation.

□   GOALS AND OBJECTIVES

A logical outcome of determining the needs of a group of language students is the specification of *goals,* that is, general statements about what must be accomplished in order to attain and satisfy students' needs. If, for instance, a group of Japanese students were doing English as a foreign language training in order to prepare for study at American universities, one goal might be to prepare them to be able to write term papers. Producing such papers is one language-related task that students might need once they start their studies in the United States, and this task can be expressed as a goal. *Objectives,* on the other hand, are precise statements about what content or skills the students must master in order to attain a particular goal. For instance, to write a term paper, the students might first need to develop several essential library skills. One such skill would be the ability to find a book in the library. To do this, the student would need several subskills: finding a particular book in the card catalog, locating the call number for that book, and finding the book by locating its call number in the stacks. The specification of objectives and the process of thinking through what is involved in achieving the program goals will lead to analyzing, synthesizing, and clarifying the knowledge and skills necessary to meet the students' language needs. Since the difference between goals and objectives clearly hinges on level of specificity, the dividing line between the two is not always clear. Nonetheless, the distinction will prove useful in planning and maintaining language programs. In fact, any discussion in a program about how to meet and satisfy students' language needs can only be as clear and precise as the objectives that result. Objectives come in many forms and may differ in degree of specificity even within a given program primarily because they can serve different student needs that themselves vary in level of specificity.

□   LANGUAGE TESTING

The next logical step in curriculum development is the development of tests based on a program's goals and objectives. This is not necessarily a simple step. The goals and objectives of a program may require extensive test development for widely different purposes within a program, for example, placement of students, language proficiency testing, diagnostic testing, and achievement testing—all of which can be very complex to develop. The strategy explained in Chapter Four on testing, however, simplifies these processes considerably. The method I advocate here for test development requires the use of two different types of tests: *norm-referenced tests* intended to compare the relative performance of students to each other; and *criterion-referenced tests* intended to measure the amount of course material that each student has learned. These two types of tests can then be used to serve different purposes within the program. Development of such tests can amount to a considerable amount of work.

However, investing resources, time, and energy for the development of a sound testing program is necessary and worthwhile in the long run. For curriculum planning, the dividends are enormous in terms of what we can learn about the previous two steps in the curriculum development process (that is, needs analysis and goals/objectives). By learning as much as possible about needs and objectives early in the process, planners can minimize waste in the crucial, and often expensive, materials development stage that follows.

As I will argue in Chapter Four on testing, the processes of developing and refining tests is by no means magical nor is it particularly easy. Nonetheless, sound tests can be used to unify a curriculum and give it a sense of cohesion, purpose, and control. Tests can be used to drive a program by shaping the expectations of the students and their teachers. In short, tests are a very crucial element in the curriculum development process.

☐ MATERIALS DEVELOPMENT

With at least preliminary sets of needs analyses, objectives, and tests in hand, curriculum planners are in the unusual position of being able to deal rationally with the problem of materials. It is relatively easy to adopt, develop, or adapt materials for a program that is well defined in terms of needs analyses, objectives, and tests. In fact, the decision as to which strategy to use (adopt, develop, or adapt) in putting materials in place is itself made easier. Can already existing materials be adopted to fill the needs of the students? Or, if there are no ready-made materials available, should they be created from scratch? Or should existing materials be adapted to meet the students' needs and the program's objectives? And if adaptation must take place, will the process be minor in scale or a major undertaking? Having clear-cut needs analyses, objectives, and tests will be of considerable help to planners in the materials development process.

I will not prescribe a particular type of materials or materials based on a particular philosophy of teaching or theory of language (although my personal biases may show through). In other words, I believe that decisions regarding the approaches, syllabuses, techniques, and exercises should always be left up to the individuals who are on site and know the situation best. What I will advocate is a strategy in which students' needs, objectives, tests, teaching, and program evaluation will all be related to each other and to the materials. As a consequence of these relationships, materials choices and use will be affected by what is learned from each of the other components of a program and will in turn have an effect of their own on those other components. The main point I wish to make is that materials can be handled rationally—whether adopted, developed, or adapted—perhaps for the first time in some language programs.

□ LANGUAGE TEACHING

Contrary to what might at first seem to be true, the system I advocate for curriculum development allows teachers more freedom than usual in the classroom to teach as they feel appropriate. Of course, the teachers and students should be aware of what the objectives for a given course are and how the testing will be conducted at the end of the course. To those ends, teachers need support and also need to be intimately involved in the process of curriculum development and revision. Drawing on the strength found in numbers, each teacher can be helped by the fact that other teachers, administrators, and students are drawn into defining students' needs and course objectives. This process has traditionally fallen solely on the teacher's shoulders. Teachers have also been responsible for selecting or developing course tests and materials.

In this book, all curriculum processes are described as group efforts. The primary reason for this emphasis is that most teachers, as individuals, are in no position to do such tasks well, because they lack the time and the expertise to do an adequate job. Hence, objectives, tests, and materials development should all be group efforts drawing on the expertise, time, and energy available from everyone involved in the program. This kind of support can help teachers do a superior job at what they are hired for: teaching.

Given a reasonably high level of program support, the teacher can be left alone to concentrate on the most effective means for teaching the courses at hand. The teacher and only the teacher should make judgments about the particular students in a given class. These judgments can be very important as the teacher deals with the myriad cognitive, affective, and personal variables that will be interacting for the particular students at a particular time to form the unique characteristics of a given class. By sorting through all of this complexity, whether consciously or not, and modifying the approaches, syllabuses, techniques, and exercises, the teacher can adapt and maximize the learning of the class as a whole, as well as the learning of most of its individual members. These are such demanding tasks that teachers should not be expected to do their own needs analyses, set objectives, create tests, and adopt, develop, or adapt materials. Teachers must be supported in their jobs to whatever degree that is possible.

The system of curriculum development and maintenance advocated in this book will provide such support.

□ PROGRAM EVALUATION

Evaluation might be defined as the systematic collection and analysis of all relevant information necessary to promote the improvement of the curriculum and to assess its effectiveness within the context of the particular institutions involved. Such a definition would be very similar to that given above for needs analysis. Indeed, the evaluation process should be a sort of ongoing needs assessment, but one based on considerably more and better information. A needs analysis is typically conducted in the initial stages of curriculum development and must rely on interview procedures, questionnaires, linguistic analyses, conjecture, and a good deal of professional judgment. Evaluation, on the other hand, can take advantage of all the above information and tools to assess the effectiveness of a program, but can also utilize all the information gathered in the processes of (1) developing objectives; (2) writing and using the tests; (3) adopting, developing, or adapting materials; and (4) teaching.

Program evaluation, then, might be defined as the ongoing process of information gathering, analysis, and synthesis, the entire purpose of which is to constantly improve each element of a curriculum on the basis of what is known about all of the other elements, separately as well as collectively. Such a continuing process of evaluation makes possible the assessment of the quality of a curriculum once it is put in place as well as the maintenance of that curriculum on an ongoing basis. Curriculum that is viewed as a product is inflexible once finished. Curriculum that is viewed as a process can change and adapt to new conditions, whether those conditions be new types of students, changes in language theory, new political exigencies within the institution, or something else. This process is known as *systematic curriculum development.*

EXAMPLE LANGUAGE PROGRAMS

Near the end of each chapter in this book, I will offer examples to illustrate the concepts discussed in the chapter. These examples will be drawn from two organizations: the Guangzhou English Language Center at Zhongshan University and the English Language Institute at the University of Hawaii at Manoa. These two programs were selected because they both have systematically designed curriculums; because I have intimate knowledge of both of them; and because they represent two distinct types of institutions. One is an English as a foreign language institution and the other is in an English as a second language setting. These two programs will be briefly described here in order to provide background for the discussions presented in later chapters.

□   GUANGZHOU ENGLISH LANGUAGE CENTER, ZHONGSHAN UNIVERSITY

The Guangzhou English Language Center (GELC) was located on the campus of Zhongshan University, known in China as Zhongshan Daxue, or simply Zhongda. Zhongda is in the city of Guangzhou in Guangdong Province in the southern part of the People's Republic of China (PRC). GELC was established in 1980 as a cooperative project between the UCLA/China Exchange Program, Zhongda, and the PRC Ministry of Education. GELC was set up as an independent unit separate from the Foreign Languages Department at Zhongda—though there was considerable cooperation between the two institutions. GELC was initially staffed by nine Americans hired and sent by UCLA to work with seven Chinese faculty members selected from the foreign languages department. GELC was set up as a five-year pull-out program: two Chinese teachers would attend UCLA each year to pursue further graduate-level training in ESL and would then return to Zhongda to replace two of the American teachers. The goal was to end up with an all-Chinese faculty after five years (with one American remaining to serve as a resident native speaker informant and EFL consultant).

During the two years that I was at GELC, 1980 to 1982, the primary function of GELC was to provide English language instruction to Chinese scientists who were bound for the United States or other English-speaking countries, either as visiting scholars or as graduate students. The emphasis in the program was on the use of English for science and technology in academic settings. The approach was generally communicative and the syllabuses were generally organized around the functions and skills that students would need to effectively use English in their studies. The techniques and exercises used to achieve these goals were worked out by the teachers, individually and in groups. GELC offered courses in five skill areas: listening, speaking, reading, writing, and culture. These courses were conducted at three levels (cleverly labeled A, B, and C) which we considered low intermediate, intermediate, and advanced (see Figure 1.3). Notice that there was no component labeled grammar. While grammar was included as needed within each of the skill courses, this lack of a course called grammar was a direct expression of our view of the communicative approach.

Initially, only students with scores on the Test of English as a Foreign Language (TOEFL) above 450 were accepted into GELC; one of our goals was to ensure that GELC would bring their overall proficiency levels up to 550 or higher on the TOEFL so that the students could satisfy North American university English requirements. In Figure 1.3, the TOEFL score range is shown to the left of the courses. Notice that the TOEFL range extends down as low as 400 because, as the program progressed, the overall proficiency of the incoming students dropped to about 400 (with a few arriving at a much lower level). The declining proficiency levels were a reality with which we had to deal. Initially,

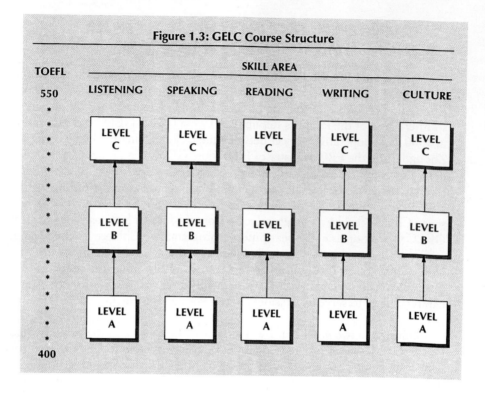

Figure 1.3: GELC Course Structure

we attempted to place students at various levels in the program, but, because the communicative skills and strategies that we taught were so new to the students, we soon found ourselves placing all new students into the A Level and requiring them all to progress through the three levels of the program.

Assignment to GELC courses was mandatory. Each of the five courses required 50 minutes per day (with 10 minute breaks), five days per week. A minimum of one hour per day of language laboratory was expected of each student and liberal amounts of homework were assigned. Each term lasted 10 weeks (300 hours of instruction including the language laboratory time), and it took three terms to complete Levels A, B, and C (for a total of 900 hours of instruction). In general, the courses were taken very seriously by the students; from the Western perspective, these students were an unbelievably dedicated, hardworking, and talented group of individuals.

☐ ENGLISH LANGUAGE INSTITUTE, UNIVERSITY OF HAWAII AT MANOA

The English Language Institute (ELI) is a subunit of the Department of English as a Second Language and is located on the 300-acre campus of the University of Hawaii in the Manoa Valley, a residential section near the state capital and

Waikiki, on the island of Oahu. The University of Hawaii at Manoa (UHM) is a public educational institution (founded in 1907) and currently has an enrollment of more than 20,000 students. The ELI was established more than 35 years ago. In recent years, 350 to 400 students from more than 50 countries have accounted for over 800 ELI course enrollments yearly.

The primary function of the ELI is to provide English language instruction to those nonnative speakers of English who have been officially admitted to UHM and who are judged to be in need of further training in the English used in academic settings. In this program too the emphasis is on communicative language use organized around the tasks, functions, and skills that students will need to perform effectively in academic settings. The techniques and exercises that will most effectively accomplish these goals are worked out among the teachers. As Figure 1.4 demonstrates, the ELI offers courses at different levels in listening comprehension, reading, speaking, and writing. These courses are taught by graduate assistants, lecturers, and faculty members of the Department of English as a Second Language.

The ELI courses are designed for undergraduate and graduate students who are fully admitted to UHM. Since UHM has a minimum entrance score on the TOEFL of 500, 500 is typically the lowest score encountered in the ELI. In

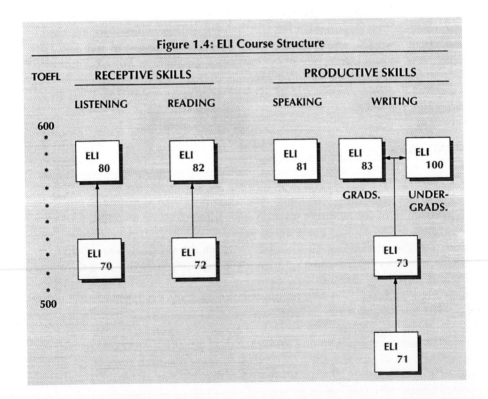

Figure 1.4: ELI Course Structure

the case of certain students (for example, graduate students who have TOEFL scores higher than 600), the ELI exempts them from further English language training. All other students, however, are tested by the ELI for English placement. After the test results have been analyzed, the students are either exempted from instruction in the ELI or are assigned to one or more of the courses offered. Assignment to ELI courses is mandatory.

All ELI courses and ESL 100 follow the University of Hawaii's regular 15-week-semester schedule. A course, which equals three credits, meets three times a week for 50 minutes each class.

Briefly, the courses in the ELI are as follows:

ELI 70	Listening Comprehension I
ELI 80	Listening Comprehension II
ELI 72	Reading for Foreign Students
ELI 82	Advanced Reading for Foreign Students
ELI 81	Advanced Speaking for International Teaching Assistants
ELI 71	Fundamentals of Writing for Foreign Students
ELI 73	Writing for Foreign Students
ELI 83	Writing for Foreign Graduate Students
ESL 100	Expository Writing

All ELI courses, with the exception of ESL 100 (which satisfies the freshman composition requirement for nonnative speakers of English), are credit-equivalent courses, which means that they satisfy financial aid and visa enrollment requirements, but do not count for graduation. For more information on this program, see the other chapters in this book or contact the English Language Institute, University of Hawaii at Manoa, 1890 East-West Road, Honolulu, HI, 96822.

SUMMARY

The various teaching activities described at the beginning of this chapter (approaches, syllabuses, techniques, and exercises) were depicted as being the responsibility of the language teachers and administrators involved. However, regardless of the choices made about approaches, syllabuses, techniques, and exercises, the systems framework for curriculum development was shown to be useful in making choices and implementing a cogent curriculum. Thus the teaching and curriculum activities were viewed as related, but fundamentally independent. Figure 1.5 shows the relationships among teaching and curriculum activities.

The teaching activities included in Figure 1.5 are shown as more or less discrete categories, indicated by the lack of arrows between boxes, whereas clear interrelations are shown among the curriculum activities, indicated by bidirectional arrows. In fact, the arrows are meant to show that each component affects all others. In addition, the reader should recognize that all teaching activities

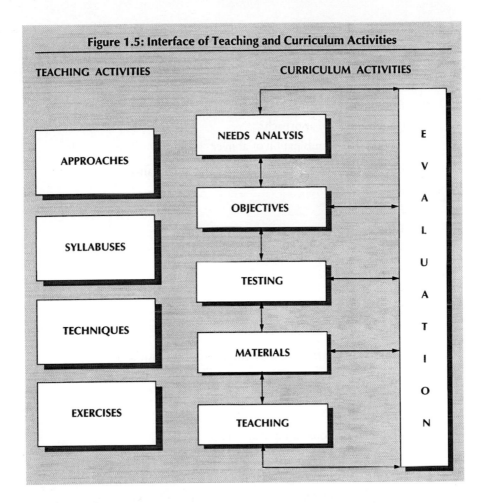

Figure 1.5: Interface of Teaching and Curriculum Activities

and curriculum activities are also likely to interact in real language programs even if I fail to supply arrows in Figure 1.5.

The chapter ended with brief descriptions of the Guangzhou English Language Institute at Zhongshan University and the English Language Institute at the University of Hawaii at Manoa. These descriptions serve as background for examples that will be used in the remaining chapters.

■ ■ ■ CHECKLIST

The following checklist is designed to help you decide what types of approaches, syllabuses, techniques, and exercises are favored in a particular language teaching situation.

- □ Approaches: How are the needs of the students viewed or defined?
  - □ Classical approach?
  - □ Grammar-translation approach?
  - □ Direct approach?
  - □ Audiolingual approach?
  - □ Communicative approach?
  - □ Other? Or a combination of above?

- □ Syllabuses: How are the materials and teaching organized?
  - □ Structural?
  - □ Situational?
  - □ Topical?
  - □ Functional?
  - □ Notional?
  - □ Skills?
  - □ Task?
  - □ Other? Or a combination of above?

- □ Techniques: How is the language presented to the students?
  - □ Bridging activities
  - □ Directed dialogue
  - □ Discussion
  - □ Grammar demonstration dialogue
  - □ Idea frame
  - □ Lecture on rules of language
  - □ Object-centered lesson
  - □ Verb-centered lesson
  - □ And others? Or combinations of the above?

- □ Exercises: How is the language practiced (check those applicable)?
  - □ Autonomous interaction
  - □ Chain dialogue
  - □ Cloze procedure
  - □ Conversion
  - □ Copying
  - □ Expansion drill
  - □ Fill-in
  - □ Matching

- □ Multiple-choice
- □ Pattern drill
- □ Proofreading
- □ Replacement
- □ Response drill
- □ Restatement
- □ Rosetta procedure
- □ Sentence combining
- □ Sentence modification
- □ Speed writing
- □ Substitution drill
- □ Transformation drill
- □ Translation
- □ True-false
- □ And others? Or combinations of the above?
- □ Packaged pedagogy?
  - □ Counseling-Learning?
  - □ Dartmouth?
  - □ Natural Way?
  - □ Silent Way?
  - □ Suggestopedia?
  - □ Total Physical Response?
  - □ Other? Or some combination of the above?

The following checklist is designed to help evaluate informally the presence of the main curriculum elements in a language program.

- □ Is there a component of the curriculum for needs analysis? (see Chapter Two)
  - □ Are documents available that give estimates of what the students need to learn when they leave the program?
  - □ Are these documents accessible and easy to read?
  - □ Do the needs of the students as perceived by the administrators and teachers match?
- □ Is there a component for goals and objectives? (see Chapter Three)
  - □ Are the goals and objectives for each course within the program available?

- □ Are these documents accessible and easy to understand?
- □ Are the goals listed separately from the objectives?
- □ Does each statement of an objective indicate what the students will be able to do at the end of the course?

□ Is there a testing component? (see Chapter Four)
- □ What types of tests does the program use?
  - □ Norm-referenced tests?
  - □ Criterion-referenced tests?
- □ Are the existing tests adequate for the types of decisions that must be made (for instance, admissions or placement decisions)?
- □ Are the existing tests adequate for determining the degree to which the objectives have been met?

□ Materials (see Chapter Five)
- □ How were the current materials acquired?
  - □ Adopted?
  - □ Developed?
  - □ Adapted?
- □ Do these materials match the majority views on approaches, syllabuses, techniques, and exercises?
- □ Do the materials match the language learning needs of the students in the program?

□ Teaching (see Chapter Six)
- □ Are teachers free to make necessary judgments about the students in their particular classes?
- □ Does the curriculum provide support for the teachers without interfering with the teaching/learning processes?

□ Evaluation (see Chapter Seven)
- □ Are there mechanisms within the curriculum to gather, analyze, and synthesize information?
- □ Are these mechanisms used to constantly improve all of the other elements of the curriculum?

■ ■ ■ TERMS

approaches (as defined in this book)
criterion-referenced tests
curriculum

mixed syllabuses
needs analysis
norm-referenced tests

curriculum activities
curriculum design
eclecticism
evaluation
exercises (as defined in this book)
goals
layered syllabuses
methods (as defined in this book)

objectives
program evaluation
syllabus (as defined in this book)
systematic curriculum development
teaching activities
techniques (as defined in this book)
testing

■ ■ ■ REVIEW QUESTIONS

1. How did the categories provided by Richards and Rodgers (1982) (approach, design, and procedure) differ from Anthony's (1963) earlier classifications?

2. How do McKay's (1978) definitions for three types of syllabuses relate to the articles in the above question?

3. How is an approach defined in the chapter? Can you name five approaches?

4. Can you name the seven types of syllabuses discussed in this chapter? How are syllabuses different from approaches?

5. How are techniques different from exercises (as the terms are used in this book)?

6. What is the purpose of a needs analysis? Why would needs analysis activities logically end in the formulation of at least some tentative statements of goals and objectives?

7. How do goals differ from objectives as they are defined in the chapter? Why might it be necessary to allow a wide variety of different types of objectives, some very specific, as well as others that are more general?

8. How do norm–referenced tests differ from criterion–referenced tests? Which would you be most likely to use to measure students' achievement of the objectives of a program? Which would you use for placement?

9. Would you prefer to adopt, develop, or adapt the materials for a new curriculum, or would you prefer a combination of all three strategies? Why might it be better to apply any of those strategies with a group of teachers rather than alone?

10. How might the curriculum activities described in this chapter help teachers to better perform their jobs? What potential political problems do you foresee in such a situation?

11. How are program evaluation and testing conceptualized differently in this chapter? How are needs analysis and program evaluation similar? How are they different?

12. What are the four sorts of teaching activities discussed in this chapter? What are the six curriculum activities also introduced here? How do these two sets of activities relate to each other in terms of what they are and who does them?

■ ■ ■ APPLICATIONS

A1. Look again at the descriptions provided for the GELC program and the ELI at UHM (in the "Example Language Programs" section above). Briefly write out the type of approach and syllabus that you think was used in each program. Also, note the place in the text where you find the information that supports your view.

A2. Next make a note of the strategy that was utilized to select the techniques and exercises used to promote student learning within the chosen approach and syllabus. List some of the techniques and exercises that you would use under similar circumstances?

A3. Choose one of the two example programs and sketch out a systematic program design for it, including needs analysis, goals and objectives, testing, materials, teaching, and evaluation (see Figure 1.2). From the descriptions in this chapter, add as many details about each of these curriculum components as you can.

B1. Write down all the different types of things that you do in your teaching situation. Now try to separate them into those things that are essentially teaching activities and those that are basically curriculum activities. Which teaching activities are most closely related to approaches? Syllabuses? Techniques? Exercises? Which curriculum activities are most closely related to needs analysis, goals and objectives, testing, materials, teaching, and program evaluation? Can you now add other activities that you do in each category? Did you have any idea how many different activities were involved in your job?

B2. Think about the language program that you work in, or one that you know about. Sketch out the ways that the program addresses needs analysis, goals and objectives, testing, materials, teaching, and program evaluation. Are the teachers helped by the program administrators with these activities or are they solely responsible not only for teaching but also for curriculum activities? How might the situation that you are thinking about be improved?

Chapter 2

Needs Analysis

INTRODUCTION

In general terms, needs analysis (also called needs assessment) refers to the activities involved in gathering information that will serve as the basis for developing a curriculum that will meet the learning needs of a particular group of students. In the case of language programs, those needs will be language related. Once identified, needs can be stated in terms of goals and objectives which, in turn, can serve as the basis for developing tests, materials, teaching activities, and evaluation strategies, as well as for reevaluating the precision and accuracy of the original needs assessment. Thus needs assessment is an integral part of systematic curriculum building. This chapter discusses the parameters necessary to perform a successful needs analysis, whether the analysis is intended to guide the creation of a new curriculum or to reevaluate existing perceptions of the students' needs. Since sound needs analysis forms a rational basis for all the other components of a systematic language curriculum, examining the aims, procedures, and applications of needs assessment will create a sound foundation for further discussion of the curriculum.

Needs analysis (in the formal and technical sense) is relatively new in language teaching circles. However, needs analyses have been conducted informally for years by teachers who wanted to assess what language points their students needed to learn. Indeed, the various activities I labeled "approaches" in the previous chapter are different expressions of this desire to figure out what students need to learn. Information sources for such informal needs assessments might include scores on an overall language proficiency test, facts gathered from a background questionnaire that asks where and for how long students have had previous language training, or impressions gleaned from teacher and student interviews about the students' cognitive and linguistic abilities. Thus, two points seem immediately obvious when thinking about needs analysis. First, informal needs analysis is not a new thing; indeed, good teachers since the birth of the teaching profession have been conducting some form of needs assessment. Second, needs analysis involves the gathering of information to find out how much the students already know and what they still need to learn.

In more formal terms, needs assessment is defined by Richards, Platt, and Weber (1985, p. 189) as "the process of determining the needs for which a learner or group of learners requires a language and arranging the needs according to priorities. Needs assessment makes use of both subjective and objective information (e.g., data from questionnaires, tests, interviews, observation)." The definition then goes on to prescribe topic areas on which information should be obtained. These will be discussed below.

Notice that the needs described in this definition are those of the learners involved and also notice that the students' language requirements are to be delineated and sequenced on the basis of both subjective and objective information. In another definition of needs assessment, Stufflebeam, McCormick, Brinkerhoff, and Nelson (1985, p. 16) point out that it is "the process of determining the things that are necessary or useful for the fulfillment of a defensible purpose." A key phrase in this broader definition is "defensible purpose." This definition is attractive because it implies that the needs that are isolated must be defensible and form a unified and justifiable purpose.

Pratt (1980, p. 79) states that "needs assessment refers to an array of procedures for identifying and validating needs, and establishing priorities among them." The key phrases that make this definition different from the others are "array of procedures" and "validating needs." The first phrase indicates that a variety of information-gathering tools should be used. The second implies that needs are not absolute, that is, once they are identified, they continually need to be examined for validity to ensure that they remain real needs for the students involved.

The definition I will use in this book is meant to combine the best features of all three of these definitions, as well as to include elements that have either been left out or glossed over in other definitions. Like needs analysis itself, this definition can never be considered a perfect, finished product: it is a working definition designed to facilitate the process of needs assessment as part of language curriculum design. In this book, the phrases *needs analysis* and *needs assessment* will be used interchangeably to refer to the systematic collection and analysis of all subjective and objective information necessary to define and validate defensible curriculum purposes that satisfy the language learning requirements of students within the context of particular institutions that influence the learning and teaching situation.

In order to accomplish all this and actually perform a needs analysis, certain systematic steps must be followed. The remainder of this chapter will elaborate on these steps and provide suggestions for a reasonable set of procedures and steps to accomplish each. There will be three basic steps:

1. Making basic decisions about the needs analysis
2. Gathering information
3. Using the information.

The last of these steps will be demonstrated through examples drawn from the GELC program and ELI.

MAKING BASIC DECISIONS ABOUT THE NEEDS ANALYSIS

Before any needs analysis can take place, curriculum planners must make certain fundamental decisions. Who will be involved in the needs analysis? What types of information should be gathered? Which points of view should be represented? And how might points of view and program philosophy interact?

□ WHO WILL BE INVOLVED IN THE NEEDS ANALYSIS?

Four categories of people may become involved in a needs analysis: the target group, the audience, the needs analysts themselves, and the resource group. While certain individuals may find themselves playing roles in several of these categories, the roles are quite different even when the same person occupies more than one.

The *target group* is made up of those people about whom information will ultimately be gathered. The usual target group is the students in a program, but sometimes the teachers and/or administrators are also targeted.

The *audience* for a needs analysis should encompass all people who will eventually be required to act upon the analysis. This group usually consists of teachers, teacher aides, program administrators, and any governing bodies or supervisors in the bureaucracy above the language program.

The *needs analysts* are those persons responsible for conducting the needs analysis. They may be consultants brought in for the purpose, or members of the faculty designated for the job. In addition to conducting the needs analysis, this group will probably be responsible for identifying the other three groups. The needs analysts as individuals and as a group must be willing to divide up, share, and delegate responsibilities or the entire needs assessment process may prove unrealizable.

The *resource group* consists of any people who may serve as sources of information about the target group. In some contexts, parents, financial sponsors, or guardians may be included as sources of valuable information about the target group. In other cases, outsiders (such as future employers or professors from the students' content courses) may provide valuable information about the target language that students will eventually need to use.

As an example, consider the roles involved in a language needs assessment for foreign students attending a British university. The foreign students themselves would be the target group. The audience would be the instructors and administrators at the university who would provide English training and support services, as well as senior administrators at the university's higher levels. The needs analysts might be a group of three private consultants hired for the purpose. The resource groups might include two types of people: native English-speaking students at the university, who could be observed to determine what types of language and language skills are necessary for academic success at the university, and professors on various faculties, who could provide information about what they feel native speakers need to do with the language, as well as what they think the language weaknesses are for nonnative speakers of English. However, membership in all of these groups might vary from situation to situation. Indeed, in this example, the instructors and administrators in the English teaching institution might serve in the resource group, as well as in the target and audience groups.

Care must be taken in identifying the target group, the audience, the needs analysts, and the resource people so that important individuals or groups are not forgotten in the process. Imagine the problems that could arise, for instance, if the students themselves were never asked what they saw as their language needs, if the authorities in charge of funding were not informed of decisions based on needs analysis, if there was confusion about who was conducting the analysis, or if an important source of information was left out. Since membership in these groups may differ from program to program, the issue should be addressed early and definitively by those responsible for the needs analysis.

□ WHAT TYPES OF INFORMATION SHOULD BE GATHERED?

The previous paragraph may have given the impression that needs analysis is a difficult process. Indeed, it is far from simple, due largely to the fact that overall philosophies and points of view can vary considerably between programs and among individuals.

Four Philosophies of Needs Assessment

According to Stufflebeam (1977, cited in Stufflebeam, McCormick, Brinkerhoff, & Nelson 1985), four divergent philosophies can arise in a needs analysis: the discrepancy, the democratic, the analytic, and the diagnostic. The importance of such philosophies lies in the fact that they will affect the types of information that will be gathered. For instance, the *discrepancy philosophy* is one in which needs are viewed as differences, or discrepancies, between a desired performance from the students and what they are actually doing. This might lead to gathering detailed information about what is needed to change students' performance based on the observed difference between the desired correct pronunciation of the English phoneme /p/ and the incorrect phoneme /b/ the students are producing in place of it. A discrepancy can, of course, also be considerably broader and more complex, as in a need to change students' abilities in academic English from an existing low level to a level sufficient for success in a British university.

The *democratic philosophy* is one in which a need is defined as any change that is desired by a majority of the group involved. Whether this group consisted of the students themselves, their teachers, program administrators, or the owners of a private, for-profit language school, the democratic philosophy would lead to a needs analysis that would gather information about the learning most desired by the chosen group(s).

In the *analytic philosophy* a need is whatever the students will naturally learn next based on what is known about them and the learning processes involved: that is, the students are at stage x in their language development, and they next need to learn $x + 1$ or whatever is next in the hierarchy of language development. Thus this philosophy might lead to a survey of the existing literature on second language acquisition in search of the hierarchical steps involved in the language learning process.

Finally, a *diagnostic philosophy* proposes that a need is anything that would prove harmful if it was missing. This philosophy might lead to an analysis of the important language skills necessary for immigrants to survive in their adopted country. Thus a study might be conducted concerning the daily needs of immigrants and then be extended to the types of language required to accomplish such survival needs.

□ WHICH POINTS OF VIEW SHOULD BE TAKEN?

The philosophy adopted by a particular program or group of needs analysts can clearly affect the types of information gathered in the analysis. However, even when all analysts share a single philosophy, the listing of needs may grow to unmanageable proportions. Consider the diagnostic philosophy and the example I proposed of a needs analysis for the survival language needed by immigrants. Let's make the general example very specific: the immigrants are Southeast Asians living in the state of Florida in the United States. A little thought indicates that immigrants will probably need the language necessary to rent an apartment, buy food, read a bus schedule, buy a bus ticket, pronounce street names clearly so they can ask directions, apply for a job, open a bank account, write a check, read and pay bills, buy a car, pass a drivers test, check into a hospital, buy a prescription, read a legal document, understand a political speech, and so forth. In fact, immigrants must know how to do many, many other things with the language. Thus, even when needs analysts share a philosophy—in the example, the diagnostic philosophy—they can end up generating a long and cumbersome list of needs. The only way to control the dimensions of such a list is to recognize that some needs are more pressing than others. For instance, most people would consider the need to use language to find lodging or to buy food more important, or at least more urgent, than the need to read legal documents or the need to understand political speeches.

Unfortunately, many of the needs that are initially perceived as important may not turn out to be so. One of the tasks of the needs analysts, then, is to sift through all their early ideas and information and then narrow the scope of their investigation. The sifting may begin by sorting through and clearly delimiting the ways that needs will be examined, and, by doing so, limiting the types of needs that will ultimately be explored. Fortunately, three basic dichotomies exist that can help narrow the choices of what to investigate in a needs analysis. The point of view taken on each of these dichotomies will in turn be related to and influenced by the philosophy that is dominant in a given program.

Situation Needs Versus Language Needs

The first dichotomy is one that distinguishes between two types of information found in any language program. Some information will center on the program's human aspects, that is, the physical, social, and psychological contexts in which learning takes place. Needs related to this type of information will be labeled *situation needs* in this book. Such needs are usually related to any administrative, financial, logistical, manpower, pedagogic, religious, cultural, personal, or other factors that might have an impact on the program.

The second sort of information is about the target linguistic behaviors that the learners must ultimately acquire. These target linguistic behaviors will be labeled *language needs* in this book. Information in this category would include details about the circumstances in which the language will be used, the dimensions of language competence involved, the learners' reasons for studying the language, their present abilities with respect to those reasons, and so forth.

This distinction between situation needs and language needs is not a clear-cut dichotomy because the two categories are often interrelated. Nonetheless, both types of information are important if a needs analysis is to be useful and effective. Since it is not humanly possible to gather *all* possible information on either type of needs, analysts must make decisions as to the balance that will be maintained between the physical, psychological, and social needs of the target group, on the one hand, and their linguistic requirements, on the other. Needs analysts must consider this balance in defining their viewpoints. Are language needs more important than situation needs, or should a balance be struck between the two? Because the distinction between situation and language needs is so fundamental to the results that are obtained and the curriculum that evolves, the concept will resurface and be amplified below—particularly in relationship to the information gathering processes. When needs analysts are confronted with the masses of information that can emerge in a needs analysis, keeping the distinction between situation needs and language needs in mind will be particularly useful for sorting through the information and finding useful patterns.

Objective Needs Versus Subjective Needs

Brindley (1984) provides another dichotomy related to the types of information in a needs analysis: objective needs versus subjective needs. *Objective needs* are those needs determined on the basis of clear-cut, observable data gathered about the situation, the learners, the language that students must eventually acquire, their present proficiency and skill levels, and so forth. *Subjective needs* are generally more difficult to determine because they have to do with "wants," "desires," and "expectations" (Brindley 1984, p. 31). This distinction between objective needs and subjective needs should not be confused with the two types of data, quantitative and qualitative, that could be gathered on either objective or subjective needs. In other words, quantitative data can be gathered on both subjective and objective needs, and so too can qualitative data. The distinction between objective and subjective needs has to do with the observability of the needs, not with the type of data that are gathered on them. For instance, students' "wants" and "desires" can be quantified in a questionnaire, but can they be observed objectively?

As is the case with situation needs and language needs, needs analysts will probably want to use information about both subjective needs and objective needs. The balance that is struck will affect many other fundamental choices in the needs analysis process, for example, which instruments and procedures to use, how to employ them, which results to believe, which to discard, and so on.

Linguistic Content Versus Learning Processes

Another dichotomy that is important to keep in mind while sorting through the information in a needs analysis is that between specifying needs in terms of the content that the students must learn versus specifying needs in terms of learning processes. The *linguistic content* position tends to favor needs analyzed objectively from a language needs perspective and spelled out in linguistic terms, whether they be phonemes, morphemes, grammatical structures, case rules, utterances, functions, notions, discourse markers, or whatever. The *learning process* position leans toward needs specified from a situation needs perspective; these tend to be more subjectively analyzed needs in the affective domain, such as motivation and self-esteem. The distinction between content and learning processes is hardly a new one. It is roughly equivalent to Widdowson's (1981, p. 2) dichotomy between the "goal-oriented definition of needs" and the "process-oriented definition of needs"; or between Brindley's (1984, pp. 31–32) "language content" and "learning content" duality; or between Nunan's (1985) "content" and "methodology" parameters. Regardless of the label applied, responsible needs analysts will use whatever is valuable in both positions, drawing on the strengths of both as appropriate for the program in question.

□ HOW MIGHT PHILOSOPHY AND POINTS OF VIEW INTERACT?

Once decisions have been made about what positions a particular needs analysis will take with regard to the dichotomies I have just discussed, their interrelations must be considered. These dichotomies will interact with one another as shown in Figure 2.1. A decision regarding one dichotomy in Figure 2.1 can easily have an effect on the balance chosen for another dichotomy. For example, consider what would happen in an analysis if language needs were viewed as much more important than situation needs. This viewpoint would probably affect the balance taken between objective and subjective needs (with a resulting shift toward the objective) as well as the balance between linguistic content and learn-

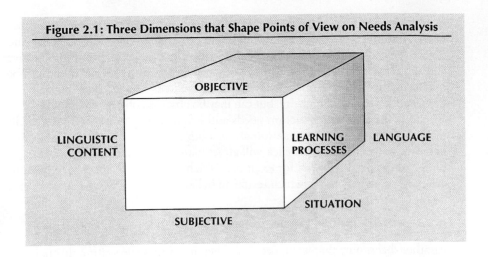

Figure 2.1: Three Dimensions that Shape Points of View on Needs Analysis

ing process needs (with a shift toward the linguistic content). Although for simplicity's sake I have discussed the three dichotomies as if they are separate, they should be viewed as three interrelated aspects of developing an overall program viewpoint on the types of needs that will be assessed. This decision would in turn have to be consistent with whatever balance of philosophies was selected earlier.

The philosophies and dichotomies have been presented here in such a way that none is advocated over the others because the decisions about which roads to follow in a particular language program depend on the personalities and institutions affecting that program. Nonetheless, early decisions about these issues can save an enormous amount of backtracking, wasted energy, and frustration.

GATHERING INFORMATION

Richards, Platt, and Weber (1985, p. 189) suggest that a needs assessment seeks information on:

1. the situations in which a language will be used (including *who* it will be used *with*)
2. the objectives and purposes for which the language is needed
3. the types of communication that will be used (e.g., written, spoken, formal, informal)
4. the level of proficiency that will be required.

As a starting point, these categories might suffice, but this list is incomplete and far too prescriptive for my purposes in this book. As I noted earlier, the needs analysts (in consultation with the teachers and administrators in the particular program) must delineate the areas of consequence for information gathering and must do so clearly and early. In the process, the analysts should remain flexible enough to allow for new areas of investigation to develop and old ones to be discarded as the process of needs assessment proceeds. The choices made depend on the philosophy of the needs analysts, as well as their points of view on the various types of information that can be examined. Once all that is clarified, the fundamental techniques used for gathering information are relatively straightforward. Such techniques are simple because they all involve, in one way or another, finding answers to relatively simple questions.

□ TYPES OF QUESTIONS

In the process of gathering information, different types of questions should be considered. Rossett (1982) identified five categories of questions designed to identify the following: problems, priorities, abilities, attitudes, and solutions.

Problems

The broadest questions are those that have to do with problems. The purpose of these questions is to identify the problems that are being experienced by the people under assessment in the target group. Questions of this type tend to be very open-ended and exploratory like the following:

1. What problems have you been having with your English when you talk to native speakers at work? (Addressed to the students)
2. What do you think the most pressing problems are for your language students? (Addressed to language teachers)
3. What do you feel is the greatest source of difficulty with English among the foreign students in engineering? (Addressed to subject matter teachers)
4. What do you think are the greatest fiscal, organizational, and/or physical impediments to learning for the students in your language program? (Addressed to program administrators)

Priorities

Questions of priority investigate which topics, language uses, skills, and so on are considered most important for the target group to learn. Such questions can be asked of any of the resource groups in the program. At a gross level, questions might be asked to find out whether reading, writing, listening, speaking, or grammar skills were considered most essential. Or with regard to each of these skills, needs analysts might be most interested in determining which of the subskills are viewed as most important. For instance, in writing, any of the following elements might be considered *most* important: using correct spelling and punctuation, organizing information well, doing library research before writing, or proofreading. Naturally, priorities may differ within the program. After all, students, teachers, and administrators will not necessarily see the world from the same perspectives (see Nunan 1986 for more on differences between students' views and teachers' views). However, the very act of finding out that such differences exist can be a useful first step in helping the needs analysts, and therefore the program as a whole, to reconcile such differences by means of a set of manageable compromises.

Abilities

Ability questions focus on the students themselves, usually to determine the abilities of the students at entry. As I will explain in more detail in Chapter Four, such questions will usually be answered by using pretests designed either to measure the overall language proficiency of students or to diagnose their specific weaknesses. In either case, such information is exceedingly important for establishing a baseline or starting point for the program, as well as for delineating the range of abilities among the students. Both of these issues are in turn important for planning the starting level, scope, and sequence of a program.

Attitudes

To ignore the attitudes and opinions of any of the groups in a program is at best an act of arrogance and at worst an act of political suicide. Attitude questions are created to uncover information about participants' feelings and attitudes toward elements of the program. These might include questions addressed to the students on how well they like studying "grammar points" as opposed to language functions such as "seeking information on the telephone." The same question might be rephrased slightly to elicit the teachers' attitudes, for example, "Do you feel that students learn English better and more efficiently by studying grammar points, language functions, or some combination of the two?" These are, of course, only examples of a class of questions that can reveal interesting and profound differences in attitudes among the participants in a program. Like other points of contention within a program, the more information available, the better the chance that a compromise will arise to resolve the potential conflict.

Solutions

The last class of questions elicits ideas for solutions to perceived problems in terms of what changes might bring about compromise and resolution. Such questions can also prove politically sound because solutions that are perceived as having come from within the program will tend to have greater backing and continued support than solutions that are perceived as imposed from above or from

Table 2.1   Procedures Available to Needs Analysts

Records analysis

Advisory meetings   Self–rating

Diagnostic testing

Achievement testing   Case studies

Diary studies

Behavior observation

Interactional analysis

Inventories   Individual interviews

Group interviews

Proficiency testing

Delphi technique

Letter writing   Literature review

Interest group meetings

Review meetings

Biodata surveys   Systems analysis

Opinion surveys

Judgmental rating   Q sort

Placement testing

outside the program. Such questions will probably come late in the needs analysis process after problems have been more clearly identified.

□ TYPES OF INSTRUMENTS

Table 2.1 lists 24 different procedures for gathering needs analysis information. Initially, this array may seem bewildering, but closer inspection will reveal patterns. For instance, notice that there are four types of testing, each of which is considered a separate procedure in Table 2.1. Surely these forms of testing are related, and can therefore be considered as one type of instrument. Similarly, the procedures within each of the six categories shown in the second column of Table 2.2 (from Brown 1989a) are related and can be considered similar enough to form a single type of instrumentation.

Table 2.2 also indicates that three of the categories of instrumentation (existing information, tests, and observations) leave the needs analysts more or less in the position of being an outsider passively looking in on the existing program (as the needs analysis process goes on). The other three (interviews, meetings, and questionnaires) seem to pull the needs analysts into the process of actively gathering or drawing out information from the participants in the program. These differences in the needs analysts' roles can have important consequences with

Table 2.2   Roles, Instruments, and Procedures for Needs Analysis (adapted from Brown 1989a)

NEEDS ANALYST'S ROLE	INSTRUMENTATION	PROCEDURES
Outsider looking in	Existing information	Records analysis Systems analysis Literature review Letter writing
	Tests	Proficiency Placement Diagnostic Achievement
	Observations	Case studies Diary studies Behavior observation Interactional analysis Inventories
Facilitator drawing out information	Interviews	Individual Group
	Meetings	Delphi technique Advisory Interest group Review
	Questionnaires	Biodata surveys Opinion surveys Self-ratings Judgmental ratings Q sort

regard to the way different categories of instrumentation (and the results based on them) are viewed by the target group, audience, resource group, and needs analysts alike. However, I will now turn to a more detailed discussion of each of these types of instrumentation before commenting further on them.

Existing Information

Existing information is the easiest category to explain. The purpose of this set of procedures is to utilize any preexisting information that may be available. Existing information can include data sources within a program (such as files or records that may be on hand when the needs analysis begins), or external data sources (such as library resources or letters exchanged with other existing programs with similar students).

Internal records might take the form of records on new and past students, financial records, teacher evaluations, and so forth. In general, the procedures in this category seem fairly straightforward. However, it is important to realize that there are several ways to analyze such records. A simple *records analysis* might explore trends in individual program components, for example, enrollments, profits, materials selection, or students' evaluations of the physical conditions and teaching. A more complex *systems analysis* would be similar but would be carried out on a larger scale. Here, various components and subcomponents, as well as their interactions, would be defined, delineated, and analyzed together, rather than as separate parts of the program. For example, a needs analyst might examine past students' evaluations of a language program's physical plant and teaching quality to determine whether they are related to levels of enrollment and profit. Existing records can be used in many ways, so, if available, they should not be overlooked as a valuable source of information, particularly for insights into the history and background of a language program.

Since language teaching goes on all over the world, important sources of information may exist outside the particular program in question. If, for instance, a group of Chinese students requires training in English for scientific purposes in American university settings, it would be useful to find out about programs that have the same general aims. One way to begin the search for such programs would be to conduct a *literature review*. Library resources in the form of books, journals, and newsletters might lead to information about similar programs and about the language learning needs of their students. Even if such programs are not precisely the same as the one in question, they still may provide the needs analysts with useful information. Perhaps the literature search reveals information about a program for training Arab scientists in English. Arab scientists are not Chinese scientists, but both groups presumably share similar needs in terms of learning English as a second language specifically for scientific purposes. Or perhaps an article on a course for preparing Taiwanese students in general academic English might provide useful information about setting up a program for Chinese scientists because, though not specifically designed for scientists, the Taiwanese program described in the article includes data concerning the English-language needs of Chinese students who attend American universities. A literature review will seldom uncover a program that has precisely the same types of students with exactly the same situation and language needs, but such a review can provide information that will diminish the need to completely reinvent the wheel each time a needs analysis is conducted.

Information found in the literature may then lead to *letter writing*. In other words, human connections can be made with the programs that have been discovered in the course of the literature review. People in other programs may or may not be receptive to taking the time to share information and ideas, but, if established, positive contacts can provide a wealth of information. Remember that the people in those other programs are very much like you and may prove equally eager for contact and sharing of ideas.

Tests

Testing will be covered in more depth in Chapter Four. Nevertheless, the issue must also be addressed here because tests are an indispensable source of information in a needs analysis (in addition to being an integral part of the curriculum that will result). Whether the purpose of measurement is *proficiency, placement, diagnosis,* or *achievement,* tests can provide a wealth of information about the general ability levels of the students, about possible ability groupings that will make sense within a program, about specific problems that students may be having with the language, and about their achievement in previous programs. However, as I explain in Chapter Four, the information gained from tests will be most useful if the tests are of high quality.

Observations

This category of instrumentation usually involves watching an individual or a small number of individuals, and recording the behaviors that occur. The behaviors of interest will normally be language and classroom behaviors (see Allwright 1983 or Chaudron 1988 for overviews on classroom observation and research, or Long 1984 for application of observations to curriculum), which might be recorded in informal notes, or more formally as an ethnographic study (for more on ethnography, see Watson-Gegeo 1988, Johnson & Saville-Troike 1992, and Davis 1992). Such a study might turn out to be a *case study* if the linguistic characteristics or behaviors of a selected individual (or perhaps several individuals) were recorded. For example, the lecture language of several native-speaking engineering professors might be studied as part of a needs analysis for an English program catering to university-bound nonnative engineering students. If the individual involved was also the investigator, self-observations might take the form of a *diary study.* This has occurred, for example, when linguists have recorded their feelings and thoughts as they went through the process of learning a language (for example, Schumann & Schumann 1977; Bailey 1980). However, it might also be revealing if the students in a language program were asked to do such introspection. *Behavior observation* is a more formal procedure in the sense that a checklist is usually developed to investigate particular verbal behaviors or actions. This checklist is then applied to the observation process. Such a procedure might be useful in observing the frequencies of certain language formulas or functions in native speech, or in investigating any one of numerous other linguistic characteristics. If a checklist or other recording procedure is applied to the purpose of studying language behaviors as interactions between people, the study would be termed an *interactional* one. Consider how interesting it might be to study the need for teachers to correct students' errors. An analysis could be done by using a checklist to determine the frequency of different types of correction coupled with notes on how students reacted to each instance of correction. The last type of procedure, the *inventory,* is used to record a count of physical objects (as in determining how many of each book a language program has) or to account for objects on a checklist of what is expected to be present (for example, a "good" program should have one classroom per 35 students, one teacher for every 100 students, two textbooks per student, one janitor for every 500 students, and so forth). While the language aspects of a program should certainly not be overlooked, neither should the physical constraints of the situation be underestimated. Thus a "simple" inventory can sometimes be important in a needs analysis.

Interviews

Interview procedures are a fairly open-ended type of instrumentation. *Individual interviews* allow for gathering personal responses and views privately. This confidentiality can, in turn, lead to insights into the "real" opinions of the participants involved. Unfortunately, interviews are time-consuming. As such, interviews may best be used to explore what issues and questions should be pursued in a later follow-up using more structured procedures such as questionnaires, behavior observations, and so on. *Group interviews* might appear to be one way around the time problem, but it is important to remember that the information given in a group interview is not confidential. For political or interpersonal reasons, it may turn out that the opinions expressed when people are interviewed in a group situation are different from their views when expressed in individual, confidential interviews. Indeed, the contrasts in the opinions of people who have been interviewed both individually and in a group format can themselves prove illuminating.

Meetings

Meetings differ from group interviews in their purpose. Whereas group interviews may help the needs analyst to gather information from the group, meetings are more likely to be structured so that the participants can accomplish certain tasks. However, observing the process of the group while it is meeting and trying to accomplish a task may provide useful information about the people and program in question. The *delphi technique* is a meeting, or series of meetings, in which the task to be performed is reaching a consensus. For example, the opinions of a group of teachers might be elicited on a questionnaire. Then, based on the overall results, a meeting would be convened to discuss differences in opinion, minority opinions, and means for reaching a consensus. The delphi technique might be used to help teachers agree on an overall philosophy for the needs analysis, to build a consensus on the goals and objectives of the curriculum, and so forth. (For more on the delphi technique, see Uhl 1990.)

Advisory meetings can be set up in the early stages of a needs analysis to inform the staff and faculty about what a needs analysis is: its purposes, the techniques used, and perhaps the benefits to be gained. They can be conducted by specialists from outside the program or, more effectively, by the needs analysts themselves, who will be personally involved in the process. Most language teachers can benefit from learning more about curriculum development in general and needs analysis in particular. The teachers in a program are also more likely to be cooperative if they are treated with respect and included in the process.

Interest group meetings are generally convened to air differences that arise in a program. These differences in views may be between individuals or between large interest groups within the program. Teams can be convened to argue the relative merits of different program philosophies, different views of students' needs, different views on how much detail must be given in objectives, and so forth. The overall purpose is to resolve the differences through compromise or consensus (the delphi technique discussed above may help).

Review meetings are conducted to draw participants into the process of sifting through and analyzing the information gathered from other procedures. This form of meeting can facilitate many types of needs analysis decision making. For example, decisions can be made about what information to include, what to ignore, what relative weights to give to the different types of information, how to deal with conflicting information, and so forth. Review meetings can prove to be particularly valuable because they allow the needs analysts to add to the available labor pool (for analysis, synthesis, and decision making) and help to foster a sense of involvement in the needs analysis.

Questionnaires

Sometimes interviews and meetings reveal issues and questions that need to be pursued on a broader scale. Written questionnaires can prove helpful in this type of situation because questionnaires are more efficient for gathering information on a large scale than are many of the other procedures I have discussed. Nonetheless, the sorts of questions that can be posed on a questionnaire range enormously. Moreover, questionnaires can be designed to accomplish any of the following purposes. *Biodata surveys* are used to elicit facts about the background of each of the participants. Such facts can include each student's age, place of birth, sex, marital status, number of years of language study, and the like. *Opinion surveys* are considerably more complex because they are designed to uncover opinions and attitudes. A series of questions might be developed to determine what teachers think about the existing program, its objectives, the materials, tests, and so forth. Another useful type of information can be gathered using *self-ratings*. This procedure requires individuals to rate their own abilities, interest levels, motivations, and so on. Self-ratings are particularly useful for obtaining practical insights into the self-image of individuals. Participants might also be asked to do *judgmental ratings* in which they give their evaluation of various aspects of the program. For instance, students might be asked to judge the effectiveness of the program materials in terms of how useful and/or interesting they are. Finally, the *Q sort* combines several of the procedures defined above because it asks individuals to give their own attitudes, views, and opinions, but also to rank them in terms of importance.

Questionnaires of all kinds may turn out to be very useful in gathering large-scale information on the needs of students (for more on developing such instruments, see Babbie 1973; Bailey 1982; Henerson, Morris, & Fitz-Gibbon 1987; and Oppenheim 1966).

□ SELECTING AND CREATING PROCEDURES

Three characteristics must be considered when using any information-gathering procedures. Only then can the advantages and disadvantages of the different categories of procedures be explored.

Characteristics of Procedures

The three characteristics of sound information-gathering procedure are reliability, validity, and usability. Reliability and validity have numerous technical definitions that are beyond the scope of this book. (See Brown 1988 for a single chapter-length discussion of these issues, or Brown (forthcoming) for much more detail on these topics.) Nonetheless, reliability, validity, and usability can also be viewed as commonsense notions.

Reliability will be defined here as the consistency with which a procedure obtains information. Any procedure—whether it be a ruler for measuring length, a scale for determining weight, or a questionnaire for ascertaining attitudes—should obtain approximately the same results every time it is used to measure the same person or object. Otherwise, the results become useless or, at best, hard to interpret. Thus reliability must be considered when selecting or creating a procedure for analyzing needs. For instance, if a needs analyst wants to use a classroom interaction checklist, the reliability of the procedure should first be considered. Such reliability can be checked statistically or by commonsense examination of what happens when the procedure is used. If the results obtained are the same, or at least very similar, when it is used repeatedly or by different analysts, such consistency is an indication that the procedure is fairly reliable.

The *validity* of a procedure will be defined here as the degree to which it is measuring what it claims to measure. If a questionnaire purports to be a measure of the level of student motivation, it is important that it be just that, not a reflection of something entirely different. Again, there are statistical techniques that can be used to study this question, but at the very least each procedure involved in a needs analysis should be carefully examined question by question to determine two things: to what degree does it appear to measure what it claims to be measuring, and to what degree is that measurement appropriate for the particular needs assessment being conducted? If the answer to either question is dubious, the procedure should be revised to make it more valid or the procedure should be discarded (regardless of how reliable it may have appeared to have been at first).

Finally, the concept of *usability* must be considered. In most cases, this issue has to do with the degree to which a procedure is practical to use. Is it relatively easy to administer, to score, and to interpret? Asking such questions in the early stages of a needs analysis can save a great deal of trouble later. Even the most reliable and valid procedures can prove impractical in some situations. For example, in conducting a language needs analysis for a group of workers on an oil rig, the analysts may want to gather data on the actual language used in communication between foremen and workers on the rig site. However, practical realities (noise, danger, security, and so on) might make this impossible, so an alternative procedure might have to be used (for example, role-play situations designed to elicit target language behaviors).

Clearly, reliability, validity, and usability are interrelated and should probably be considered to be equally important. In other words, a procedure must logically be reliable, valid, and usable within a given context before it can be effectively used in a needs analysis.

Advantages and Disadvantages of Different Procedures

One statement about the observation of human behavior seems fairly safe: such observations are never perfect. In fact, all the procedures discussed here are imperfect, at least to some degree. Fortunately, they are imperfect in different ways, that is, each of these procedures has different strengths and different weaknesses. Thus if analysts use various combinations of procedures, they will create a stronger overall information-gathering process. In other words, multiple sources of information should be used in a needs analysis—although the specific combination appropriate for a given situation must be decided on the site by the needs analysts themselves (probably after input from program administration, faculty, and perhaps students). Table 2.3 may prove useful in sorting out which types of procedures can be most useful for answering the different types of questions defined above. These questions are separated into those with the most bearing on situation needs versus language needs.

□ CONSIDERATIONS SPECIFIC TO LANGUAGE NEEDS ANALYSIS

Table 2.3 shows which instruments may be appropriate for situation needs analysis, language needs analysis, or both. Other forms of analysis that are specific to the study of students' language needs have been borrowed from applied linguistics: discourse analysis and text analysis.

Table 2.3 Instruments, Procedures, and Appropriate Types of Questions

INSTRUMENTS AND PROCEDURES	APPROPRIATE FOR ADDRESSING					
	SITUATION NEEDS					LANGUAGE NEEDS
	PROBS	PRIOR	ABIL	ATTIT	SOL	
Existing information						
Records analysis	X		X			
Systems	X				X	
Literature review	X				X	
Letter writing	X				X	
Tests						
Proficiency	X		X			
Placement	X		X			
Diagnostic	X		X			
Achievement	X		X			
Observations						
Case studies	X					X
Diary studies	X					X
Behavior observation	X					X
Interactional analyses	X					X
Inventories	X	X				
Interviews						
Individual	X	X	X	X	X	X
Group	X	X	X	X	X	X
Meetings						
Delphi technique	X				X	X
Advisory	X	X				
Interest group	X	X				
Review	X	X	X	X	X	X
Questionnaire						
Biodata survey	X					X
Opinion survey	X			X		X
Self-ratings	X		X	X		X
Judgmental ratings	X	X		X		X
Q sort	X			X		X

Discourse Analysis

Direct observations and data collection on the language used in particular settings and for specific purposes may prove useful in studying students' language needs. Examples of such settings and purposes include the language used on oil rigs (discussed above), for job interviews, for university lectures, and in doctor-patient encounters. The focus of such investigations is to document the language and communication features commonly found in each setting. Initially, decisions have to be made about the units of analysis to use in studying the data (for example, whether to examine speech acts, sentence types, functions, clauses, grammatical constructions, morphemes, or vocabulary). The units of analysis will in turn reflect the needs analysts' views of the nature of language and language learning (that is, their theory of language expressed in the types of approaches discussed in Chapter One) and how the data are to be used. Such an analysis can isolate the kinds of language and communication activity the learners will ultimately have to understand or produce, and eventually generate objectives, tests, and instructional materials based on those activities. (See Sinclair & Coulthard 1975; Coulthard 1979; Hatch & Long 1980; Edmondson 1981; Hoey 1983; Crombie 1985; Cook 1989; McCarty 1991; and Coultard 1992, for more on discourse analysis.)

One way of using discourse analysis to study students' needs is described in the elaborate model provided in Munby (1978, pp. 190–98). He suggests the following nine parameters as the framework for a needs analysis:

1. participant: biographical facts and language background
2. purposive domain: the specific purposes for which the language will be used
3. setting: physical and psychosocial characteristics of the setting
4. interaction: the social relationships involved
5. instrumentality: medium, mode, and channel of communication
6. dialect: regional, class, and temporal
7. target level: language characteristics required and under what conditions
8. communicative event: events and functions
9. communicative key: attitude and tone.

The approach advocated by Munby is described in a book of 232 pages so my brief summary of a section from that book necessarily fails to capture it all. In general, Munby's framework emphasizes the subjective side of needs analysis because it relies heavily on the analyst's intuitions. Nevertheless, it offers a useful framework for observing and sorting through information about the types of discourse that students will eventually need to use.

Text Analysis

If the learners will encounter the target language primarily in print—that is, for purposes of reading or writing—text analysis may help in determining what the students will ultimately have to read or write. Many different genres and types of texts may come under scrutiny (for example, scientific discourse, newspaper editorials, or social science journal articles) in this form of analysis. Again, the units of analysis chosen (for instance, cohesive devices, rhetorical features, readability, or vocabulary) will tend to reflect the needs analysts' understandings of the nature of different kinds of texts and the analysts' belief systems with regard to the nature of language and language learning.

For example, in examining the textbooks used by undergraduates in science courses, an analyst might decide that the purpose of the analysis is to generate information on the vocabulary level of the textbooks, and/or the ratio of scientific vocabulary to general vocabulary, and/or the kinds of expository writing found in textbooks, and/or the kinds of topics covered. The analysts' biases will definitely affect the results of needs analyses in general and text analysis in particular. (See van Dijk 1977 or de Beaugrande & Dressler 1981 for more on text analysis.)

EXAMPLE NEEDS ANALYSES

The various needs assessment instruments and procedures discussed earlier can generate a large quantity and a wide variety of data. Such information provides a useful starting point for developing or evaluating a language program. I should stress, however, that data have little meaning in themselves. Data must be analyzed, interpreted, and evaluated before the resulting information can be applied to the practical realities of curriculum development. The applications of informal and formal needs analysis that were conducted at GELC and in the ELI at UHM should help to clarify how such needs analysis information can be used. However, the actual uses to which such information will be put in other programs may vary tremendously.

□ GUANGZHOU ENGLISH LANGUAGE CENTER, ZHONGSHAN UNIVERSITY

In the summer of 1980 the planning for GELC began at UCLA for a fall 1980 start-up in China. This program was somewhat unusual in that we had the luxury of designing the program from the very beginning without the baggage of established practices and prejudices to interfere. Three of the key Chinese faculty came to UCLA to work with us Americans in designing the program that we would put in place at Zhongda. At the outset, the needs analyses were relatively informal. Somehow by instinct we managed to think about both the language needs of our future students and the situation needs that we ourselves would have once we arrived in China. As such, our efforts may serve as a good example of areas to analyze in setting up a new program from scratch.

Existing Information

In preparation for the summer planning activities with our Chinese colleagues, a number of the American faculty had taken a course at UCLA on English for Specific Purposes (ESP), which had helped us to locate and sort through the literature on the topic. We found many useful articles in the literature—especially those about scientific discourse and about existing English for Science and Technology (EST) programs. In addition, we wrote letters and made phone calls to institutions that could share information on similar programs. These efforts saved us from having to reinvent everything from scratch.

Tests

We also knew, in very general terms, what to expect from the students who would be coming to GELC. By agreement with the Ministry of Education, the students had all been tested on a reduced version of the UCLA English as a Second Language Placement Examination (ESLPE), from which we were able to estimate the students' proficiency levels in terms of TOEFL scores. Initially, only students with estimated TOEFL scores higher than 450 were accepted. Since TOEFL was not administered in China at that time, we thought it wise to assemble a number of tests that we could use on site to roughly predict students' TOEFL scores. In addition, we planned to use retired versions of the ESLPE for placing the students into levels once we arrived on site. No provisions were made at this point for diagnostic or achievement testing.

Observations

At UCLA we were also in a position to do some useful observations of our own. For instance, during much of 1980 two teams consisting of three graduate students in the TESL master's degree program at UCLA were engaged in analyzing lecture discourse and reading texts in engineering English for the purpose of developing tests. This process involved doing interviews and holding meetings with engineering professors and students. Another team, of teachers this time, was analyzing the interactive discourse recorded in a set of videotaped panel discussions by scientists on various science topics. A third team was preparing videotaped lectures on the philosophy of science which were then analyzed for discourse elements that might be useful for teaching the listening skill. All available EST textbooks were collected and analyzed in terms of what I would now call approaches, syllabuses, techniques, and exercises to determine which ones would be appropriate for our program. Our Chinese colleagues were particularly helpful in gauging the level of materials that would be appropriate, in telling us about the learning styles that we would encounter, in estimating the relative strengths to expect in the skill areas, and so forth.

As to our situation needs, all necessary equipment, supplies, textbooks, and resource books needs had to be anticipated. We began by looking through the catalogs used at UCLA for purchasing supplies and equipment. We compiled a basic list of our program equipment and supply needs and held meetings to decide on other items that might be necessary. Since most of our initial purchases required "hard" currency (that is, U.S. dollars instead of PRC yuan), they had to be sorted out in advance. We also relied heavily on our Chinese colleagues to tell us what might be purchased in China using Chinese currency so as to minimize our hard currency purchases. Next, all the supplies and equipment were ordered, inventoried, and shipped. We also made a list of purchases that we could more sensibly make in Hong Kong just before entering the PRC, and also compiled a list of items that we could get in the PRC.

In addition, personal living requirements had to be considered. Housing for the Americans was planned and built in China; travel arrangements through Hong Kong to Guangzhou were planned and arranged; hard currency personal appliances such as hot water heaters, space heaters, and refrigerators were selected, bought, and shipped; and all necessary visas, shots, and family arrangements were made. Our Chinese colleagues were of immeasurable help in estimating all these situation needs in addition to serving as Chinese language teachers and friends.

To say the least, the summer of 1980 was a very busy one for this group of language teachers. Our focus was split between what our students' language needs would be and what we ourselves would need in that situation in order to deliver instruction. At times, launching this program in the PRC seemed only marginally simpler than delivering an equally large group of astronauts to the moon.

Once we arrived at Zhongda and began teaching, we realized that our views of the situation needs were inaccurate in many ways, but these problems were easily solved by buying equipment or supplies from the local economy, by improvising, or—as a last resort—by making trips to Hong Kong for purchases. More importantly, we found that our perceptions of the students' language needs were also inaccurate in many areas.

Naturally, we continued to draw on secondary sources, tests, and linguistic analyses for information on the students' language and situation needs, but we were now in a position to do needs assessment of a more primary nature. For instance, we began to administer tests for estimating TOEFL scores on a regular basis. These helped us to understand our students' needs in global terms. We also conducted classroom observations on informal and formal levels that helped us to zero in on specific problems that our Chinese students were encountering.

Meetings

Consonant with Chinese traditions, meetings were a dominant and useful part of gathering information on the needs of our students. These included weekly teachers meetings, regular seminars/workshops to discuss ESP issues, weekly meetings for each skill area, and weekly meetings for the multiple sections of each course. The number of meetings we attended seems staggering in retrospect, but they did not seem out of line at the time because we were teaching only three hours per day (in the morning) and were expected to spend the other half of our days in curriculum development and research activities. Thus we were being paid, in part, to attend these meetings, which were considered an essential part of the job.

We also conducted regular meetings with student representatives, who were elected from each of the classes. These meetings had three useful functions: (1) helping us to efficiently gather information on the students' views of their language and situation needs; (2) aiding us in disseminating information (including the teachers' views on various curriculum issues) to the students; and (3) providing a vehicle for venting any student discontent and anger before it could become destructive. In short, these student representative meetings provided a way to make the students understand that they had a voice in the program and a stake in its success.

Questionnaires

One particularly useful result of these student representative meetings was a bilingual questionnaire that was developed jointly by the teachers and the student representatives. This questionnaire was designed to investigate the students' attitudes toward various aspects of the program—particularly materials, teaching, and logistical issues. However, describing how we used this questionnaire begins to trespass on the discussion of program evaluation (which is, after all, a sort of ongoing needs analysis) so I will postpone this discussion until Chapter Seven. However, three quick observations are warranted before I move on to the ELI example.

First, the GELC example I have just described suggests a series of orderly and organized needs assessment activities. From the perspective of those conducting these analyses, however, there was more of an air of chaos and hysteria, which is hard to convey in prose. Nevertheless, our focus remained clear throughout: we wanted to determine the students' language needs. We were also unusually aware of situation needs because so many of us (teachers and students alike) came together at Zhongda from other places.

Second, one of the dramatic mistakes that we made (at least from my point of view) was that we waited for almost six months before trying to shape the needs analysis information into tentative sets of goals and objectives. We did eventually see the error of our ways, as I will explain in the "Example Objectives" section of the next chapter.

Third, early in the process, we realized that determination of students' needs was an ongoing (never-ending) process and that a wide variety of different information sources would prove important—from literature review and discourse analysis on the formal end of a continuum, to discussions in the hall and rumor control at the other end. We also realized that it was important to remain open and flexible, and never to view the curriculum as a finished product. This flexibility may initially have been due to the particular (or is it *peculiar?*) personalities involved rather than to any special foresight on our parts. Nonetheless, flexibility proved invaluable as the program developed and necessarily changed.

□ ENGLISH LANGUAGE INSTITUTE, UNIVERSITY OF HAWAII AT MANOA

The needs assessments conducted in the ELI were done under quite different conditions. The ELI was a long-established institution, wherein curriculum development had become stagnant and seemed to need a boost. At UHM, we had the luxury of being associated with a master's program, from which we could draw talent and energy in the form of graduate student projects. Because I was coteaching a course in Language Curriculum Development, teams of master's students could be encouraged (but not required) to do needs analyses and objectives setting for ELI courses. The first time this course was offered, two graduate students did an outstanding job of analyzing the academic listening needs of ELI students at UHM (see Kimzin & Proctor 1986). Their paper not only served as the basis for developing the tests, materials, and teaching in listening, but also functioned as a model for the other needs analyses that were performed later (for instance, see Asahina & Okuda 1987; Weaver, Pickett, Kiu, & Cook 1987; and Brown, Chaudron, & Pennington 1988, for foreign teaching assistant speaking skills; see Loschky, Stanley, Cunha, & Singh 1987; and Asahina, Bergman, Conklin, Guth, & Lockhart 1988, for academic reading; and Power 1986, for academic writing). Hence a brief summary of Kimzin and Proctor (1986) will give a feeling for what all of the needs analyses in the ELI were like.

Literature Review

Kimzin and Proctor first turned to a search of the literature on teaching academic listening with the purpose of finding information on the state of the art and on what had previously been done to teach academic listening in other programs. Their discussion cited Rothkopf (1970), G. Brown (1977), Robin, Fox, Martello, and Archable (1977), Richards (1983), Ur (1984), Dunkel (1985), Murphy (1985), Works (1985), and others.

Several in-house reports that had some bearing on the issues involved were also located. They were Harper, Gleason, and Ogama (1983) on the listening needs at UHM, and Mason (1985) on general needs in the ELI at UHM. Both of these proved somewhat dated, but useful as a starting point.

Table 2.4   ELI Student Survey According to Class Types (Kimzin & Proctor 1986)

CLASS TYPE	# OF 70/80 STUDENTS
1. Large lecture: 100% lecture, 0% discussion	41
2. Small lecture: 80% lecture, 20% discussion	23
3. Seminar-type: 50% lecture, 50% discussion	30

Initial Survey

Before they actually began extensive research at UHM, Kimzin and Proctor conducted a quick survey during the spring of 1986 in one ELI 70 class and one ELI 80 class ($N = 52$) to identify the types of content area courses the students were taking in addition to their ELI requirements (see Tables 2.4 and 2.5).

Case Studies

Based on these survey results, Art 474, Physics 274, Public Health 777, and Economics 150 were chosen for further investigation because they were considered representative courses in the popular areas of liberal arts, science, and business. These courses ranged in type from small seminars to large (150-student) lecture situations. Case studies were conducted in each course in order to specify the listening, note-taking, and discussion skills needed for these particular types of classes and fields of study.

Each class was observed twice and tape recorded. Then interviews were conducted with each of the course instructors, as well as with ELI students con-

Table 2.5   ELI Student Survey According to Content Areas (Kimzin & Proctor 1986)

CONTENT AREA	# OF 70/80 STUDENTS
1. Liberal Arts	31
2. Science	25
3. Business	20
4. Engineering	13
5. Mathematics	4

currently enrolled in the courses. Kimzin and Proctor carefully recorded and analyzed all of this information and included many relevant documents in their appendices. For instance, the Class Observation Form and Instructor and Student Interview Guides were all appended to their needs analysis report.

During the case studies the needs analysts chose to focus on the following: (1) the actual difficulties both the instructors and their foreign students may have in content classes, (2) students' preferred learning styles, and (3) students' coping strategies. Thus each of the classes was analyzed in detail for various aspects of lecture style and discourse, both of which were felt to be important aspects of the language needs of our students. The interviews conducted with the instructors and the ELI students provided information that was much more closely related to the situation needs. Most of the information obtained in these case studies (whether from observations or interviews) was presented in narrative form for each of the four courses in turn. This case-study approach in conjunction with the information obtained in the literature review proved to be useful for gaining insights into the lecture-listening processes involved in a variety of settings, as well as for formulating tentative goals, microskills, and objectives for the ELI listening courses.

Questionnaires

The needs analysts next administered an ELI student questionnaire that was an attempt to ensure that the tentative goals, microskills, and objectives were consistent with the foreign students' self-perceived listening needs and not biased too much by the expectations of the needs analysts and the teachers. To that end, one section of ELI 70 and three sections of ELI 80 were surveyed ($N = 67$). Along with biodata information, the questionnaire provided a checklist that listed 27 tentative microskills under the following categories: lecture-listening, note-taking, and discussion skills. Students were asked to check *yes, no,* or *not sure* to questions about the need for each skill and the degree to which the skills were presently taught in their ELI courses. This questionnaire was also appended to the needs analysis report.

Table 2.6 offers a summary of the biodata information that was collected, and Table 2.7 offers a summary of the students' perceptions with regard to the lecture-listening category of their listening needs. Other tables displayed the results for note-taking and discussion skills. Notice how clearly the results are summarized in Table 2.7 for both types of questions and how the responses are also ranked in order of importance.

Meetings

A particularly important meeting proved to be one attended by the needs analysts, the ELI administrators, current and future instructors, a professional note

Table 2.6   ELI 70 and ELI 80 Student Biodata (Kimzin & Proctor 1986)

$N = 28$

Native Language:

10	Chinese	(36%)	1	Samoan	(4%)
5	Vietnamese	(18%)	1	Tamil	(4%)
3	Indonesian	(11%)	1	Lingala/French	(4%)
3	Korean	(11%)	1	Kikngo	(4%)
1	Japanese	(4%)	1	Man`de	(4%)
1	Thai	(4%)			

Age:

  18 to 57 years
  Mode = 24 years; Mean = 26.3 years

Sex:

  25 Males   (86%)
   3 Females (11%)

Time in U.S.:

  6 months to 7 years
  Mode = 6 months; Mean = 3.2 years

Semesters at UH:

15	1 semester	(54%)	3	3 semesters	(11%)
9	2 semesters	(32%)	1	4 semesters	(4%)

Semesters at other American universities:

14	0 semesters	(50%)	3	5 semesters	(11%)
2	1 semester	(7%)	1	6 semesters	(4%)
2	3 semesters	(7%)	1	8 semesters	(4%)
5	4 semesters	(18%)			

Academic major:

8	Engineering	(29%)	5	Social sciences	(18%)
4	Science	(14%)	3	Humanities	(11%)
8	Liberal arts/ undeclared	(29%)			

Current student status:

18	Undergraduate	(64%)
10	Graduate	(36%)

Table 2.7 ELI Students' Perceptions of Listening Skills (Kimzin & Proctor 1986)

RANK	SKILL NEEDED IN ALC COURSES		SKILL PRACTICED IN ALC COURSES	RANK
		A. Listening to Lectures		
1	25 (86%)	Identify the main ideas	18 (67%)	7
1	25 (86%)	Identify persuasive state-- ments and supporting details	21 (75%)	1
3	23 (82%)	Understand meanings of new vocabulary and terms	20 (77%)	3
4	22 (76%)	Identify cause-and-effect relationship	19 (70%)	5
5	21 (72%)	Identify supporting ideas	21 (72%)	1
5	21 (72%)	Identify comparisons and contrasts	20 (69%)	3
7	20 (69%)	Identify the major topic	17 (61%)	8
8	19 (66%)	Understand an explanation of a graph, chart, or formula	10 (36%)	11
9	18 (64%)	Understand colloquial sayings and idioms	19 (70%)	5
10	17 (61%)	Understand lecturer's body language	15 (56%)	9
11	13 (46%)	Recognize cultural references to understand words	14 (52%)	10

taker, and a business English consultant. The primary purpose of this meeting was to discuss tentative goals, microskills, and objectives as they had been formulated from all of the above information. As Kimzin and Proctor (1986, p. 30) put it:

> At this point within the research project, there was a need to obtain feedback from the ELI staff on whether the proposed microskills were representative of listening behaviors in university courses and whether they were valid for ALC [academic listening comprehension] instruction. We also felt that the instructors' comments would indicate either general acceptance or rejection of a skills-based curriculum.

Summarizing the Results

The final product of this needs assessment process was a list of goals, organized as shown in Table 2.8 and listed in great detail as shown in the excerpt given in Table 2.9. Here, goals were meant to provide general descriptive statements that outline course aims, and objectives were meant to be the means by which microskills could be operationalized with the ultimate aim of reaching the overall goals. These goals, microskills, and objectives, in turn, would provide the listening courses with a solid basis for test development, materials development, and teaching. This list was the best available at the time because it was based on a wide variety of information sources, as well as professional judgment within the ELI. However, I must note that no such list of objectives should ever be considered perfect and finished. In fact, in the ensuing years, the ELI perceptions of students' needs have shifted considerably and so have its objectives. Nevertheless, Kimzin and Proctor (1986) provided a foundation. None of the curriculum development that has been accomplished in recent years in the ELI would have been possible without the hard work of all those graduate students cited above, who put their hearts and souls into trying to figure out the language and situation needs of our students.

SUMMARY

In this chapter a number of basic decisions were discussed because they must be addressed before even starting a needs analysis: Who will be involved? What types of information will be gathered? A variety of potential tools were also listed in six categories: existing information, tests, observations, interviews, meetings, and questionnaires. All these tools shared three important characteristics that must be considered in selecting or creating them: reliability, validity, and usability. Discourse and text analysis were also discussed because of their particular

**Table 2.8   Goals and Instructional Categories for
Academic Listening Courses at UHM (Kimzin & Proctor 1986)**

ELI 70 GOALS		ELI 80 GOALS
#1	Students will be able to follow the basic ideas of a lecture.	#1	Students will be able to synthesize arguments within a lecture.

A.   Lecture organization
B.   Cohesion
C.   Vocabulary
D.   Lecturer's style

| #2 | Students will be able to use effective note–taking skills. | #2 | Students will be able to devise and reference a note–taking system compatible with their academic needs. |

A.   Taking notes
B.   Using notes

| #3 | Students will be able to effect learning by actively participating in academic situations. | #3 | Students will be able to develop coherent arguments in class discussions and in oral presentations. |

A.   Classroom discussions
B.   ELI 70: Student-Teacher conferences
     ELI 80: Oral presentations

importance in language needs assessment. The chapter ended with an explanation of how needs analyses were conducted in the GELC and ELI programs. The uses to which such information can be put will be further amplified in the remainder of this book.

Table 2.9   Abridged Goals, Objectives, and Microskills for ELI 70
(Kimzin & Proctor 1986)

GOAL #1   STUDENTS WILL BE ABLE TO FOLLOW THE BASIC IDEAS OF A LECTURE.

MICROSKILLS	JUSTIFICATION SOURCES

A. *Lecture Organization*

70/1 **Identify the major topic.**

Case studies
  Art 474 p. 20
Student questionnaire
  Ranked 8th out of 11
Richards (1983)
  Item 2
Harper et al. (1983)
  Item 1.0

OBJECTIVE: Identify 2 out of 3 major topics within a 30-minute academic lecture by writing a 1- to 3-sentence explanation for each topic with 80% accuracy.

70/2 **Identify main ideas.**

Case studies
  Art 474 p. 22
Student questionnaire
  Ranked 7th out of 11
Richards (1983)
  Item 3
Harper et al. (1983)
  Item 1.1

OBJECTIVE: Identify 3 out of 5 main ideas within a 30-minute academic lecture by correctly answering 4-item multiple-choice comprehension questions with 80% accuracy.

70/3 **Identify supporting details.**

Case studies
  Art 474 p. 22
Student questionnaire
  Ranked 1st out of 11
Richards (1983)
  Item 3
Harper et al. (1983)
  Item 1.1

OBJECTIVE: Identify supporting details within a 30-minute academic lecture by marking statements as true or false with 90% accuracy.

■ ■ ■ *CHECKLIST*

The following checklist will serve as a good point of review for the concepts involved in needs analysis as well as a guide for actually performing the steps in a needs analysis:

- □ Have the basic decisions been made before starting?
  - □ Who will be involved?
    - □ Target group?
    - □ Audience?
    - □ Needs analysts?
    - □ Resource groups?
  - □ What types of information will be gathered?
    - □ Discrepancy philosophy?
    - □ Democratic philosophy?
    - □ Analytic philosophy?
    - □ Diagnostic philosophy?
  - □ Which points of view will be taken?
    - □ Situation versus language needs?
    - □ Objective versus subjective needs?
    - □ Linguistic content versus learning processes?
  - □ Have possible interactions between philosophies and viewpoints been considered?

- □ How will information be gathered?
  - □ Have all five types of questions been considered?
    - □ Problems?
    - □ Priorities?
    - □ Abilities?
    - □ Attitudes?
    - □ Solutions?
  - □ Have a variety of different types of instruments been employed?
    - □ Tests?
    - □ Existing records?
    - □ Observations?
    - □ Interviews?

☐   Meetings?

☐   Questionnaires?

☐ Have the important characteristics of measurement been considered in selecting or creating those instruments from at least a common-sense point of view?

    ☐   Reliability?

    ☐   Validity?

    ☐   Usability?

☐ Have the advantages and disadvantages of each type of instrument been considered in choosing which to use?

☐ Have the factors specific to language needs analysis been considered?

    ☐   Discourse analysis?

    ☐   Text analysis?

☐ How will the information be used to make decisions about each of the following?

    ☐   See Chapters Three through Seven

■ ■ ■ *TERMS*

abilities questions	achievement tests
advisory meetings	analytic philosophy
attitudes questions	audience group
behavior observation	biodata surveys
case studies	delphi technique
democratic philosophy	diagnostic philosophy
diagnostic tests	diary studies
discourse analysis	discrepancy philosophy
group meetings	individual meetings
interactional analysis	interactional observation
interest group meetings	inventories
judgmental ratings	language needs
learning process	letter writing
linguistic content	literature review
needs analysis	needs analyst group
needs assessment	objective needs
opinion surveys	participant

placement tests
problems
Q sort
reliability
review meetings
situation needs
subjective needs
target group
validity

priorities
proficiency tests
records analysis
resource group
self-ratings
solutions
systems analysis
usability

■ ■ ■ REVIEW QUESTIONS

1. Who should be involved in a needs analysis? Target group? Audience? Resource group? Needs analysts? All parties involved? Why?

2. What philosophy is the most effective in a needs analysis? Discrepancy philosophy? Democratic philosophy? Analytic philosophy? Diagnostic philosophy? Some combination of these philosophies? Why?

3. What position is most appropriate for each of the following viewpoints? Situation versus language needs? Objective versus subjective needs? Linguistic content versus learning processes? Why?

4. How might answers to question two affect answers to question three, and vice versa?

5. Frame at least two needs analysis questions (ones that would appropriately be asked of students) for each of the following question categories: problems, priorities, abilities, attitudes, and solutions.

6. What are the fundamental differences between situation and language needs in terms of the procedures that will be used to collect information on them?

7. What are the three important characteristics necessary for developing quality needs analysis instruments? Are these necessarily statistical concepts?

8. What are the advantages and disadvantages of each of the following categories of needs analysis instruments? Existing information? Tests? Observations? Interviews? Meetings? Questionnaires?

9. What are the factors specific to language needs analysis? How can those factors be investigated through use of text or discourse analysis?

10. How should the information gleaned from a needs analysis be used? What types of decisions should be based on these perceptions? Is the needs analysis ever finished?

■ ■ ■ APPLICATIONS

A1. Look back at the "Example Needs Analyses" section and choose either the GELC or the ELI program description. Apply the checklist provided in the "Summary" to that description insofar as it is possible.

A2. How would you rate the quality of the needs assessment in the example program that you chose? How would you improve it? Would it make a difference if you had unlimited resources? What differences?

B1. Do an informal needs analysis for some language course or program in which you are involved.

B2. Better yet, form a team and work together with others on a formal needs analysis for some language course or program with which you are involved.

Chapter 3
Goals and Objectives

INTRODUCTION

In some quarters, the view is taken (often with an air of sarcasm) that any ESL/EFL program that is not ESP (English for Specific Purposes) is ENOP (English for No Obvious Purpose). In other words, the purpose of any language program should be clear to the participants and to the outside world. Since purposeful curriculum is a central idea in systematic curriculum design, the focus of this chapter will be on transforming the information gathered in a needs analysis into usable statements that describe the purpose(s) of a program. The chapter will address the following topics: (1) the nature and relationships among needs, goals, and objectives; (2) the processes involved in specifying instructional objectives; (3) arguments for and against the use of objectives; and (4) example goals and objectives.

NEEDS, GOALS, AND OBJECTIVES

The process of needs analysis can generate a tremendous amount of information that must be sorted and utilized in some way within the curriculum. One way to use this information is to apply what has been learned in the needs analysis for the formulation of program goals and objectives.

☐ GOALS

Program *goals* are defined in this book as general statements concerning desirable and attainable program purposes and aims based on perceived language and situation needs. In a brand-new program, these perceptions may be based solely on a formal needs analysis; in a well-established program, such perceptions will more likely be based on information gathered along the way during the ongoing evaluation process. In deriving goals from perceived needs, four points should be remembered:

1. Goals are general statements of the program's purposes.
2. Goals should usually focus on what the program hopes to accomplish in the future, and particularly on what the students should be able to do when they leave the program.

3. Goals can serve as one basis for developing more precise and observable objectives.

4. Goals should never be viewed as permanent, that is, they should never become set in cement.

The primary reason for this last point is that the needs being addressed are only *perceived* needs and such perceptions may change. In fact, actual changes may occur in both language needs and situation needs if new and different types of students enter the program. This happened at GELC when our initial population of students, who were mostly experienced Chinese scientists older than 35, gradually shifted and became a population mostly made up of students in their 20s who had just finished undergraduate studies. The difference in student ages itself caused some significant changes, but the fact that the older cohort of students had been educated before the Chinese Cultural Revolution, while the younger cohort had been educated during or after it, caused even more radical adjustments. All in all, the language learning needs of the students changed rather dramatically, and so did our goals.

Goals may take many shapes. They may be language and situation-centered as in the three goals included in the statement: "In our program, the students will learn how to fill out forms in French, read a menu, and order a meal." They may be functional, like in the statement: "The goal of our course is that the students will be able to converse in social German with a focus on greetings, conversational openers, polite rejoinders, and farewells." They may be strictly structural, like in the statement: "The center's aim is to help students learn the grammatical system of French."

A curriculum will often be organized around the goals of the program. Thus the goals and syllabuses of a program may be related. However, the needs analysis might indicate needs that have more to do with attitudes and feelings than with syllabus-related linguistic systems (see the discussion of cognitive and affective domains later in this chapter). One such goal might be that "the students will gain an appreciation of French culture." Another goal might be that "the program fosters acceptance of cultural differences between countries." Goal statements are attempts to delineate in general terms what the program hopes to accomplish within the time allotted.

The process of defining goals makes the curriculum developers and participants consider, or reconsider, the program's purposes with specific reference to what the students should be able to do when they leave the program. Thus goal statements can serve as a basis for developing more specific descriptions of the kinds of learning behaviors the program will address. These more specific descriptions are sometimes called instructional objectives.

□ OBJECTIVES

If curriculum goals are defined as statements of the desirable and attainable curriculum purposes and aims based on the perceived language and situation needs of the participants in a program, what makes objectives different? *Instructional objectives* will be defined here as specific statements that describe the particular knowledge, behaviors, and/or skills that the learner will be expected to know or perform at the end of a course or program. Direct assessment of the objectives at the end of a course will provide evidence that the instructional objectives, and by extension the program goals, have been achieved, or have not been achieved.

Consider the following "objectives" that were stated for an upper-level ESL for academic purposes class at a well-known American university:

> By the end of the course, a student will be able to:
> 1. Prepare a term paper (including footnotes, bibliography, title page, and so forth).
> 2. Take notes on a lecture.
> 3. Answer questions following such a talk.

In all fairness, it must be pointed out that the course had 17 other "objectives," which varied considerably in level of specificity. Nevertheless, a statement like "a student will be able to prepare a term paper" is far too general to fit the definition of an objective as I have given it here.

The three "objectives" do match the definition I have given for curriculum goals. Looking just at the first one, it seems reasonable to want the students in an upper-level academic English program to be able to write a term paper. If the needs analysis indicates that writing a term paper is indeed a need, then such a goal should be stated—but as a goal, not as an objective. Only after considerable analysis of the performances and skills involved in the process of doing a term paper could instructional objectives be stated. These objectives would then serve as building blocks that would lead to accomplishing the broader curriculum goal.

The primary question, at a very practical level, is whether the difference between goals and objectives is clear. Consider, for instance, whether the following seem more like curriculum goals or instructional objectives:

> By the end of the course, the students will be able to:
> 1. Understand conversational English.
> 2. Correctly underline sentences that function as examples within 600 word passages of 11th grade reading level on general science topics three out of four times.
> 3. Develop oral language skills that will prepare them to participate in class discussions, make oral presentations before an audience, and respond to questions, as well as continue to improve through self-evaluation of speech.
> 4. Find and write down the library call numbers for 10 books found in the card catalog when supplied with only the author and title with 90 percent accuracy.

The odd-numbered items in this list seem to me to be curriculum goals while the even-numbered ones are probably specific enough to be considered instructional objectives. The level of specificity is the single-most-distinguishing characteristic between goals and objectives. The examples illustrate that the level of specificity is not a simple function of the length of the statement. For instance, statement three (a goal) is quite lengthy, yet it is so general in content that it must be a goal.

In distinguishing between goals and objectives, it is probably easiest to consider the extremes. Ask yourself if the statement is closer to a very general goal or to a very specific instructional objective. The trick is to decide whether the statement is closer to the general or the specific end of the continuum. At the most general extreme, consider the course descriptions that are found in many U.S. university catalogs. For instance, the description of ELI 80 at the University of Hawaii at Manoa includes the following statement: "Intensive work in understanding lectures, taking lecture notes, writing examinations, and study skills" (UHM 1987, p. 81). On a continuum from general to specific, it seems clear that this description contains four very general goals for the ELI 80 course. Similar goals are stated in the catalog descriptions for the other seven ELI courses. These eight course descriptions, taken together, could be said to form a set of goals for the entire ELI program.

At the other extreme on the continuum are very specific instructional objectives. These are easy to spot because they are specific, and they are specific because they have the three essential characteristics indicated by Mager (1975, p. 23), that is, they include three components:

1. Performance (what the learner will be able to do)
2. Conditions (important conditions under which the performance is expected to occur)
3. Criterion (the quality or level of performance that will be considered acceptable)

What are Mager's three components in the following instructional objective?

By the end of the course, the students will be able to write the full forms of selected abbreviations drawn from pages 6–8 of the course textbook with 80 percent accuracy.

The performance part of the objective probably includes the fact that the students "will be able to write the full forms of selected abbreviations." This is what they are expected to be able to do. The conditions under which the performance is likely to occur include the fact that the students are only responsible for certain abbreviations (that is, those on pages 6–8). The criterion level of acceptable performance is set at 80 percent accuracy for this objective. The form of an instructional objective is almost always like the example given above, so with practice such objectives become increasingly easy to recognize and understand. Remember: instructional objectives occupy the very specific end of a continuum at the opposite end from general goals.

Now reconsider the four example statements:

1. Understand conversational English.
2. Correctly underline sentences that function as examples within 600–word passages of 11th grade reading level on general science topics three out of four times.
3. Develop oral language skills that will prepare them to participate in class discussions, make oral presentations before an audience, and respond to questions, as well as continue to improve through self-evaluation of speech.
4. Find and write down the library call numbers for 10 books found in the card catalog when supplied with only the author and title with 90 percent accuracy.

Statements two and four are instructional objectives because they are closer to that more specific end of the continuum and because they contain the characteristics described by Mager. In contrast, statements one and three are goals because they are much closer to the general end of the continuum and lack the characteristics Mager advocates for precision. Knowing about Mager's three characteristics—performance, conditions, and criterion—can help not only in distinguishing between the goals and objectives of other institutions, but also in formulating clear and concise objectives for a language program.

Statements of the aims and purposes of a language program can take many alternative forms. However, such statements will all fall somewhere along a continuum that has very general goals on one end and strict instructional objectives on the other end. In some cases, as in the college catalog example I just discussed, it is useful to have statements of general goals. In other cases, it is necessary to produce more precise statements like those at the other end of the continuum. Thus in developing curriculum, it may prove necessary for planners to derive objectives from goals, or vice versa. In either case, the activity will force curriculum developers to think about the purposes of the program at several levels of specificity.

□ FROM GOALS TOWARD OBJECTIVES

Developing statements of perceived needs into program goals, and these in turn into clear objectives, is an effective way to clarify what should be going on in the language classroom. Once having thought through what will be taught in each classroom, planners can make efforts to coordinate across courses and throughout an entire language program. In other words, the process of converting perceptions of students' needs into goals and objectives provides the basic units that can in turn be used to define and organize all teaching activities into a cogent curriculum. Once objectives are in hand, the basic elements of the students' needs can be analyzed, assessed, and classified to create a coherent teaching/learning experience. In short, objectives provide the building blocks from which curriculum can be created, molded, and revised.

Logically, this process of restating needs in terms of program goals and then breaking them down into precise instructional objectives will begin with a careful examination of the needs of the students as discovered in any available needs analysis or program description documents. Consider, for example, the results of a needs analysis conducted by Schmidt (1981). Using a case study approach to needs assessment, she found English for academic purposes (EAP) needs as follows:

1.   The need to understand the implicit relationships between terms in a table or outline presented in lectures.
2.   The need to be able, in reviewing the notes, to understand the implicit relationship in order to fill in the connecting prose that ties the main parts of an entire concept together.
3.   The need to be able to deal simultaneously with a new concept and new vocabulary presented in a lecture in order to express that concept in her notes in English.
4.   The need to be able to express generalizations or definitions in an essay exam, instead of simply giving an example.
5.   The need to be able to do all of the above under time pressure.

The perceived needs found by Schmidt can be changed into statements of course (or program) goals with relative ease. For instance, with a few minor changes, the following program goals might be created:

By the end of our program, the students will be able to:
1.   Understand the implicit relationships between terms in a table or outline presented in lectures.
2.   Understand the implicit relationship in order to fill in the connecting prose that ties the main parts of an entire concept together.
3.   Deal simultaneously with a new concept and new vocabulary presented in a lecture in order to express that concept in notes in English.
4.   Express generalizations or definitions in an essay exam, instead of simply giving an example.
5.   Do all of the above under time pressure.

However, this example of converting perceived needs into goals may be deceptively easy. In other situations the perceived needs may be specified in great detail. As a result, the detailed needs may have to be classified and collapsed into general categories before they can be expressed as general course or program goals. In still other situations, the perceived needs may be stated so generally that they must be narrowed and better defined before useful program goals can be derived from them. In all situations, however, the overall purpose is to state the needs of the students in terms of realizable goals for the course or program.

With goal statements in hand, the next step for planners is to determine if it is necessary and possible to narrow the scope even further by breaking the goals down into logical subunits that will help to clarify what it is that the students should be able to do by the end of each course. One way to do this is to break the goals into their smallest units and classify them together into a set that might work well together as objectives.

Let's once again examine the goals that were derived above from Schmidt's (1981) needs analysis:

1. Understand the implicit relationships between terms in a table or outline presented in lectures.
2. Understand the implicit relationship in order to fill in the connecting prose that ties the main parts of an entire concept together.

These two goals can be analyzed into three parts: one related to tables, another about outlines, and a third focused on essays. These parts can then be reorganized into three potentially related objectives as follows:

By the end of the course the students will be able to identify implicit relationships between parts of a concept: in a table, in an outline, or in an essay.

Breaking goals down into their basic components and logically reorganizing those components into classes of more specific potential objectives can also lead to rethinking initial perceptions concerning students' needs. For instance, the classifications created above might spur rethinking other ways that implicit relationships may be important. In a teachers' meeting, perhaps the suggestion arises that examples of implicit relationships should be introduced through use of flow charts because the arrows would help the students to see the relationships with relative ease. Perhaps another teacher points out how implicit relationships in a table may be expressed in the prose accompanying the table. Thus the group may decide to expand on the initially perceived needs in order to fulfill those needs or may indeed change views on what the students actually do need. This latter possibility would probably require confirming the reality of the newly perceived needs by conducting further needs assessment.

In the end, this group of curriculum developers might derive five potential objectives from the two goals given above as follows:

By the end of the course the students will be able to identify implicit relationships in academic English between parts of a concept: in a flow chart, in a table, and in an outline, as well as in the prose describing a chart or table and in an essay.

Another group of curriculum developers, even in the unlikely event that they came up with the same perceived needs, might decide that students really only need to understand the implicit relationships in tables because the connections are so patently clear in outlines. Thus the scope of the originally perceived needs can be reduced or completely abandoned on the basis of differing points of view, attitudes among the curriculum designers, new information about the students, or directives from higher up in the administration of a program. In other words, the same perceived language needs in different programs (or even in the same program but at different times) may result in entirely different end results because of situation needs and constraints, or because of differences in views on approaches, syllabuses, techniques, and exercises held by different groups of language educators. In all cases, the aim should be to isolate and state potential objectives (based on the goals) with as much precision as makes sense in the context. The curriculum developers will then be in a position to use the guidelines I offer in the next section to formulate still clearer instructional objectives.

The steps involved in narrowing the perceptions of students' needs to realizable program goals and, further, to instructional objectives can be summarized as follows:

1. Examine the needs of the students as discovered and presented in the needs analysis documents.
2. State the needs of the students in terms of realizable goals for the program.
3. Narrow the scope of the resulting goal statements:
    a. By analyzing them into their smallest units
    b. By classifying those units into logical groupings
    c. By thinking through exactly what it is that the students need to know or be able to do to achieve the goals
4. State the smaller more specific goals as objectives with as much precision as makes sense in the context using the guidelines given in the remainder of this chapter.

This transition from needs to goals to potential objectives is far from a scientific one. In truth, all curriculum developers must eventually recognize the political nature of what they are doing and make the best of it. To do this, curriculum specialists will have to abandon any illusions they have concerning "scientific" ways to determine the language and situation needs of the participants in a program and any beliefs that these needs can be realized as sets of perfect objectives for the students to achieve. Needs analyses are far from perfect. Any needs analysis is at best an attempt to make sense out of the complexity and confusion that makes up the field of language teaching. One way that the disarray of our profession can be reduced is by finding new possibilities and patterns in the things that we think the students need to learn. However, any such attempt is necessarily filtered through the perceptions of those conducting the analysis. In addition, deriving goals and objectives from those perceived needs and implementing them as instruction changes the shape of those perceptions, even as they emerge. All of this emphasizes the tentative nature of needs analysis and the impermanence of curriculum, but, in my view, this impermanence does not detract from the usefulness of such endeavors as a process.

GETTING INSTRUCTIONAL OBJECTIVES ON PAPER

Working out the goals and objectives of a program based on the perceived needs of the students can be an interesting and productive process in itself. However, sooner or later, the results of these efforts must be formalized and written down.

□ SOURCES OF IDEAS FOR OBJECTIVES

A number of sources are available to help formulate objectives from the goals of a program. These include other programs and their curriculums, the books and journals that constitute the language teaching literature, and educational taxonomies that were worked out as far back as the 1950s.

Other Language Programs

Sometime during the process of formulating goals and objectives, or earlier during the needs analysis stage, letters can and should be written to similar programs. Any statements of goals and objectives or any course descriptions that those programs are willing to share can be very useful: redundancy of effort will be avoided, and new, creative ideas for student needs, goals, and objectives may come to light. Ultimately, our field would benefit from a clearinghouse for language teaching objectives similar to organizations that have surfaced in the past few decades in the education field (for example, the International Objectives Exchange in Culver City, California). In the interim, we will have to rely on the good will of our colleagues.

The Literature

Other sources of ideas for filling out the goals and objectives in a program are the numerous published accounts of similar efforts around the world. Examination of the books and journals devoted to language teaching, especially with an eye for topics like needs analysis, goals and objectives, and curriculum development, will lead to the realization that language teachers have been working on these issues for years. For example, ideas for objectives might come from a wide assortment of books and articles ranging from Steiner's (1975) book on objectives to the Finocchiaro and Brumfit (1983) or Nunan (1991) books on curriculum development, and from the Findley and Nathan (1980) article on using objectives to teach communicative competence to the Richards (1983) article on listening comprehension.

One particularly rich source of ideas for objectives is the van Ek and Alexander (1980) book, which was prepared for the Council of Europe. This important document details the objectives for a functional unit credit system of language teaching for adults. Curriculum developers will find that this book is a rich source for detailed lists of different situations in which adults are likely to use language and the language functions that are apt to be useful in those situations. Unlike the situational syllabuses I discussed in Chapter One, the situations delineated in van Ek and Alexander are described in terms of the social and psychological roles in language use, settings, topics, and so forth. Table 3.1 shows part of the list of useful language functions that van Ek and Alexander suggest. Their book also provides lists of the useful vocabulary and grammar (called "exponents" in this case) for teaching adult students, and devotes three chapters to discussion of objectives and one to behavioral specifications (in the form of the examples shown below in Table 3.7).

The point I wish to make is not so much that this article or that book is the final answer to a curriculum designer's dreams, but rather that there are many resources available to anyone ready to search them out. While I am writing this book, other useful articles and books are no doubt being produced, so I advise my readers to take the time to look for this type of information. Early efforts in this area may save a great deal of energy in the long run.

Taxonomies

In sorting through all the information on students' needs, and program goals and objectives, the kinds of factors you are dealing with in language learning programs can be grouped into two very broad categories. More or less parallel to the distinction I made in Chapter Two between language and situation needs are the generally accepted distinctions between the cognitive and affective goals of education—sometimes called the cognitive and affective domains. H. D. Brown (1988) provides a good introductory source for information on these two domains as they apply to language teaching.

In a language program, the *cognitive domain* appropriately refers to the kinds of language knowledge and language skills the students will be learning in the program. In other words, any *cognitive goals* in language teaching might better be termed *language goals,* that is, the language learning content of the program.

The cognitive domain was defined and outlined in 1956 by Bloom, whose book has become the standard model for such taxonomies, particularly as they relate to the cognitive domain. An outline of his main categories of human cognitive activities is provided in Table 3.2. These categories may not cover all conceivable classifications and divisions, but they can help language teachers to think through what adult students should be able to do. For example, in working out objectives for the ELI at the University of Hawaii at Manoa, we found ourselves having difficulty differentiating the lower-level listening course, ELI 70, from the upper-level course, ELI 80. Our goals were to provide the students with the language knowledge and listening skills necessary for them to compete in the academic community. However, we were having problems distinguishing the knowledge and skills that were intermediate level (ELI 70) from those that were advanced (ELI 80). We solved our problem by having our students work

---

Table 3.1   Functional Syllabus (adapted from van Ek and Alexander 1980)

1.0   Imparting and seeking factual information
    1.1   Identifying
    1.2   Reporting (including describing and narrating)
    1.3   Correcting
    1.4   Asking.

2.0   Expressing and finding out intellectual attitudes
    2.1   Expressing agreement and disagreement
    2.2   Inquiring about agreement or disagreement
    2.3   Denying something
    2.4   Accepting an offer or invitation
    2.5   Declining an offer or invitation
    2.6   Inquiring whether offer or invitation is accepted or declined
    . . .
    2.24   Stating that permission is withheld.

3.0   Expressing and finding out emotional attitudes
    3.1   Expressing pleasure, liking
    3.2   Expressing displeasure, dislike
    3.3   Inquiring about pleasure, liking, displeasure
    3.4   Expressing surprise
    3.5   Expressing hope
    3.6   Expressing satisfaction
    . . .
    3.19   Inquiring about want, desire.

4.0   Expressing and finding out moral attitudes
    4.1   Apologizing
    4.2   Granting forgiveness
    4.3   Expressing approval
    4.4   Expressing disapproval
    4.5   Inquiring about approval or disapproval
    4.6   Expressing appreciation
    4.7   Expressing regret
    4.8   Expressing indifference.

5.0   Getting things done (suasion)
    5.1   Suggesting a course of action
    5.2   Requesting others to do something
    5.3   Inviting others to do something
    5.4   Advising others to do something
    5.5   Warning others to take care or to refrain from doing something
    5.6   Instructing or directing others to do something

6.0   Socializing
    6.1   To greet people
    6.2   When meeting people
    6.3   When introducing people and when being introduced
    6.4   When taking leave
    6.5   To attract attention
    6.6   To propose a toast
    6.7   When beginning a meal

Table 3.2 Outline of Bloom's (1956) Taxonomy of the Cognitive Domain

1.0   Knowledge
    1.1   Knowledge of specifics
        1.11   Knowledge of terminology
        1.12   Knowledge of specific facts
    1.2   Knowledge of ways and means of dealing with specifics
        1.21   Knowledge of conventions
        1.22   Knowledge of trends and sequences
        1.23   Knowledge of classifications and categories
        1.24   Knowledge of criteria
        1.25   Knowledge of methodology
    1.3   Knowledge of universals and abstractions in a field
        1.31   Knowledge of principles and generalizations
        1.32   Knowledge of theories and structures

2.0   Comprehension
    2.1   Translation
    2.2   Interpretation
    2.3   Extrapolation

3.0   Application

4.0   Analysis
    4.1   Analysis of elements
    4.2   Analysis of relationships
    4.3   Analysis of organizational principles

5.0   Synthesis
    5.1   Production of unique communication
    5.2   Production of a plan, or proposed set of operations
    5.3   Derivation of a set of abstract relations

6.0   Evaluation
    6.1   Judgments in terms of internal evidence
    6.2   Judgments in terms of external criteria

on the same skills at both levels but apply them to different types of cognitive tasks. Referring to Bloom's taxonomy, we decided to reorganize our objectives for ELI 70 around the first three levels of Bloom's taxonomy (that is, 1.0 Knowledge, 2.0 Comprehension, and 3.0 Application) and to tasks related to those three levels. ELI 80 was then reorganized to reflect the last three levels of cognitive activity (that is, 4.0 Analysis, 5.0 Synthesis, and 6.0 Evaluation). Drawing on the Bloom listing of cognitive objectives within each of these categories (in combination with what we had learned through the needs analysis for the courses), we were able to separate the two courses into two sets of distinct objectives, and to do so in ways that never would have crossed our minds without Bloom's taxonomy. In other words, our needs analysis was fine, but it was also useful to consider another point of view (in this case, Bloom's).

The *affective domain* refers to those aspects of learning that are related to feelings, emotions, degrees of acceptance, values, biases, and so forth. *Affective goals* would be those goals in a program that are designed to alter or increase such affective factors. Consider the idea of happiness. If one of the goals of a program is to make the students happy, that goal would clearly be in the affective domain. However, while contributing to student happiness is an admirable goal which may represent sincere hopes on the part of teachers, student happiness would only be an appropriate program goal if it was consciously addressed in the program, that is, if it was going to be dealt with in some specific, defined way.

Where there are goals, there are also potential objectives. Affective domain objectives may not necessarily be stated in a form that describes performance, conditions, and criterion as suggested by Mager for instructional objectives. For example, in order to cope successfully in a particular setting, students may need to change certain attitudes and learning strategies. The situation analysis might focus on the feelings that learners have about the value of different kinds of learning activities (for examples, see Nunan 1986), or their preferred and customary learning styles. For example, in a speaking class at the GELC we wanted to make extensive use of pair-work and group-work activities to help the students develop fluency in English. The learners came from a teacher-centered educational background, and were therefore loath to accept the idea that working with another learner, rather than with the teacher, was useful. In essence, the needs analysis had revealed that learners needed pair and group activities, yet obviously they had negative feelings about the use of these kinds of activities. For this specific group of learners, who were unfamiliar with pair-work and reluctant to take part in such activities, it was necessary to develop the following instructional goal: "Learners will willingly participate in pair-work activities and recognize the effectiveness of pair-work as a learning activity."

In short, objectives in the affective domain often address the processes of learning rather than the language content and may be fairly general in nature. Thinking in terms of making affective objectives as precise and clear as possible will nevertheless be useful because the aim is always to state goals as objectives that are as unambiguous as possible and communicate what it is the students should be able to do at the end of the course or program. The single most important resource for thinking about this type of objective, as well as for organizing and presenting them, is Krathwohl, Bloom, and Masia (1956). A brief outline of the taxonomy presented in that book is given in Table 3.3.

Another taxonomy that proved useful in developing the objectives for our reading courses (ELI 72 and 82) at the UHM is the one Bennett (1972) offers. This taxonomy of reading objectives is briefly outlined in Table 3.4. It was originally designed for native speakers of English, but nevertheless proved useful for refining and organizing our ESL reading objectives. Notice in particular that the last level, 5.0 Appreciation, attempts to deal with reading skills that border on being more affective than cognitive in nature.

Table 3.3 Outline of the Affective Domain Taxonomy (outlined from Krathwohl et al. 1956)

1.0   Receiving (Attending)
    1.1   Awareness
    1.2   Willingness to receive
    1.3   Controlled or selected attention

2.0   Responding
    2.1   Acquiescence in responding
    2.2   Willingness to respond
    2.3   Satisfaction in response

3.0   Valuing
    3.1   Acceptance of a value
    3.2   Preference for a value
    3.3   Commitment

4.0   Organization
    4.1   Conceptualization of a value
    4.2   Organization of a value system

5.0   Characterization by a value or value complex
    5.1   Generalized set
    5.2   Characterization

□ SOUND INSTRUCTIONAL OBJECTIVES

Having broken down the perceptions of the students' needs into goals and potential objectives, and having organized them on the basis of all available information, the next step for planners is to state them as clear and unambiguous instructional objectives. Writing lucid statements of what students will be able to do at the end of a course is not as easy to do as it might at first seem. For example, my overall goal in this chapter is to help the reader develop the skills necessary to define and write clear instructional objectives (a "need," at least in my perception). In order to transform my goal into potential objectives, I must first break it into the smallest separable units, group those units logically, and then express them as a set of instructional objectives—a set that reflects my analysis of the tasks involved in the goal. The following objectives have resulted from this process:

> By the end of this chapter, the readers will be able to perform each of the following tasks with 90 percent accuracy:
>
> 1. Distinguish between curriculum goals and instructional objectives
>
> 2. Recognize complete or incomplete instructional objectives
>
> 3. Recognize vaguely stated instructional objectives as well as clearly stated ones
>
> 4. Write clear and complete performance objectives—including subject, performance, conditions (if necessary), a measure, and criterion level

Table 3.4 Outline of a Taxonomy of Reading Objectives (from Bennett 1972)

1.0   Literal comprehension
    1.1   Recognition
        1.11   Recognition of details
        1.12   Recognition of main ideas
        1.13   Recognition of a sequence
        1.14   Recognition of comparison
        1.15   Recognition of cause–and–effect relationships
        1.16   Recognition of character traits

    1.2   Recall
        1.21   Recall of details
        1.22   Recall of main ideas
        1.23   Recall of a sequence
        1.24   Recall of comparison
        1.25   Recall of cause-and-effect relationships
        1.26   Recall of character traits

2.0   Reorganization
    2.1   Classifying
    2.2   Outlining
    2.3   Summarizing
    2.4   Synthesizing

3.0   Inferential comprehension
    3.1   Inferring supporting details
    3.2   Inferring main ideas
    3.3   Inferring sequence
    3.4   Inferring comparisons
    3.5   Inferring cause-and-effect relationships
    3.6   Inferring character traits
    3.7   Predicting outcomes
    3.8   Interpreting figurative language

4.0   Evaluation
    4.1   Judgments of reality or fantasy
    4.2   Judgments of fact or opinion
    4.3   Judgments of adequacy and validity
    4.4   Judgments of appropriateness
    4.5   Judgments of worth, desirability, and acceptability

5.0   Appreciation
    5.1   Emotional response to content
    5.2   Identification with characters or incidents
    5.3   Reactions to the author's use of language
    5.4   Imagery

As I pointed out previously, Mager (1975) suggested three components necessary for the formulation of good objectives:

1. *Performance:* An objective always says what a learner is expected to be able to *do.*
2. *Conditions:* An objective always describes the important conditions (if any) under which the performance is to occur.
3. *Criteria:* Wherever possible, an objective describes the criterion of acceptable performance by describing how well the learner must perform in order to be considered acceptable.

The essential criterion that Mager holds up to objectives is "Do they communicate?" To that end, Mager's rules will be expanded in this chapter to ensure the creation of language objectives that do communicate. Thus the type of instructional objectives described here will contain five elements, each of which will be discussed in terms of language teaching: subject, performance, conditions, measure, and criterion.

Subject

While it may seem like quibbling to specify subject as an element of an objective, it is necessary in order to stress the importance of thinking of objectives in terms of what the *students, learners,* or *workshop participants* will be able to do at the end of the course, program, or workshop. The subject will not always be the same in every situation. In fact, the objectives I stated at the beginning of the last section referred to what the *readers* would be able to do by the end of this chapter. Thus the subject of an objective may vary considerably, and while this may only be a necessary consideration at the beginning of the objectives specification process, it is still important. Often, this part of objectives is handled at the beginning of the list in the following, or similar, format:

> By the end of the third level course, the students in the Wonderland Language Program will be able to:
> 1. . . . . . . ,
> 2. . . . . . . ,
> 3. . . . . . .
>   and so forth.

Notice that this statement is indeed dealing with the "students" but there is more to the *subject* than the word "students." The statement also tells us something about who the students are, that is, third level students in the Wonderland Language Program, who will be at the end of that third level when we expect our objectives to be accomplished. Such information, though seemingly trivial, turns out to be important in clarifying objectives if people outside of the program ever look at them. The subject description becomes particularly important if the objectives are to be compiled across levels or skills, or if they are to be shared among language programs.

Performance

The performance component as described by Mager answers the question: "What will the subject be able to do at the end of the course?" The focus of language objectives should be on what the learners *can do* with the language. This *can-do* focus is remarkably consistent with contemporary notions of language teaching, wherein the central concern is with helping students to communicate in the language when they are finished with their training. Thus at UHM, we often find ourselves trying to teach language skills that the students will actually be able to use, that is, language skills to help them function, or *do* things, in their content courses at the University of Hawaii at Manoa (perhaps as described in Table 3.2).

Note also that the statement of expected performance is couched in *terminal* terms. If needs have been established, they can usually be conceptualized in terms of what the student should be like, or be able to do, when he or she has finished a given course. Objectives that are framed in such terms will reflect qualities, skills, or knowledge that each student should attain by course end without necessarily specifying the route by which she or he will get there. Thus objectives can allow for differences among teachers as well as among individual students' learning styles. In other words, statements that may at first appear rigid and formalistic can be made maximally flexible and responsive to individual differences by ensuring that the objectives are specified in terms of end performances. Of course, there should always be room for variation in this rule. Some language programs have found that the mapping of the route to the terminal objectives through the use of "interim," "enabling," or "daily" objectives is useful. In my opinion, there is really no difference between this view and the notion of terminal objectives: the terminus is simply being brought forward and the course or program being viewed in shorter terms. Personally, I prefer to take a longer view of curriculum.

There is one last consideration crucial to clearly stating the performance part of an objective. The verb used to describe the expected behavior must be as clear and unambiguous as possible. Mager (1975, p. 20) lists a number of verbs that he calls "slippery words," that is, terms open to misinterpretation. They are listed along with words that he considers better in Table 3.5. A quick comparison of the two lists in Table 3.5 reveals that the primary difference is that the verbs in the right-hand column are far more readily observable than the others. Gronlund (1985) provides additional lists of useful verbs for various types of behaviors, two of which are of particular interest in language programs: language behaviors and "study" behaviors. These are shown in Table 3.6.

Table 3.5   Mager's (1975) Words to Watch

WORDS OPEN TO MANY INTERPRETATIONS	WORDS OPEN TO FEWER INTERPRETATIONS
to know	to write
to understand	to recite
to *really* understand	to identify
to appreciate	to sort
to *fully* appreciate	to solve
to grasp the significance of	to construct
to enjoy	to build
to believe	to compare
to have faith in	to contrast

Table 3.6   Other Useful Words to Use (adapted from Gronlund 1978)

LANGUAGE BEHAVIORS

Abbreviate	Edit	Punctuate	Speak	Tell
Accent	Hyphenate	Read	Spell	Translate
Alphabetize	Indent	Recite	State	Verbalize
Articulate	Outline	Say	Summarize	Whisper
Call	Print	Sign	Syllabify	Write
Capitalize	Pronounce			

"STUDY" BEHAVIORS

Arrange	Compile	Itemize	Mark	Record
Categorize	Copy	Label	Name	Reproduce
Chart	Diagram	Locate	Note	Search
Circle	Find	Look	Organize	Sort
Cite	Follow	Map	Quote	Underline

Conditions

Thinking through what the students must be able to perform is useful, but often the clarification of what it means "to perform" will only occur when the conditions that surround the performance are described. Consider the following objective:

By the end of level C, the students at the Guangzhou English Language Center will be able to:

1. Write missing elements on the appropriate lines in a graph, chart, or diagram from information provided in a 600-word 11th grade reading level general science passage.

Clearly, the subjects of this objective are contained in the lead-in material before the colon. The expected performance is to "write missing elements . . . in a graph, chart, or diagram from information provided in a . . . passage." The conditions under which the performance will take place involve a number of considerations. How will the students know which are the missing elements and where they are in the chart, and so forth? ("on the appropriate lines") What length, difficulty, and topic will be involved in the reading passage? ("600-word 11th grade reading level general science passage") These are all conditions that might dramatically affect the difficulty of the task. Hence they must be clearly thought through and concisely stated.

Looked at another way, the statement of conditions is actually the clarification of what it means to perform whatever is being required of the students. However, it is essential to remember that no objective will ever be perfectly stated, because of the nature of language and language learning. That is not to say that the attempt should not be made. The conditions stated above do help to clarify what is meant by the objective. But there will probably always be gaps in the statement of objectives because of what we do not know or understand about the nature of language learning. If the example above seems absolutely clear consider the following: What exactly is a graph? A chart? A diagram? Do they differ in complexity? What is 11th grade readability? And what is general science? Before giving up entirely, however, consider how much more clearly a course can be designed to meet the students' needs if such objectives are worked out to the best of our abilities—be they ever so imperfect. Also, contemplate for a moment how many language programs have absolutely no provision for thinking through the needs of the students or the goals and objectives of the courses. Is it not preferable to make the attempt to state even imperfect objectives that reflect the students' needs and program goals—especially in view of the fact that there are ways to improve on them as the program continues to develop (see Chapter Seven)?

Measure

The key to the *measure* part of an objective is to ask how the performance will be observed or tested. In the objective described above, the students' performance on the objective could be verified by observing that they are able to write the correct words in the blanks provided. Thus, the *measure* is that part of an objective that states how the desired performance will be observed. Such observations may take the form of a test-item specification (for example, "in multiple-choice format") or they may be more like the task description given above. Unlike what many critics of the use of objectives might think, such measurement is in no way limited to pencil-and-paper types of test questions like multiple-choice, true or false, matching, and so forth (though these may all turn out to be appropriate). The only limitations are in the minds and creative abilities of those who are developing the objectives. Teachers who can break free of traditional measures and think in terms of the students' needs are much more likely to create measures based on tasks that the students will ultimately need to accomplish with the language.

Criterion

Stating the level of accuracy that will be considered sufficient to succeed (or pass) on a given objective can be problematic. Unfortunately, there are only "rules of thumb" to go by in setting such levels. What rationale can there possibly be for accepting a criterion of 75 percent but not 74 percent? "Tradition" might serve as one answer, but not a very satisfying one. More problematic, some students will inevitably succeed on some objectives but fail on others. The point is that language educators are called upon to make decisions about their students' lives. Hence, cut points and the collapsing of scores across objectives are issues that must be faced, and criterion levels within the objectives may become very important. Be they ever so nebulous, such statements of criteria for success will force administrators, teachers, and students alike to face what the criteria mean, think about them, and perhaps revise cut-point decisions right along with the rest of the curriculum.

PROS AND CONS OF CURRICULUM OBJECTIVES

The idea of instructional objectives evolved from the belief that educational institutions could be made more effective if human enterprises could be analyzed scientifically. The preparation of students for various human endeavors could then be provided systematically in school curriculums. Specifications for these school activities would become the objectives of education (Bobbitt 1924). Tyler (1949, pp. 59–60) refined these notions by proposing guidelines for developing objectives. He believed that educational goals were best stated as objectives that would describe changes in student behavior.

Mager (1962) provided a definition for instructional objectives by specifying the three essential characteristics: performance, conditions, and criteria. The number of characteristics has been expanded in this book to include subject, performance, conditions, measure, and criterion (perhaps because of my language teacher compulsion for complete sentences including subject, verb, and object).

□ BATTLE LINES ARE QUICKLY DRAWN

However, not everyone in the language teaching field agrees with the idea of using instructional objectives. Like the continuum from very general goals (as in a college catalog) to very specific instructional objectives, there seems to be a continuum of attitudes among language teachers that ranges from abhorrence of anything resembling an instructional objective (for example, Tumposky 1984) to strong advocacy of their use (for instance, Steiner 1975). I will argue that most curriculum developers must find, or even foster, a compromise position somewhere between the extremes. The main complaints that arise with regard to objectives are (1) that objectives are associated with behavioral psychology; (2) that some things cannot be quantified; (3) that objectives trivialize teaching; (4) that objectives limit the teacher's freedom; and (5) that language learning simply cannot be expressed in objectives. Let us consider each of these issues in turn.

Association With Behavioral Psychology

Among the first to admit the negative attitudes toward objectives was Mager, who pointed out in the second edition of his book (1975, p. 23) that: "During the early sixties we talked about behavior, rather than about performance. This turned out to be an unfortunate choice of terms. A number of people were put off by the word, thinking that objectives necessarily had something to do with behaviorism or with behaviorists. Not so." Though association with behavioral psychology might be a positive factor for those who still strongly advocate the audiolingual approach, most language teachers react negatively to the idea. However, since the association is not real, this issue is easily resolved. It is just necessary to realize, as Mager (1975, p. 23) explained, that "Objectives describe performance, or behavior, because an objective is specific rather than broad or general, and because performance, or behavior, is what we can be specific about." To avoid the negative impact of the *behavioral* objectives label, they have been called instructional objectives in this book.

Some Things Just Cannot be Quantified

One of the most common arguments raised against objectives is that it is impossible to express the goals of many teaching activities in terms of objectives. The examples given usually center around literature and art, particularly with reference to appreciating such works. The contention is that it is difficult to describe the types of behavior expected of a student who is supposed to read and discuss a sonnet by William Shakespeare, or who has just viewed some impressionist paintings.

In answer, some might take the position that any teaching that is undefinable has no value (a position that itself has little constructive value). The reading taxonomy shown in Table 3.4 (under level 5.0) does provide some positive guidelines in the area of creating objectives for appreciation of literature. But I am certainly not advocating that all learning activities be expressed as strict and narrow behavioral objectives. I spent two years at the Oberlin Conservatory of Music, hold baccalaureate degrees in both French and English literature, and certainly understand the value of discussing music, poetry, and art. But the discussions that I experienced in literature classes were often rambling and unfocused. The class discussion might well have been more stimulating if the literature teachers had taken the time and made the effort to explore for themselves and their students just what it was that the students were expected to be able to do when they completed the course and to check whether or not the students could, in fact, do those things when the course was completed. Perhaps the goals and objectives would necessarily be somewhat less precise than many of the examples given in this book. At the least, they could be expressed in experiential terms like "The students will read at least 10 of e.e. cummings's poems aloud and think about the intonation patterns and rhythms of what they read in addition to the meaning." This is a way of defining what the students will experience in terms that are verifiable. The teacher can give clear directions that encourage the students to listen to the intonation patterns and rhythms of the poems and then monitor whether or not the reading aloud takes place through taping, in-class reading in groups, and so on.

The teacher might equally well believe that "every American university student needs to experience William Faulkner's short story 'The Bear.'" This experience is also potentially verifiable. The typical way to check if students have read something is to give a short quiz on it or to ask students to write an in-class essay. The choice of test versus essay, or even oral examination, will depend, in large part, on what the teacher, or curriculum designer, feels the students need to be able to do with the short story once they have read it. Reading "The Bear" is another kind of experience that can be stated as an objective and for which the performance can be verified.

Perhaps the teacher thinks that the students should not only read the story, but also understand that the "gun," the "fyce," and the "bear" all have symbolic value. This objective too is observable in a quiz or essay. Of course, the teacher may want to clarify what conditions pertain, for instance, whether the students should be allowed to assign their own values to these symbols or if the values should be prescribed.

In short, it may be true that instructional objectives with the five components described in this book will not be possible, necessary, or desirable in all situations. However, the attempt to define what the students need to be able to do with the literature (or artwork, or piece of music) they encounter and what it is that the teacher wants the students to be able to do as a result of such encounters certainly cannot hurt and might provide some structure to the teaching process that would help both the students and the teacher understand what it is that is expected of them.

Similarly, there may be other cases within the language classroom where teachers want to address intercultural, or affective domain, issues. The teacher may feel that there are certain tasks and learning activities that learners should experience because of the intrinsic value of these experiences. Common sense dictates that the experiences be verified in some way or other so that the students will actually participate in and take the activities seriously. Perhaps a simple checklist will suffice, or a quiz, an essay, or an oral interview. Language (and literature) teachers tend to do these things anyway. Why not do them in a more organized manner? Such specifications may not be as precise as instructional objectives. However, the more specific they are, the more useful they will be.

Objectives Trivialize Instruction

Another criticism raised about objectives is that they trivialize education by forcing teachers to focus only on things that can be expressed as objectives. Like so many criticisms of objectives, the trivialization charge is an argument against a position that no sensible educator would ever take. Nobody that I have encountered is advocating the use of the smallest, most trivial units as objectives to define the language teaching and learning processes. My discussion of literature objectives should head off any accusations that trivial units are the focus in this book. The problem is not that objectives necessarily trivialize teaching: the problem is that objectives, as stereotyped in the minds of some teachers, would do so if anyone were naive enough to actually advocate using them in that strict and narrow form.

Admittedly, part of the trick in successfully using objectives is to decide on the proper level of specificity for each of the objectives as they apply to a language course and the needs of the participants in that course. But what level of specificity is adequate? The answer that I usually give in the programs with which I am associated is parallel to Chomsky's famous stricture that a grammar, to be adequate, should generate all and only the grammatical sentences of the language (Chomsky 1957, p. 13). The objectives for a language program should express all and only the instructional intentions and purposes of that program. They should be observable but not trivial. And they should fit the program. How specific should the objectives be? Only the curriculum developers and/or teachers familiar with the program can decide that. However, attempting to decide on the appropriate level of specificity for objectives to meet the students' needs can lead teachers to think about and clearly define a language curriculum—perhaps for the first time in that program's history.

Objectives Curtail a Teacher's Freedom

The charge has also been leveled that objectives interfere with the teacher's freedom, in particular, with the teacher's freedom to respond to problems and ideas that arise spontaneously out of the process of teaching. From my perspective, limiting the teacher's initiative in the classroom would be foolish indeed. The teaching of language is a very complex task. Students vary in countless ways in their abilities and in the ways they learn language (or anything else). Only the individual teacher's trained and experienced mind can deal successfully with this degree of complexity and efficiently foster language learning and acquisition in as many students as possible.

With this view in mind, objectives begin to take on the aura of a necessity. Given the complexity of the task of language teaching, the teacher should not also be expected to be an expert in needs analysis, goals and objectives setting, testing, materials development, and evaluation. Certainly, the teacher should have substantial input into the development of all these curriculum elements. Nevertheless, the collective wisdom of all the teachers (as helped by the curriculum developers and supported by the administrators) would logically be more appropriate, energizing, and creative in developing curriculum than the sum of each teacher trying to do so on his or her own. The process of developing curriculum should maximize the effectiveness of the teacher in the classroom by giving him or her help with all the petty yet important organizational, production, and logistical elements of the program—thereby freeing him or her to concentrate on delivering instruction in the best ways available according to his or her professional judgment.

Since the statement of objectives is central to the curriculum process as defined in this book, the development of consensus among the teachers is essential, particularly about what the students need to learn, which goals are important, which objectives are necessary to meet the program goals, and what the level of specificity should be for each objective. Such processes should be initiated early in the curriculum development process and should become part of any ongoing review mechanisms that are used for keeping the curriculum alive and healthy (see Chapter Seven).

Language Learning Cannot be Expressed in Objectives

Valette (1980, p. 157) pointed out that objectives are often linked to a view of language learning that sees language proficiency as the sum total of mastering a vast array of discrete items: "Language learning . . . is not the sum of myriad parts: it is not by learning 1000 grammar rules, 1000 verb forms, and 3000 items of vocabulary, for instance, that one can suddenly read, speak, or understand the language." Perhaps I should point out in print that the structuralist point of view, described and dismissed by Valette, is probably held by a majority of the language teachers in the world today. Structural syllabuses make sense to many teachers whether those of us in academia like it or not. For such teachers, this quotation from Valette might in fact constitute an argument in favor of objectives. Even for teachers who hold other views of language teaching, her argument provides yet another example of how criticism of objectives is often based on characteristics that objectives do not necessarily have. Yes, objectives are often linked to structural syllabuses in the minds of critics, but a quick look at van Ek and Alexander (1980; also see Table 3.1 and Table 3.7) will reveal that objectives can also be closely linked to functional syllabuses. In fact, they can be connected to any approach or syllabus that is favored in a particular language program. The only limits on the use of objectives are the resources and creativity of the curriculum developers and teachers involved

Tumposky (1984) suggests that objectives are inappropriate in view of the nature of foreign language learning, since language is creative and unpredictable. She indicates that objectives are best reserved for lower-order skills. A similar criticism was reflected in the first charge noted above that more complex and creative aspects of learning cannot be reduced to objectives. Here, as elsewhere in Tumposky's article that decries the "cult of efficiency," she sets up stereotypical characteristics of the worst, most restrictive conceivable objectives and then argues against their use.

□ OBJECTIVES DO NOT BITE

Of course, in the hands of the educational equivalent of Darth Vader, objectives would be rigid, narrowly defined, restrictive, and dangerous. In general, however, people who advocate and use objectives inhabit the same planet as those who do not. In fact, they might be in the next classroom dealing with the same types of students who have the same needs, but trying to express those needs in terms of what they think the students should be able to do at the end of instruction. Such teachers usually find that objectives are most effective when a variety of different types are used and when the level of specificity for different objectives is allowed to diverge. Some objectives, even a majority, may be best described in the fairly specific instructional objective format, while others may be better characterized in less specific experiential objectives, at least until the language teaching profession better understands how to define them.

The difference between the two teachers is that the teacher next door who uses objectives is at least attempting to define what she hopes to teach the students to do. She may never get it completely right, but at least she is attempting to do so. Teachers who are critical of objectives, often for emotional reasons, are avoiding one tool among many that might help them become better teachers. The sad thing, from my perspective, is that suspicion and contempt of the use of objectives usually arises from misunderstandings resulting from stereotypes of what an objective is, stereotypes that are narrower than would be practical in any real teaching situation, stereotypes that no sane educator would advocate. As a result, many teachers join what might be called the "cult of inefficiency" through default.

Clearly, my view is that the advantages of objectives far outweigh their disadvantages; in fact, with a little creativity, the disadvantages can be entirely avoided. The advantages are many and worth thinking about. Chief among these is the fact that current views of language proficiency focus on the students' abilities to use language for specific purposes and activities. In other words, many of us are trying to teach our students to do things with the language. These performances or behaviors are naturally linked to the kinds of instructional objectives described in this book. Hence objectives are a natural way to define the very kinds of proficiency that even the most up-to-date language programs are trying to address.

Other benefits that can be derived from the use of objectives include the following:

1. Objectives help teachers to convert the perceived needs of the students into teaching points.

2. Objectives help teachers to clarify and organize their teaching points.

3. Objectives help teachers to think through the skills and subskills underlying different instructional points.

4. Objectives help teachers to decide on what they want the students to be able to do at the end of instruction.

5. Objectives help teachers to decide on the appropriate level of specificity for the teaching activities that will be used.

6. Objectives help teachers by providing a blueprint for the development of tests and other evaluation instruments (see Chapter Four).

7. Objectives help teachers to adopt, develop, or adapt teaching materials that maximally match the students' needs (see Chapter Five).

8. Objectives help teachers to develop professionally by letting them focus on just what it is that they are trying to accomplish in the classroom (see Chapter Six).

9. Objectives help teachers to evaluate each learner's progress, as well as overall program effectiveness, by permitting the systematic study, modification, and improvement of their perceptions of students' needs, course objectives, tests, materials, teaching, and evaluation procedures (see Chapter Seven).

10. Objectives help teachers to contribute to and learn from an ongoing process of curriculum development that draws on the collective energy and strengths of all of the teachers in a program to lessen the load of each individual.

In order to realize all of these advantages and avoid the pitfalls, there are a number of points that should be remembered:

1. Objectives can range in type and level of specificity.

2. Objectives are not permanent. They must remain flexible enough to respond to changes in perceptions of students' needs *and* to changes in the types of students who are being served.

3. Objectives must be developed by consensus among all of the teachers involved. Be this agreement ever so grudging, each teacher must have some stake in the success of the objectives.

4. Objectives must not be prescriptive in terms of restricting what the teacher does in the classroom to enable students to perform well by the end of the course.

5. Because of all of the above, objectives will necessarily be specific to a particular program. Though it may help to examine the objectives of other programs, those adopted, developed, or adapted for a given program will reflect the specific needs and views of the participants in that program at a given period of time. Hence there must be provision in the evaluation process for modification of the objectives.

6. Above all else, the objectives must be designed to help the teachers, not hinder their already considerable efforts in the classroom.

Though objectives will never be perfect, the act of trying to state course or program objectives will not only add structure to satisfying the students' language needs, but will also help the program leadership and its teachers to think through what it means to teach language in all of its complexity. Objectives can be used to guide the teaching of language without interfering with the techniques and exercises chosen by the teacher in the classroom.

However, the process of writing satisfactory objectives is difficult, and writing them alone, in isolation from other teachers, is even more difficult. At least one second opinion should always be solicited on any goal specification or instructional objectives project. But my experience indicates that teamwork is even better because it allows the teachers who must ultimately teach the objectives to be directly involved in the process. At the very least, teachers should always be extensively consulted.

Another point that is often missed by those who criticize instructional objectives is that objectives are only a part of the overall process of curriculum development. This means two important things: objectives do not stand alone and objectives are not set in cement. Objectives are only a small part of the curriculum process and, if they are not closely linked to the other components (that is, to needs, goals, tests, materials, teaching, and evaluation), they are meaningless. Within this relationship, objectives are part of a process and therefore must be alterable. If the tests for certain objectives show that the students can already perform those objectives with 100 percent accuracy at the beginning of a course, the curriculum developers must be willing to discard them and rethink the perceived needs of the students. Likewise, if some objectives turn out to be unattainable by the end of the course, they should be modified to reflect pedagogical realities. In short, objectives are only one tool in the curriculum process, albeit a valuable one, that must never be viewed as a finished product but rather as a flexible aid in the never-ending process of developing and refining a language program.

EXAMPLE GOALS AND OBJECTIVES

Once written, a collection of objectives is just an agglomeration unless they are somehow organized and presented so that they can be utilized for further curriculum development. One way to present objectives is shown in Table 3.7. Notice how this brief excerpt from van Ek and Alexander (1980) is organized under one of their general topic areas, health and welfare. It is then divided into subtopics: parts of the body, positions of the body, and so forth. To the right, the performance objectives are presented as a continuation of the sentence at the top: "Learners should be able to deal with various aspects of health and welfare" —which is really a goal statement. This kind of clear organization can help teachers and students to understand a set of objectives.

□ GUANGZHOU ENGLISH LANGUAGE CENTER, ZHONGSHAN UNIVERSITY

Table 3.8 shows some of the performance objectives for the Level B Reading course at GELC in 1982. In terms of format, note that a footnote is used to convey a great deal of the information that pertains to all of the objectives. Notice also that this information seems to be addressed to the students. We felt that these objectives reflected what we wanted the students to be able to do at the end of the course, and therefore we saw no reason to keep them secret. The objectives were distributed and explained on the first day of class so that students would know where the teachers thought the students ought to be headed in the course.

**Table 3.7   Extract of Objectives Format
(adapted from van Ek & Alexander 1980)**

7. Health and welfare
    Learners should be able to deal with various aspects of health and welfare:

7.1	parts of the body	refer to some parts of the body where simple gesture does not suffice to locate the source of pain, disorders, etc.
7.2	positions of the body	refer to and inquire about positions and movements of the body, sitting, standing, lying down, etc.
7.3	ailments/accidents	report illness, injury, accident; say whether they have been ill before and whether they have been operated upon; say whether they have to take medicine regularly, if so, what medicine.
	. . .	
7.9	emergency services	ask for police or the fire department, ask for an ambulance, a doctor, ask for the consul.

Table 3.8   Example Objectives from GELC Reading Level B Course* (GELC 1982)

The students should be able to do the following:

1. Skim a 600-word passage for six minutes, then answer multiple choice factual questions (without the passage) with 60 percent accuracy.

2. Answer multiple factual questions on a 600-word passage in six minutes with 70 percent accuracy.

3. Answer multiple factual questions about a graph, chart, or diagram in three minutes with 70 percent accuracy.

4. Take notes in outline format on a 600-word passage including main ideas and subideas (i.e., at least two levels) with 70 percent accuracy.

. . .

9. Fill in connectors (provided) in the appropriate blanks in a 600-word passage with 70 percent accuracy.

10. Write labels for missing elements in a graph, chart, or diagram from information provided in a 600-word passage with 70 percent accuracy.

11. Fill in meanings (provided) for the prefixes and stems given in appendix in Long et al (1980) with 70 percent accuracy.

. . .

14. Fill in meanings of unknown words based on sentence level context with 70 percent accuracy.

15. Identify sentences which function as examples in a 600-word passage with 70 percent accuracy.

16. Identify sentences which function as analogies in a 600-word passage with 70 percent accuracy.

* All reading passages will be on general science topics and will be at grade 11 reading level, which is equal to junior year (next to last) ability in U.S. high school, or approximately the *red* cards in your 4a SRA reading cards. The multiple–choice questions will each give you three choices.

Table 3.9 presents a set of objectives from the GELC Level C (or most advanced) Writing course. Coordinated by Ann Hilferty, the writing teachers had agreed on, or at least come to a consensus on, these objectives. Notice how a special format was invented to show the relative importance, or weight, of each objective, as well as the degree to which the teachers had agreed to focus on fluency, accuracy, or content for each objective. Note also that these objectives are stated in more general terms than those shown in Table 3.8 for reading. This group of teachers chose to express the upper-level writing skill objectives in this way because of the unique combination of backgrounds, personalities, and classroom styles of the teachers involved. Reasonably, then, this format was judged a success in the course for which it was designed.

The objectives from the GELC Level A Culture course (see Table 3.10) were even more general in nature. The teachers felt that these cultural topics were the important ones to cover and that the students only needed passive

Table 3.9   Example Objectives from GELC Writing Level C Course (adapted from GELC 1982)

These objectives describe all the tasks which each student should be able to perform by the end of the course. Test questions and graded assignments will be drawn from this list to determine each student's course grade. A score of 60 points is needed to pass the course.

WEIGHT	OBJECTIVE	PERCENT OF SCORE		
		FLUENCY	ACCURACY	CONTENT
5 pts.	1. WRITING WITH FUNCTIONS: Write a 100-word paragraph in 15 minutes using one function selected from the following list: Define, Compare, Paraphrase, Exemplify, Contrast, Process description, Classify, Request, Physical description, State purpose, Cite, Cause and effect	50	00	50
2 pts.	2. NARROWING A TOPIC: Given a composition topic, write a statement of purpose which narrows the topic.	00	25	75
15 pts.	3. IN-CLASS COMPOSITION: Write a 400-word composition in 45 minutes on an assigned topic.	25	25	50
	. . .			
3 pts.	7. ERROR IDENTIFICATION AND CORRECTION: Identify and correct the errors in a 400–word student composition.	00	100	00
5 pts.	8. ACADEMIC NOTE: Write a 50-word note to a fictional colleague which performs one assigned function, selected from the following list: a. Make an appointment. b. Apologize for not being able to keep an appointment. c. Reschedule an appointment because the other person failed to come. d. Schedule a professional meeting. e. Ask to be excused from a professional meeting. f. Thank a professor for dinner in his/her home.	00	25	75
5 pts.	9. ACADEMIC LETTER: Write a 150–word letter (to a fictional professor at an American university) which performs one assigned task, selected from the following list: a. Describe a research project. b. Suggest an exchange of papers and information. c. Recommend a friend for work or study.	00	25	75
	. . .			

Table 3.10 Example Objectives from GELC Culture Level A Course (GELC 1982)

Students should be able to answer true-false questions on the following topics with 70 percent accuracy:

CULTURE

5%	1.	Definition of "culture." (Lecture Notes 1)

FAMILY

10%	1.	Definitions and statistics for the following types of families: nuclear, single–parent, blended, and extended. (Lecture Notes 4; Video-tapes)
5%	2.	Rate and causes of divorce in the U.S. (Lecture Notes 4)
5%	3.	Roles and responsibilities for the different family members. (Video-tapes; *Beyond Language* [Levine & Adelman 1982], pp. 111–12)

WORK

10%	1.	Different attitudes toward work. (*Beyond Language*, pp. 185–89)
5%	2.	Definitions of the following terms: white collar; blue collar; minimum wage; salaries; hourly. (Videotapes, *Beyond Language*, pp. 194–95)
5%	3.	The normal work schedule.
5%	4.	High prestige/low prestige jobs. (*Beyond Language*, p. 191)
5%	5.	High salary/low salary jobs. (*Beyond Language*, p. 194)

SCHOOL

5%	1.	Basic organization of the American education system: elementary, junior high, senior high, and college. (*Visiting the USA* [Lanier 1973], chapter 5)
5%	2.	Differences between private and public education (*Visiting the USA*, chapter 5)
10%	3.	Values underlying our education system. (Lecture Notes 3)
10%	4.	Education vocabulary. (*Beyond Language*, pp. 163–64)
10%	5.	Teacher/student expectations. (*Beyond Language*, pp. 160–61)
5%	6.	Definitions of the following terms: lecture, seminar, discussion section.
100%		Total

knowledge about them; thus they needed only to be able to answer true–false questions about the topics. At other levels, the same group of teachers decided that more precise objectives would be more appropriate. The following are three examples taken from the Level C Culture course:

Students should be able to:

5%	1.	Answer matching questions about the information provided by the graduate catalog, class schedule, weekly calendar, and Office of International Students with 70 percent accuracy. (Lecture: Sources of Information about a University)

......

5%	9.	List three factors to consider when choosing a bank, with 67 percent accuracy. (Lecture: Banking and Money Matters, II–A)
10%	10.	Fill in a blank check with 100 percent accuracy. (Lecture: Banking and Money Matters, IV)

......

The Level C Culture course objectives do provide considerably more detail. Notice how the criterion (accuracy) levels vary from objective to objective. In the case of objective nine, there are three things that must be listed. Apparently, the teachers felt that the students should be able to list at least two correctly. In objective 10, however, the teachers evidently considered accuracy a much more important issue, perhaps because writing checks in the United States is a crucial survival skill and doing so inaccurately can cost money.

Table 3.11 is different from the others in that the listening teachers, coordinated by Margaret Graham, felt that the objectives should be organized around global functions like *Directions and Spatial Relations, Numbers and Numerical Relations,* and the like. Remember that GELC was catering to the language needs of Chinese postgraduate scientists. So the functions chosen may be quite different from those appropriate for other programs.

□ ENGLISH LANGUAGE INSTITUTE, UNIVERSITY OF HAWAII AT MANOA

The format shown in Table 3.12 was worked out for the ELI by Kimzin and Proctor (1986) based on the needs analysis discussed in Chapter Two (see Tables 2.8 and 2.9). Recall that their needs assessment was for the upper-level ESL listening course in the ELI at the UHM. Notice how different these objectives are in format from those shown in Table 3.11 for the same skill in another program. Kimzin and Proctor chose to organize their objectives around the main goals described in their assessment of the listening needs of students at UHM following the pattern of microskills presented in Richards (1983).

SUMMARY

The various formats shown in this chapter for presenting objectives were all derived in one way or another from the basic conceptualizations provided by Mager. In all cases, they attempt to be as clear as possible, but obviously the

Table 3.11 Example Objectives from GELC Listening Level A Course (adapted from GELC 1982)

At the end of Level A Listening, the students should be able to do the following:

DIRECTIONS AND SPATIAL RELATIONS

1. Given an oral statement containing spatial direction, they will identify the space indicated on a map, diagram, chart, or graph by answering in written form an oral question about what is located or written in that space with 80 percent accuracy.

. . .

5. After filling in numbers on a chart, they will listen to directions and read the chart in order to answer four to eight oral questions with 60 percent accuracy.

NUMBERS AND NUMERICAL RELATIONSHIPS

1. Given an oral statement containing a number up to nine digits, they will demonstrate 80 percent comprehension of the number by writing it into a blank with one repetition.

. . .

4. Given oral clues, they will be able to distinguish differences between addition, subtraction, multiplication, and division problems with 100 percent accuracy.

TIME AND TEMPORAL SEQUENCE

1. Demonstrate comprehension of the following concepts: Greenwich Mean Time, telling time, frequency adverbs, sequence, punctual versus durative, and adjectival use of time by answering 24 oral questions with 60 percent accuracy.

. . .

5. Given 10 oral problems involving times, names, and other facts, they will answer in written form with 60 percent accuracy.

. . .

Other units included **Dates and Chronological Order, Measurements and Amounts, Proportion, Comparison and Contrast,** and **Getting the Facts.** Each unit had between two and seven objectives associated with it.

degree to which clarity is possible varies widely even in the example programs discussed here. The sample objectives were originally included in this chapter to provide examples that can be applied in other language teaching situations. However, these objectives also serve as evidence of the tremendous variation that can occur in the level of generality and in the content of language program objectives. Clearly, objectives can (and probably must) vary from program to program, as well as in different courses within a program. The students' needs are apt to differ in various situations, so the goals and purposes are also apt to vary. More to

**Table 3.12 Example Objectives from UHM Listening Course, ELI 70
(adapted from Kimzin & Proctor 1986)**

GOAL #1

Students will be able to follow an argument, theme, or thesis of a lecture.

Microskills:

A. Lecture organization
   1. Identify cause-and-effect relationships.
   2. Identify comparisons and contrasts.
   3. Cite premises in persuasive arguments.
   4. Recognize supporting details in persuasive arguments.
   5. Understand explanation or a model (graph, chart, diagram, or formula).

B. Cohesion
   1. Recognize commonly used formulaic expressions.
   2. Recognize commonly used idioms.
   3. Identify anaphoric and cataphoric references.
   4. Recognize cohesive devices showing cause and effect, comparison and contrast, and persuasion.

C. Vocabulary
   . . .

D. Lecturer's style
   . . .

[Other goals included **Students will be able to devise a complex notetaking system,** and **Students will be able to present a coherent argument in small groups and seminar-type discussions.**]

Example performance objectives:

A.1. Indicate the cause-and-effect relationships in a 50-minute academic lecture by inserting an appropriate word or phrase in the blanks provided with 80 percent accuracy.

. . .

A.3–4. Indicate what the premise is in a 50-minute persuasive argument by underlining the key words or phrases in a 500-word summary with 80 percent accuracy.

the point, from a political perspective, the characteristics of the teachers and what they are willing and able to do will differ across situations, or even across time within a particular setting.

For those reasons, instructional objectives must be viewed as flexible, temporary, and revisable so that they can be tailored to different contexts and respond to changes over time in the needs of the students or in the physical and human resources of the program. Objectives can provide a useful tool that allows teachers to work out, often for the first time, what they want their students to be able to do when they are finished with the course. Objectives are a central part of any systematic curriculum development, but they can and should range in level of generality according to what is being taught and who is teaching it. Objectives can be creative, but only as creative as the people formulating and using them. Thus, boring and trivial objectives may not be so much a result of the use of objectives, as the result of a lack of imagination and creativity in the curriculum developers.

Remember also that instructional objectives are inherently political in nature. If they are presented to the faculty as a fait accompli, they may be resented, resisted, and gradually destroyed. When they are a result of faculty cooperation and consensus building, objectives stand a much better chance of success. Without goals and objectives, a program may have no clear purpose and direction. With goals and objectives, at least a tentative definition exists of what the program has to offer the students and what it is that a group of professional language teachers are trying to achieve.

■■■ CHECKLIST

The following checklist will serve as a review for this chapter, as well as a useful reference when thinking about objectives:

□ Have program goals been specified?

  □ Is each goal sufficiently comprehensive?
  □ Is each goal justified?
  □ Will each goal actually be addressed during instruction?
  □ Does each goal express what the learner will achieve?
  □ Can each goal be achieved?
  □ Have both the content and process of learning been addressed?
  □ Do the goals reflect the program's view of language proficiency?
  □ Have both cognitive and affective goals been specified?

□ Have instructional objectives been developed?
  □ Have the instructional objectives been specified clearly?
  □ Are there distinct differences in the level of specificity between the program goals and the instructional objectives?
  □ Have each of the following elements been considered in developing the objectives:

  □ Subject?
  □ Performance?
  □ Measure?
  □ Conditions?
  □ Criterion?

□ Have the objectives been reviewed:
  □ By a second party?
  □ By a team of objectives writers?
  □ By the teachers who must ultimately teach them?

□ Most crucially, how can the objectives continually be made to better match the needs of the students, the teachers, and the program as an institution? [see Chapters Four and Six on testing and evaluation, respectively]

■ ■ ■ *TERMS*

affective domain	affective goals
behavioral objective	cognitive domain
cognitive goals	conditions
criterion	goals
instructional objective	language goals
measure	performance
performance objective	subject
taxonomy	terminal

■ ■ ■ *REVIEW QUESTIONS*

1. How does setting program goals fit together with the needs analysis? Should goal statements reflect the perceived needs? Why might the goals be a bit different from the needs as originally perceived?

2. How do program goals differ from instructional objectives? What steps should be followed to convert general program goals into more specific instructional objectives? How specific should the objectives be? Would there be differences among the objectives in terms of level of specificity?

3. How are the following three types of information useful as sources of ideas when putting potential objectives on paper, organizing them, and filling in gaps: other language programs, literature review, and taxonomies?

4. Should course objectives be primarily related to the cognitive domain or to the affective one? If objectives are drawn from both domains, which set would most likely be stated in more general terms?

5. What are the three characteristics that Mager insists be included in a behavioral, or an instructional, objective? Why are they important for clear objectives? What two characteristics have I added? Why were they added? Do you think they are necessary to ensure that objectives be as unambiguous as possible?

6. Are behavioral objectives related to behavioral psychology?

7. Some types of learning goals are difficult to express as objectives. Do you feel that the attempt to clarify such outcomes in some form of objectives should be abandoned? Why or why not?

8. Do you feel that there is any justification for developing objectives that trivialize instruction or limit teachers' freedom in the classroom? Why or why not?

9. Can you list five of the 10 benefits (listed in the chapter) that can be derived from the process of specifying goals and objectives? Do you think these benefits are worth the extra effort involved?

10. What warnings were given in the chapter to help you avoid some of the pitfalls that may arise in specifying goals and objectives?

■ ■ ■ *APPLICATIONS*

A1. Look back at the Example Goals and Objectives section where the GELC program objectives are described. Apply the checklist given above in the "Summary" to any or all of the example objectives supplied in that description.

A2. How would you rate the quality of the objectives that you examined in A1? How would you improve them? How would you test or observe each objective? What techniques and exercises would you use to teach each one? Is there a relationship between teaching and testing as you have conceived of them for each objective?

B1. Find or jot down the goals for a program or course that you are involved in and develop them into a set of objectives that are as specific and unambiguous as possible.

B2. Better yet, get a team of teachers together and try to specify the goals and objectives for a language course or program in which you all teach. You may find that you need to do some form of needs analysis before this is possible.

Chapter 4

Testing

INTRODUCTION

Once program objectives have been established, testing is, or should be, a natural next step in the process of curriculum design. In this chapter I will begin by exploring the most important types of decisions that must be made in most language programs: proficiency, placement, diagnosis, and achievement. Next I will discuss the various types of tests that should be adopted, developed, or adapted in order to make such decisions responsibly. Tests will be examined in terms of whether they are norm-referenced or criterion-referenced tests, which differ fundamentally in the ways they are applied to different types of decisions. Then I will outline a strategy for creating successful tests within a language program—including suggestions for integrating tests into the overall curriculum and using checklists to help in evaluating the quality of tests and to aid in administering those tests. I will end the chapter with a section on the testing programs in the GELC and ELI examples.

This chapter attempts to cover a great deal of ground. No single chapter can serve as a substitute for training in language testing. However, it can suggest practical steps that can be taken to set up and implement decent testing in a language program. These steps can then be improved and made more sophisticated as the program continues to develop. The rewards for a language program that develops sound tests will be commensurate with the investment of time and energy because testing is crucial in making so many different types of decisions in a curriculum.

MAKING DECISIONS WITH TESTS

Over the years four different categories of tests have traditionally been discussed in language testing books (for instance, Alderson, Krahnke, & Stansfield 1987): proficiency, placement, diagnosis, and achievement. These four categories are probably emphasized because they fit neatly with four of the fundamental types of decisions that must be made in language programs.

□ PROFICIENCY DECISIONS

Teachers sometimes find themselves in the position of having to determine how much of a given language their students have learned and retained. In such a case, general, overall language ability is the focus without reference to any particular program (and its objectives, teaching, and materials). Such information may prove necessary when students are completely new to a program, and it is necessary to get a general notion of how much of the language they know, for example, to make intelligent admissions decisions.

Consider the importance of knowing the students' general level of proficiency at the beginning of an EFL program if the program has contracted with the ministry of education of country X to develop a 30-week intensive program (30 hours per week) wherein the students will learn the English necessary to successfully pursue studies in American universities. How would the general entry and exit levels for such a curriculum be tested? Certainly, the entrance requirements of American universities would furnish one set of constraints that would provide program planners with a logical starting place for estimating where the program is headed in terms of its general proficiency goals. General proficiency is being used in this case to describe what the students should have attained by the time they finish the 30-week program. In contracting to produce students who have sufficient command of English to study in American universities, the staff of the EFL program should define the level of proficiency to meet this goal in measurable terms. Most American universities require a score of 500 or 550 on the TOEFL for admissions. This is a political reality: TOEFL is an overall English language proficiency test that is widely used to judge students for admissions decisions.

Knowing where the program is headed in terms of the general proficiency level targeted for outgoing students is only part of the solution. The proficiency levels of students when they enter the program must also be measured. Consider a situation in which the students arrive with general proficiency levels below 300 on the TOEFL. Can any ESL/EFL program reasonably expect to produce students with TOEFL scores of 500 or 550 at the end of 30 weeks of intensive instruction if they arrive with scores averaging 300? Probably not. But, then, this is a decision that must be made by the administrators, teachers, and contract negotiators involved. After study and deliberation, these language teaching professionals might decide to protect themselves and their program by requiring that incoming students have TOEFL scores of at least 450. Such a strategy would dramatically improve the chances of delivering on a contractual agreement to produce students with a score of 550 at the end of the program. In addition to contractual issues, entry and exit level proficiencies are crucial for understanding the overall boundaries of a program. What level of overall proficiency do the students have when they come to us? And what level will they have when they leave us? Answering these two fundamental questions will help planners in making many different types of curriculum decisions.

For instance, proficiency decisions can come into play in initially gauging the proper level for program goals and objectives, or when revising them. Even if the objectives have been formulated, proficiency scores, like those provided by the TOEFL, might help planners to gauge whether the goals initially set for the program were too difficult or too easy for the target group to meet.

Checking at the beginning of the curriculum development process to see if program objectives are set at the appropriate level for the students is far more productive than waiting until after the program is firmly in place, at which point costly materials, equipment, and staff decisions have already been made.

Proficiency decisions are also applied to comparing the effectiveness of different language programs. Since proficiency tests, by definition, are general in nature, rather than geared to any particular program, they can be used to compare regional branches of a particular language program, or to examine different language centers across a state, a province, or a country. However, such decisions must be made carefully because proficiency tests are not designed to measure specific types of language teaching and learning, and most definitely not the specific types of language teaching and learning that are taking place in a particular language center. Thus proficiency comparisons across programs can only be very general in nature and must be interpreted with extreme care and conscientious attention to the uniqueness of each of the programs involved and to the validity and appropriateness of the test for the types of decisions being made.

In short, *proficiency decisions* involve tests that are general in nature (and not specific to any particular program) because proficiency decisions require general estimates of students' proficiency levels. Such decisions may be necessary in determining exit and entrance standards for a curriculum, in adjusting the level of goals and objectives to the true abilities of the students, or in making comparisons across programs. Despite the fact that proficiency decisions are general in nature, they are nevertheless very important in most language programs.

☐ PLACEMENT DECISIONS

Also relatively general in purpose, placement decisions are necessary because of the desirability of grouping students of similar ability levels together in the same classes within a program. Some teachers feel that they can do better teaching when they can focus in each class on the problems and learning points appropriate to students at a particular level. Placement tests are designed to facilitate the grouping of students according to their general level of ability. The purpose of a placement test is to show which students in a program have more of, or less of, a particular ability, knowledge, or skill.

If a given program has a very wide range of levels (for instance, nine levels ranging from beginning to very advanced), a general proficiency test could conceivably serve as a placement instrument as well. However, even when measuring general traits it is important to examine the test in terms of how well it matches what is actually taught in the classrooms. If there is a mismatch between the testing and the program (as found in Brown 1981), the placement of students into levels may be based on something entirely different from what is taught in the levels of the program. Consider a situation in which a general grammar placement test is being used. If the focus of the program is on social communication at three levels, and a pencil-and-paper grammar test is used to place students into those levels, numerous problems may arise. Such a test is placing students into levels on the basis of their *written grammar* abilities. While grammar ability may be related to social language ability, there are probably other cognitive and affective factors that are more important to being effective in social communication. Some other type of oral placement procedure (for example, the ACTFL Oral Proficiency Scale described in ACTFL 1986) might more sensibly be used to separate the students into three relatively homogeneous groups for the purposes of teaching them beginning, intermediate, and advanced social communication skills.

In short, *placement decisions* should be based on instruments that are either designed with a specific program in mind or, at least, seriously examined for their appropriateness to a specific program. The tests upon which placement decisions are based should either be specifically designed for a given program (and/or track within a program) or, at least, carefully examined and selected to reflect the goals and ability levels in the program. Thus a placement test will tend to apply only to a specific program and will be narrower in purpose than a proficiency test.

□ ACHIEVEMENT DECISIONS

Sooner or later any language program will take an interest in improving its students' achievement (that is, the amount that has been learned). To make any decisions related to student achievement and how to improve it, planners must have some idea of the amount of language that each person is learning in a given period of time (with very specific reference to a particular program). To help with such decisions, tests can be designed that are directly linked to the program goals and objectives. These achievement tests will typically be administered at the end of a course or program to determine how effectively students have mastered the desired objectives. Such decisions can be made even more effectively if based on tests that are administered periodically during the program—perhaps at the beginning, middle, and end. Such multiple testing procedures are important not only to the process of developing the tests themselves, but also to the ongoing development of the curriculum, especially in terms of examining and revising program goals and objectives. The information gained in this type of testing can also be put to good use in reexamining the needs analysis, in selecting or creating materials and teaching strategies, and in evaluating program effectiveness. Thus the development of systematic achievement tests is crucial to the evolution of a systematic curriculum. A needs analysis is just a needs analysis and objectives are just so much scribbling unless some check is made to see that the needs and objectives fit the people involved and the realities of the language teaching and learning situation.

In short, *achievement decisions* are central to any language curriculum. We are in the business of fostering achievement in the form of language learning. In fact, this book promotes the idea that the purpose of curriculum is to maximize the possibilities for students to achieve a high degree of language learning. The tests used to monitor such achievement must be very specific to the goals and objectives of a given program and must be flexible in the sense that they can readily be made to change in response to what is learned from them about the other elements of the curriculum. In other words, well-considered achievement decisions are based on tests from which a great deal can be learned about the program. These tests should, in turn, be flexible and responsive in the sense that their results can be used to affect changes and to continually assess those changes against the program realities.

□   DIAGNOSTIC DECISIONS

The last category of decisions is concerned with diagnosing problems that students may have during the learning process. This type of decision is clearly related to achievement decisions, but here the concern is with obtaining detailed information about individual students' areas of strength and weakness. The purpose is to help students and their teachers to focus their efforts where they are most needed and where they will be most effective. In this book, "areas of strength and weakness" will refer to examining the degree to which the specific instructional objectives of the program are part of what students know about the language or can do with it. While achievement decisions are usually centered on the degree to which these objectives have been met at the end of a program or course, diagnostic decisions are normally made along the way as the students are learning the language. As a result, diagnostic tests are typically administered at the beginning or in the middle of a course. In fact, as I explain below, one well-constructed test (designed to reflect the instructional objectives) in three equivalent forms can serve as a diagnostic tool at the beginning and middle points in a course and as an achievement test at the end.

In short, *diagnostic decisions* are focused on the strengths and weaknesses of each individual vis-à-vis the instructional objectives for purposes of correcting deficiencies "before it is too late." Hence, diagnostic decisions are aimed at fostering achievement by promoting strengths and eliminating weaknesses.

MATCHING TESTS TO PURPOSES

Language teaching professionals make proficiency, placement, achievement, and diagnostic decisions about their students all the time. But how well do they make those decisions? And how good are the tests upon which such decisions are based? To help in developing sound tests for making important decisions, I will begin by explaining a clear-cut distinction between two major families of tests: norm-referenced and criterion-referenced. This distinction can help decision makers differentiate between norm-referenced and criterion-referenced *test items* (that is, test questions) in such a way that tests can be more effectively adopted, developed, or adapted to serve various decision making purposes.

□ NORM-REFERENCED VERSUS CRITERION-REFERENCED TESTS

The separation of tests into the norm-referenced and criterion-referenced families has had little coverage in the language testing literature (recent exceptions include Cartier 1968; Cziko 1982, 1983; Brown 1984, 1989b, 1990a, 1990b, 1992a, 1993a; Hudson & Lynch 1984; Bachman 1989); however, criterion-referenced testing has been much discussed in educational testing circles (for example, see almost any recent volume of the *Journal of Educational Measurement* or *Applied Psychological Measurement*). One definition for a *criterion-referenced test* (CRT) is:

> a test which measures a student's performance according to a particular standard or criterion which has been agreed upon. The student must reach this level of performance to pass the test, and a student's score is therefore interpreted with reference to the criterion score, rather than to the scores of other students. (Richards, Platt, & Weber 1985, p. 68)

This is markedly different from the definition for a *norm-referenced test* (NRT) given in the same source:

> a test which is designed to measure how the performance of a particular student or group of students compares with the performance of another student or group of students whose scores are given as the norm. A student's score is therefore interpreted with reference to the scores of other students or groups of students, rather than to an agreed criterion score. (Richards, Platt, & Weber 1985, p. 68)

The essential difference between these definitions is that the performance of each student on a CRT is compared to a particular standard called a criterion level (for example, if the acceptable percent of correct answers were set at 70 percent for passing, a student who answered 86 percent of the questions correctly would pass), whereas on an NRT a student's performance is compared to the performances of other students in whatever group has been designated as the norm (for example, regardless of the actual number of items correctly answered, if a student scored in the 84th percentile, he or she performed better than 84 out of 100 students in the group as a whole).

The key to understanding this difference is implicit in the terms *percent* and *percentile*. In administering a CRT, the principal interest is in how much of the material on the test is known by the students. Hence the focus is on the percent of material known, that is, the percent of the questions that the student answered correctly in relation to the material taught in the course and in relationship to a previously established criterion level for passing.

In administering an NRT, the concerns are entirely different. Here, the focus is on how each student's performance relates to the scores of all the other students, not on the actual number (or percent) of questions that the student answered correctly. Thus, in one way or another, the focus is on percentile scores, which indicate the proportion of students who scored above and below the student in question. For instance, a student with a percentile score of 54 performed better than 54 out of 100 students but worse than 46, and a student with a percentile score of 99 performed better than 99 out of 100 students but worse than one.

Percentile scores (which indicate how the students relate to each other) can be reported without any reference to the percent of questions that each of those students answered correctly. Thus, in a sense, the concepts of percentile and percent scores are independent. If a particular NRT has difficult items on it, the percent of correct answers will be low for all students, but their positions relative to each other in terms of percentile scores might be virtually the same as on an easier version of the test on which they all had higher percent scores. In short, CRTs are designed to examine the *amount* of material known by each individual student (usually in percent terms) while NRTs examine the *relationship* of a given student's performance to the scores of all other students (usually in percentile or other standardized score terms).

The definitions given earlier for CRTs and NRTs (from Richards, Platt, and Weber 1985) cover one difference between the two types of tests, that is, that the scores are interpreted differently. Because of this primary distinction, other differences occur in practice. As Table 4.1 (adapted from Brown 1984) shows, the two types of tests also differ in: (1) the kinds of things that they are used to measure, (2) the purpose of the test, (3) the distributions of scores that will result, (4) the design of the test, and (5) the students' knowledge of the test questions beforehand. Exploring each of these notions separately should help to clarify the importance of the overall distinction between NRTs and CRTs.

Used to Measure

In general, NRTs are more suitable for measuring general abilities or proficiencies. Examples would include reading ability in Spanish or overall English language proficiency. CRTs, on the other hand, are better suited to giving precise information about individual performance on well-defined learning points. For instance, in a structural syllabus, one subtest on a CRT might consist of five items testing the article system in English, a very specific learning point. But CRTs are not limited to testing grammar points. In a notional-functional syllabus, a subtest on a CRT might consist of a rating scale where judgments are made about the student's ability to seek information from another speaker, apologize for making a mistake, interrupt another speaker, and so on. CRT items can take any form. In fact, CRT items can be as varied as the imagination of the test developer allows. It is, however, important that the concepts being tested by CRT items be as specific and well defined as possible.

Table 4.1	Differences Between Norm-referenced and Criterion-Referenced Tests (adapted from Brown 1984)	
CHARACTERISTIC	**NORM-REFERENCED**	**CRITERION-REFERENCED**
1. Used to measure	General language abilities or proficiencies	Specific language points based on course objectives
2. Purpose of testing	Spread students out along a continuum of abilities or proficiencies	Assess the amount of material known by each student
3. Distribution of scores	Normal distribution	Students can all score 100 percent if they know the material or skill
4. Test design	A few long subtests with similar items throughout	Numerous short, clearly defined subtests, each testing one objective
5. Students' knowledge of test questions	Have no idea what types of questions to expect	Know exactly what content to expect on test

Purpose of Testing

As I pointed out earlier, the scores on NRTs are interpreted in relative terms, that is, a student's score is interpreted in relationship to the scores of all other students. Hence, the purpose of an NRT must be to generate scores that spread the students out along a continuum of general abilities or proficiencies in such a way that differences among the individuals are reflected in the scores.

In contrast, the scores on CRTs are viewed in absolute terms, that is, a student's performance is interpreted in terms of the amount, or percent, of material known by that student. Since the purpose of a CRT is to assess the amount of knowledge or material known by each individual student, the focus is on individuals rather than on distributions of scores. Nevertheless, as I will explain next, the distributions of scores for the two families of tests can be quite different in interesting ways.

Distribution of Scores

Because of their purpose, NRTs must be constructed to spread students out into a relatively wide distribution of scores. In other words, for an NRT to be effective some students should score very low, and others very high, and the rest everywhere in between. Indeed, the way items for an NRT are generated, analyzed, selected, and refined will typically lead to a test that produces scores that fall into a normal distribution, or "bell curve." This is necessary so that the differences among individuals will be revealed. If the group is heterogeneous with regard to the ability or proficiency being tested, that fact should be reflected in their scores.

In contrast, on a CRT, it would be perfectly acceptable, even desirable, for all of the students to score 100 percent on an end-of-term test if they had all learned all the material. Similarly, if the students had a definite need to learn the material in the first place (because they did not previously know any of it), their scores on the same test should be very low at the beginning of the term. Again, the way that CRT items are generated, analyzed, selected, and refined will lead to these very types of results. For a CRT, then, it is perfectly logical and acceptable to have a very homogeneous distribution of scores whether the test is given at the beginning or end of a period of instruction.

Test Design

The distinctly different strategies used to develop NRT and CRT items result in tests that also look different. Regardless of what facets of language are being tested, an NRT is likely to be relatively long and to be made up of a wide variety of different item types. An NRT usually consists of a few subtests on rather general language skills, for example, reading and listening comprehension, grammar, writing, and the like. These subtests will tend to be relatively long (30–50 items) and cover a wide variety of different test items.

In comparison, CRTs are much more likely to be made up of numerous, but shorter, subtests. Each of the subtests will usually represent a different instructional objective for the given course—with one subtest for each objective. For example, if a course has 12 instructional objectives, the CRT associated with that course might have 12 subtests (although sometimes only a subsample of the objectives will be tested). For practical reasons, if the number of CRT subtests is large, they will usually be kept relatively short (say, three to 10 items each).

Students' Knowledge of Test Questions

Because of the general nature of what NRTs are testing and the usual wide variety of items, students rarely know in any detail what types of items to expect. The students might know what item formats they will encounter, for example, multiple-choice grammar items, but seldom will they be able to predict actual language points.

However, on a CRT, students should probably know exactly what language points will be tested, as well as what item types to expect. If the instructional objectives for a course are clearly stated and if those objectives are the focus of instruction, then the students should know what to expect on the test. Surprises would only occur if, for some reason, the criterion-referenced tests were not properly referenced to the criteria: the instructional objectives.

Such statements often lead to protests that the development of CRTs will cause instructors to "teach to the test" to the exclusion of other more important ways of spending class time. While many elements of the teaching and learning process cannot be tested using a multiple-choice test, many other forms of observation can be used to determine whether students have accomplished the objectives. Oral interviews, pair work, group work, and other methods can all be used as testing devices to observe the degree to which the objectives of a course have been accomplished. Regardless of the form of testing, the process should be one that helps rather than constrains the teacher.

If the needs analysis reflects reality in any sense and if the goals and objectives have been constructed to reflect the perceived needs of students, then the tests (broadly defined) that result should reflect the important language points being taught. Teaching to such tests would provide a useful way of keeping the teachers and students on track, as well as for giving feedback to both groups concerning the effectiveness of the teaching and learning processes. A very useful side effect of all this is the fact that the information gained can also be enlightening with regard to the effectiveness of the needs analysis, goals and objectives, the tests themselves, the materials, the teaching, the students' study habits, and so forth. In short, CRTs can provide very useful information for the never-ending evaluation process that I advocate in the last chapter of this book.

That is not to say that I advocate the use of CRTs over NRTs. Both types of information are very important for the decision-making processes in a language program. However, the distinction remains valuable for making sure that the correct type of instrument is used for the correct type of decision.

□ DIFFERENT INSTRUMENTS FOR DIFFERENT PURPOSES

The first column of Table 4.2 indicates test qualities that vary for the four types of decisions (and parallel types of tests involved in making those decisions). Notice that the decision/test types are labeled across the top of the table and range from proficiency to placement to achievement to diagnosis. The table indicates, first, that there are differences in the degree to which the information provided by the test is general or specific. Second, the focus of each of these types of tests differs from general skills prerequisite for the program to very detailed analysis of the students' ability to perform on instructional objectives. Third, these four types of decisions/tests differ in the purposes of the decisions for which they were designed, varying from comparing individuals overall with other groups to informing students and teachers of which objectives the students can perform well and which still need work. Fourth, the types of comparisons can range from comparisons with other institutions to direct comparisons of each student's performance on each of the course or program objectives.

Fifth, the decisions are typically made at different times throughout a student's stay in a program. Proficiency decisions are usually made before entry or

Table 4.2 Matching Tests to Decision Purposes

TEST QUALITIES	TYPE OF DECISION/TEST			
	PROFICIENCY	PLACEMENT	ACHIEVEMENT	DIAGNOSIS
1. Detail of information	Very general	General	Specific	Very specific
2. Focus	General skills prerequisite to program entry	Learning points drawn from entire program	Instructional objectives of course or program	Instructional objectives of course or program
3. Purpose of decision	Compare individual overall with other groups/ individuals	Find each student's appropriate level	Determine amount of learning with regard to program objectives	Inform students and teachers of objectives that still need work
4. Type of comparison	Comparison with other institutions	Comparisons within program	Comparison to course or program objectives	Comparison to course or program objectives
5. When administered	Before entry or at end of program	Beginning of program	End of courses	Beginning or middle of courses
6. Interpretation of score	Spread of scores	Spread of scores	Degree to which objectives have been learned	Degree to which objectives have been learned
7. Type of test	NRT	NRT	CRT	CRT

at the end of the program, while placement decisions are typically made at the beginning of a program of study. Achievement decisions and testing are usually done at the end of a course or program, and diagnosis is most often done at the beginning or in the middle of a course.

Sixth and seventh, since two types of decisions, proficiency and placement, require that comparisons be made among students, the items used to develop tests for these decisions will logically be selected for characteristics that spread the students out along a continuum of abilities. Hence proficiency and placement decisions will be best served by the NRT family of tests. The other two types of decisions, achievement and diagnosis, will best be served by tests that help to determine the degree to which students have acquired the knowledge or skills required by the objectives. Items for such tests will thus be selected on the basis of characteristics indicating that they show learning over time. Those students who do not know the material or skills involved should score poorly. Those students who do know the materials or skills should have high scores. Hence achievement and diagnosis decisions will be best served by the CRT family of tests.

☐ ADOPT, DEVELOP, OR ADAPT?

Once a consensus has been built as to the purposes and types of tests to employ in a program, a strategy must be worked out to maximize the quality and effectiveness of the tests. In the best of all possible worlds each program would have a resident testing expert, whose entire job would be to develop tests especially created for and suited to that program. But even in the worst of all possible worlds rational decisions can be made when selecting commercially available tests if certain guidelines are followed. In between the two extremes of developing tests from scratch or adopting them from commercial sources is the possibility of adapting existing tests so that they are made to better fit with the purposes and objectives of the program.

Many language tests are, or should be, situation specific. That is to say, a test can be very effective in one situation with one particular group of students and be virtually useless in another situation or with another group of students. Teachers cannot simply go out and buy (or worse yet, illegally photocopy) a test and automatically expect it to work with their students. It may have been developed for completely different types of students (different in background, level of proficiency, gender, and so forth) and for entirely different purposes (that is, based on differing approaches, syllabuses, techniques, or exercises).

Though all of this may seem like a great deal of work, remember that in most language programs, any rational approach to testing will be a vast improvement over the existing conditions. My purpose in this section of the chapter will be to suggest systematic bases for getting started in adopting, developing, or adapting decent language tests for a particular and very specific language program.

Adopting Language Tests

As I just mentioned, the tests that are used for program decisions are very often bought from commercial publishing houses. Tests are also sometimes adopted from other language programs or taken straight from the current textbook. Given the wide diversity and variation in the nationalities and levels involved in the various language programs around the world, it may turn out that any test that is adopted is being applied to a population quite different from that envisioned when the tests were originally written. As a result, program decisions that can dramatically affect the lives of the students may be irresponsibly based on tests consisting of test questions that are quite unrelated to the needs of the particular group of students or to the curriculum being taught in the specific program involved.

Selecting good tests that match the specific needs of a program is therefore important. Test reviews (written by language testing specialists) are one good place to start. Such reviews can be found in the review sections of some language teaching journals, right alongside the reviews of texts and professional books. Unfortunately, test reviews appear infrequently. *Language Testing* is a journal that focuses on language tests and also provides reviews. For those in ESL/EFL, Alderson, Krahnke, and Stansfield (1987) is a useful source of test reviews for most of the major tests available at the time it was published. *The Mental Measurements Yearbook* (see Kramer & Conoley 1992) also includes some reviews of language tests.

Alternative ways to approach the task of selecting tests for a program might include: (1) taking a language testing course, (2) reading up on testing, (3) hiring a person who already knows about testing, or (4) giving one member of the staff release time to become informed on the topic. In all cases, the checklist provided in Table 4.3 will (with some background in testing) help in selecting tests that match the purposes for which they are needed.

Table 4.3 begins by considering general factual information about each test: title, author, publisher, and date of publication. However, the theoretical orientation of the test should also be reviewed. Is it in the correct family of tests (NRT or CRT)? Is it designed for the kind of decision making the program needs? Does it match the program's methodological orientation and goals? In a practical sense, does the test seem to be aimed at the correct population and designed to test the skills that the program teaches? How many subtests and separate scores will there be, and are they all useful to the program? Do the types of items reflect the productive and receptive types of techniques and exercises that are viewed as important in the program?

If the test is meant to be an NRT, are norms and standardized score equivalents provided? For any test, what descriptive information is given and does it make sense? Is the test reliable and valid? It is the publisher's responsibility to convince the user that the test is good, so look for the arguments supporting the quality of the test. Weigh those arguments carefully, and judge whether they are convincing.

Other practical considerations include the initial and ongoing costs of the test and the quality of all of the materials provided. Is the test easy to administer? What about scoring? Is that reasonably easy given the type of test questions involved? Is the interpretation of scores clearly explained with guidelines for presenting the scores to the teachers and students?

Clearly, then, a number of factors must be considered even when adopting an already published test for a program. Ideally, the program would have a resident expert, someone who can help everyone else to make the right decisions. If no such expert is available, it may be advisable to read up on the topic yourself. Books like Brown (forthcoming), Carroll & Hall (1985), Henning (1987), and Bachman (1990) provide information on language testing that should help

Table 4.3   Test Evaluation Checklist (adapted form Brown forthcoming)

A. General background information
   1. Title
   2. Author
   3. Publisher and date of publication
   4. Published reviews available

B. Theoretical orientation
   1. Test family (norm-referenced or criterion-referenced)
   2. Purpose of decision (proficiency, placement, achievement, or diagnosis)
   3. Language methodology orientation (approach and syllabus)

C. Practical orientation
   1. Target population (age, level, nationality, language/dialect, educational background, and so forth)
   2. Skills tested (for instance, reading, writing, listening, speaking, structure, vocabulary, pronunciation)
   3. Number of subtests and separate scores
   4. Type of items reflect appropriate techniques and exercises (receptive: true-false, multiple-choice, matching; productive: fill-in, short-response, essay, extended discourse task)

D. Test characteristics
   1. Norms
      a. Standardization sample
      b. Type of standardized scores
   2. Descriptive statistics (central tendency, dispersion, and item characteristics)
   3. Reliability
      a. Types of reliability procedures used
      b. Degree of reliability for each procedure
   4. Validity
      a. Types of validity procedures used
      b. Do you buy the above validity argument(s)?
   5. Practicality
      a. Cost of test booklets, cassette tapes, manual, answer sheets, scoring templates, scoring services, any other necessary test components
      b. Quality of items listed immediately above (paper, printing, audio clarity, durability, and so forth)
      c. Ease of administration (time required, proctor/examine ratio, proctor qualifications, equipment necessary, availability and quality of directions for administration, and so forth)
      d. Ease of scoring (method of scoring, amount of training necessary, time per test, score conversion information, and so forth)
      e. Ease of interpretation (quality of guidelines for the interpretation of scores in terms of norms or other criteria)

anyone to make informed selections. If the program decides to consult with an outside expert who specializes in language testing, be sure to ask if his or her expertise includes both NRTs and CRTs. While most language testers understand NRT construction and interpretation, real practical knowledge of CRT development, use, and interpretation is still relatively rare.

Developing Language Tests

In the best of all possible worlds, sufficient resources and expertise will be available in a program so that proficiency, placement, achievement, and diagnostic tests can be developed and fitted to the specific goals of the program and to the specific population studying in it. If this is the case, decisions must be made about which types of tests to develop first. Probably those that are most program-specific should be developed first. That might mean first developing achievement and diagnosis tests (which are based entirely on the needs of the students and the objectives of the specific program), while temporarily adopting previously published proficiency and placement tests. Later, a program-specific placement test could be developed so that the reasons for separating students into levels in the program are related to the things that the students can learn while in those levels. It is rarely necessary or even useful to develop program-specific proficiency tests because of their interprogrammatic nature. In other words, for purposes of reference to other programs elsewhere, an adopted test that is used by a wide variety of language programs will be most appropriate. Naturally, all of these decisions are up to the teachers, administrators, and curriculum developers in the program in question.

Adapting Language Tests

It may turn out that a preexisting test that works fairly well, but not perfectly, can be adapted to the specific testing needs of a particular program. The process of adapting a test to a specific situation will probably involve some variant of the following strategy:

1. Administer the test to the students in the program.
2. Select those items that appear to be doing a good job of spreading out the students for an NRT, or a good job of measuring the learning of the objectives with that population for a CRT.
3. Create a shorter, more efficient, revised version of the test that fits the ability levels of the specific population of students.
4. Create new items that function like those that were working well in order to have a test of sufficient length.

With the basic knowledge that can be gained from any of the language testing books listed above, these four steps should be easy. Brown (forthcoming) reviews these steps in detail for both NRTs and CRTs. Following such guidelines should enable those who are interested to adapt tests to the goals and decision-making purposes of any language program. Be warned, though, that test development is work—lots of work. However, the work is worthwhile because of the information that can be gained and the satisfaction that can be derived from making responsible decisions about students' lives.

ORGANIZING AND USING TEST RESULTS

Having decided to adopt, develop, or adapt tests (or some combination of all three), curriculum planners must next put the tests into place and begin to use them for decision making. The checklist shown in Table 4.4 will help them with the actual implementation of tests. To begin with, make sure that the purposes of administering the various tests are clear to the curriculum developers and to the teachers (and eventually to the students). This probably means that these purposes must be clearly defined in both theoretical and practical terms that are understood and agreed to by a majority of the staff. It would also be wise to check the quality of each test by using the checklist presented in Table 4.3 as a guide.

The next step is to ensure that all the necessary physical conditions for the test have been met. This might mean assuring that there is a well-ventilated and quiet place in which to administer the test and enough time in that space for some flexibility and clear scheduling. Also make sure that the students have been properly notified and signed up before the test (if necessary), and consider whether the students should be given precise information about where and when the test will be given, what they should do to prepare, and what they should bring with them. Perhaps this information should take the form of a handout or pamphlet.

Before actually administering the test, check to make sure that there are adequate materials on hand (with a few extra copies of everything). All necessary equipment should be handy and in good repair (with backups if that is appropriate). Proctors must be trained in their duties and have sufficient information to do a professional job of test administration.

After the test has been administered, provision must be made for scoring. Again, adequate space and scheduling are important so that qualified staff can be properly trained to carry out the scoring of the test. Equally important is the interpretation of the results. There must be a clearly defined purpose for the results, and provision for helping teachers use scores and explain them to their students. Ideally, there will also be a well-defined place for the results in the overall curriculum planning.

Record keeping is often forgotten in the process of test administration. Nevertheless, resources must be provided for keeping track of scores, including sufficient clerical staff, computers and software, office equipment and supplies, and so on. In all cases, ready access to the records is very important for all staff

**Table 4.4   A Checklist for Successful Testing
(adapted from Brown forthcoming)**

A. Purposes of test
   1. Clearly defined (theoretical and practical orientations)
   2. Understood and agreed upon by staff

B. Test itself (see Table 4.3)

C. Physical needs arranged
   1. Adequate and quiet space
   2. Enough time in that space for some flexibility
   3. Clear scheduling

D. Preadministration arrangements
   1. Students properly notified
   2. Students signed up for test
   3. Students given precise information (where and when test will be, as
      well as what they should do to prepare and what they should bring with
      them, especially identification if required)

E. Administration
   1. Adequate materials in hand (test booklets, answer sheets, cassette tapes,
      pencils, scoring templates, and so forth) plus extras
   2. All necessary equipment in hand and tested (cassette players, micro-
      phones, public address system, videotape players, blackboard, chalk, and
      so forth) with backups where appropriate
   3. Proctors trained in their duties
   4. All necessary information distributed to proctors (test directions, answers to
      obvious questions, schedule of who is to be where and when, and so forth)

F. Scoring
   1. Adequate space for all scoring to take place
   2. Clear scheduling of scoring and notification of results
   3. Sufficient qualified staff for all scoring activities
   4. Staff trained in all scoring procedures

G. Interpretation
   1. Clearly defined uses for results
   2. Provision for helping teachers interpret scores and explain them to students
   3. A well-defined place for the results in the overall curriculum

H. Record keeping
   1. All necessary resources for keeping track of scores
   2. Ready access to the records for administrators and staff
   3. Provision for eventual systematic termination of records

I. Ongoing research
   1. Results used to full advantage for research
   2. Results incorporated into overall program evaluation plan

members within the legal limits of confidentiality that prevail locally. However, if program administrators are to avoid becoming buried under the paperwork, provision must also be made for the eventual destruction or long-term storage of these records. Last but not least, there should be an ongoing plan for research based on the results. At a minimum, the results should be used to full advantage, which means that they should be effectively incorporated into the overall curriculum development and program evaluation plans.

EXAMPLE TESTING PROGRAMS

The examples of testing programs provided here are meant to emphasize the importance of having a well-integrated program of different types of tests that (1) assist the administrators and teachers in making decisions about the students, (2) provide feedback to the teachers, and (3) aid in examining the various elements of the curriculum. Note, however, that the two examples given here describe testing programs that operated quite differently from each other. For instance, no placement tests were used in the GELC program, whereas an extensive placement battery and interview are used in the ELI. Moreover, the diagnostic and achievement tests in the two programs, though serving roughly the same purposes, turned out to be quite different because the goals and objectives of the two programs were unique to each. All of this emphasizes once again the degree to which curriculum design, including all the elements described in this book, must to a large degree be adapted or developed for the specific program involved.

□ GUANGZHOU ENGLISH LANGUAGE CENTER, ZHONGSHAN UNIVERSITY

In the two previous chapters, I mentioned bits and pieces of the testing program at GELC. However, the GELC testing was much more than bits and pieces. When it was fully implemented, we considered it a *testing program* that had many interrelated parts including norm-referenced proficiency tests and criterion-referenced diagnostic and achievement tests. A number of benefits were garnered from these testing efforts in the area of curriculum development.

Norm-Referenced Proficiency Tests

I mentioned our agreement with the Chinese government in Chapter One. Recall that GELC was only going to accept students who had TOEFL scores in excess of 450, and that our aim was to raise their overall proficiency to 550 on the TOEFL by the time they graduated. For both of these decisions, admissions and graduation, we were concerned with the interface of our program with the outside world. In other words, we needed to know how proficient the students were when they arrived (from the outside world) as well as how proficient they were when they left our program (that is, when they went back to the outside world); these were both proficiency decisions.

Prior to the first TOEFL test administered in China in December 1981, we had to make these decisions using tests that we had equated (through something called regression analysis; see Brown [1988]) with TOEFL tests. We developed a series of tests that allowed us to predict (within a certain margin of error) how well the students would do if they were to take the TOEFL. These pseudo-TOEFL tests were administered at the beginning of the program and at the end of each 10-week session so that we could monitor the progress of the students in global proficiency terms. This pattern of tests also gave the students ample opportunities to practice taking tests similar to the actual TOEFL—a test that most of them would eventually experience.

The students were mostly bound for universities in the United States and were naturally curious, even anxious, about the TOEFL test. This anxiety caused problems when some students, after 10 weeks of study, found that their predicted TOEFL scores had dropped because of quite natural testing error. Reporting scores to the students necessitated a good deal of explanation about the TOEFL test as well as about the statistical principles behind regression analysis and the standard error of estimate. (Both of these topics are beyond the scope of this book, but can be investigated further by referring to Brown [forthcoming] or Henning [1987].) Since the students were scientists and for the most part had some background in statistics, these concepts were relatively easy to communicate with them. This proficiency testing activity further revealed to us that the students had a need that we had not adequately anticipated (that is, to prepare for taking the TOEFL). However, because of the flexibility that we were able to build in our program, this perceived need was met by adding a minor TOEFL preparation component to the Listening C course, and also by sometimes teaching this component independently. As the left side of Figure 4.1 demonstrates, proficiency testing played a large part in the GELC program.

In contrast, after a few unsatisfactory attempts, we dropped placement testing. We found that most of our Chinese students had strong grammar knowledge, but were relatively weak in using the English language for reading, writing, listening, or speaking. In other words, the students knew a great deal about the language—indeed, they sometimes asked esoteric grammar questions that baffled trained ESL teachers—but they could not communicate very well using the system about which they knew so much. As a result, one of our goals was to teach the students the functions and communicative strategies that they would need to succeed in academic settings. Thus much of the teaching and practice in class was focused on fostering fluency, whether in reading, writing, speaking, or listening. (For instance, in response to the request that I "speak more slowly," it was quite natural for me to insist instead that the student should "listen more quickly.")

Figure 4.1: GELC Testing Program

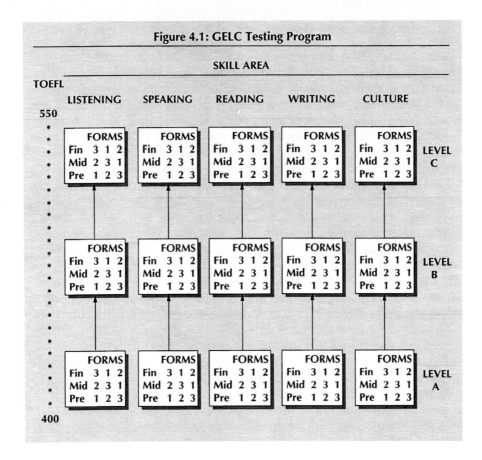

This situation had two important ramifications for our testing program. First, we realized that *all* the students could benefit from taking *all* of the courses, Levels A through C. Upon arrival, none of them had a command of the functions that we were teaching, or had sufficient fluency or adequate communicative strategies to be placed in more advanced courses with the students who had already had many opportunities to practice these skills and strategies. Thus we decided to place all students in the A Level and to have them all progress through the entire sequence of courses.

Second, we found that we could not count on the pseudo-TOEFL tests, or the real TOEFL for that matter, to reflect the types of skills that our students were learning. This meant that if we were going to develop placement tests in the future, they would have to be developed specifically for our program and its communicative goals. It also meant that if we wanted to show the gains being made by our students, we would need something more sensitive and specific to our program than overall proficiency tests.

Criterion-Referenced Diagnostic and Achievement Tests

This last realization led directly to the development of criterion-referenced tests that were based on the objectives of our courses. These tests were developed by the teachers in each skill area to directly reflect the objectives of their courses and the types of activities that were going on in those courses. Therefore, the tests could be considered very much like the final examinations that teachers almost everywhere develop (in isolation) for their courses. However, in this case, we were able to plan more carefully than most isolated teachers can because the tests were to be based on existing and relatively clear sets of objectives; we were also in a position to draw on the strength that comes from combining the talents of a number of good teachers.

Initially, we set out to create two forms of the test for each course so that we could use them as a pretest and posttest in each session. Ultimately, we aimed at having three forms of each test for each course so that we could use them as pretest, midterm, and posttest (as shown in Figure 4.1). When these tests were fully implemented, we were in a position to give the students diagnostic information objective-by-objective based on the pretest, diagnostic progress information objective-by-objective at the midterm, and achievement information objective-by-objective at the end of the course.

A quick glance back at Table 3.8 will give the reader an idea of how the reading test must have looked because the objectives in that table are the closest to describing just exactly how we would test them. Once the tests were administered, the scores were reported in percent terms to the students as diagnostic or progress reports like the one shown in Table 4.5. Such reports provided the students and teachers alike with information about which areas had already been mastered, and which areas should receive the most attention in terms of study and practice.

One problem we had to deal with was the practice effect. Brown (1988, p. 35) defines the *practice effect* as "the potential influence of the measures on each other." In this case, simply having taken one of the tests was likely to improve the students' performances on any subsequent administrations of the same test. In general, we took the view that the tests should be considered part of the teaching and that the practice effect could be considered part of the learning experience. Nevertheless, we wanted to minimize the effect that remembering specific test questions would have on subsequent tests. In other words, we did not want any student taking exactly the same form of any test more than once.

Therefore, to minimize the impact of the practice effect, we used what is called a *counterbalanced design* for administering the tests (see Figure 4.1, inside each course box). At the beginning of each course, all three forms (1, 2, and 3) of the test were administered to random thirds of each class. At the midterm, the same three forms were used but the students' names were already on the tests so that the students did not take the same form taken on the pretest. For the final achievement examination, the same three forms could be used, but again the

Table 4.5 Example Diagnosis/Progress Report for GELC Reading B*
(adapted from GELC 1982)

OBJECTIVE:	YOUR SCORE:
1. Skim a 600-word passage for six minutes, then answer multiple-choice factual questions (without the passage) with 60 percent accuracy.	_____
2. Answer multiple-choice factual questions on a 600-word passage in six minutes with 70 percent accuracy.	_____
3. Answer multiple-choice factual questions about a graph, chart, or diagram in three minutes with 70 percent accuracy.	_____
4. Take notes in outline format on a 600-word passage including main ideas and subideas (that is, at least two levels) with 70 percent accuracy.	_____
. . .	
9. Fill in connectors (provided) in the appropriate blanks in a 600-word passage with 70 percent accuracy.	_____
10. Write labels for missing elements in a graph, chart, or diagram from information provided in a 600-word passage with 70 percent accuracy.	_____
11. Fill in meanings (provided) for the prefixes and stems given in appendix in Long et al. (1980) with 70 percent accuracy.	_____
. . .	
14. Fill in meanings of unknown words based on sentence level context with 70 percent accuracy.	_____
15. Identify sentences which function as examples in a 600-word passage with 70 percent accuracy.	_____
16. Identify sentences which function as analogies in a 600-word passage with 70 percent accuracy.	_____

* All reading passages were on general science topics and were grade 11 reading level, which is equal to junior year (next to last) ability in U.S. high school, or approximately the *red* cards in your 4a SRA reading cards.

names were preassigned so that no student took the same form encountered on the pretest or midterm test. As Figure 4.1 shows, this system meant that a student taking Form 1 of the Level C Listening test on the pretest would take Form 2 at the midterm and Form 3 on the final. Similarly, a student who took Form 2 on the pretest would take Form 3 at the midterm and Form 1 on the final. The remaining students would take Form 3 on the pretest, Form 1 at the midterm, and Form 2 on the final exam. Thus no student took exactly the same test twice.

We developed such an elaborate system of tests because we felt that it was important to provide valuable diagnostic, progress, and achievement information to the students and their teachers, and to do so without causing a direct practice effect by allowing students to take the same test twice. However, we also recognized that it is important to have pretest-posttest information in developing CRTs so that the effectiveness of the items can be studied and the tests can be improved. (Unfortunately, discussing these techniques is beyond the scope of this book.)

Benefits of a Sound Testing Program

These criterion-referenced tests were not easy to develop. In fact, a tremendous amount of work was involved. However, a determined group of teachers did create these tests, and did so in multiple forms. The payoff from all this work was enormous, especially with regard to gathering information on all the elements of the curriculum design process.

First, the tests helped us to closely examine our perceptions of the students' needs. For example, we found that they could perform quite well (sometimes with 100 percent accuracy) on all the items for some of the objectives on the first day of class. When we discovered this type of situation, it became quite clear to us that our initial perceptions about some objectives were wrong and that the students did not need instruction in those objectives.

Second, after we discovered that some objectives did not need to be taught, we had the freedom to concentrate instead on the remaining objectives or to add new objectives designed to meet more advanced needs. Thus we were able to avoid wasting time teaching material that the students already knew and to focus instead on teaching what the students needed to learn. Perhaps we were succumbing to what Tumposky (1984) sarcastically calls the "cult of efficiency," but frankly I do not understand why attempting to be relatively efficient is a bad thing. We were simply trying to foster as much language learning as we could in the short 30-week period we had to work with the students. Why would we want to waste time teaching and practicing material that the students had mastered before arriving at GELC?

Third, changing the objectives due to what we learned from the tests naturally led to rethinking our materials and teaching strategies to meet the newly perceived needs of the students. Such rethinking sometimes prompted major changes, but more often took the form of incremental modifications in the materials, teaching techniques, and practice exercises that were worked out by the groups of teachers most directly involved.

The fourth and last benefit gained from our testing program was that whenever we needed to focus on program evaluation, we had a great deal of information ready to be presented. We had information about the overall proficiency of our students (norm-referenced), as well as information about what and how much the students were learning in the classroom (criterion-referenced). One form of evaluation that took place in the GELC program was the yearly report we prepared for all interested parties in China and the responsible parties in the UCLA/China Exchange Program office in Los Angeles. By the second year, we were clearly in a position to fashion a summary report that described our program in terms of student needs, program goals, objectives, how the students fit with the rest of the world in overall proficiency terms, and how much they were learning as a group in each of their classes. We were also able to suggest clear-cut changes in the program in an ongoing process of curriculum development. Thus the information gained from the testing program helped us to focus our program evaluation report (see Chapter Seven for much more on this topic).

□ ENGLISH LANGUAGE INSTITUTE, UNIVERSITY OF HAWAII AT MANOA

The testing in the ELI is both different from and similar to the testing that we did in China. The primary difference is in the placement procedures, which in the ELI are necessarily quite elaborate. Like the GELC program, all ELI testing activities are viewed as interrelated parts of a single comprehensive testing program; indeed, the various parts are even more tightly knit together in the ELI. As such, they form what we feel is a fair, flexible system of decision making.

Because the teachers and administrators in the ELI want classes that have fairly homogeneous groups of students (in terms of ability levels), placement procedures are used. But these procedures are not based solely on placement test results, as is the case in many institutions. Instead, we use four sets of procedures that help us to ensure that students are working at the level that most benefits all parties concerned: (1) initial screening procedures, (2) placement procedures, (3) first-week assessment procedures, and (4) achievement procedures.

Initial Screening Procedures

Before students are admitted to UHM, they are carefully screened by the Office of Admissions and Records. The students' previous academic records, letters of recommendation, and TOEFL scores are reviewed and only those students with total scores of 500 or higher are accepted for admissions to UHM. This information, including each student's TOEFL subtest and total scores, is transmitted to the ELI. If their scores are above 600, students are notified that they are exempted from any ELI requirement. Those students who have scored between 500 and 599 are notified that they must clear the ELI immediately upon arrival at UHM. In this way, the initial screening procedures narrow the range of English proficiencies with which the ELI must deal.

Note that even after screening decisions have been made, any student may request an interview with the director or the assistant director to have his or her particular case reconsidered. These interviews allow us some flexibility and an initial opportunity to spot students who may logically be exempted (for instance, students from India who had all their education in English-medium schools and spoke English at home). In Hawaii, there are many varied and interesting cases, particularly with immigrant youngsters, that must be dealt with on a one-to-one basis in this manner.

Placement Procedures

In most cases, however, students who scored between 500 and 599 on the TOEFL are required to take the ELI Placement Test (ELIPT) as soon as they arrive on campus. We require this test for three reasons: (1) because we want more detailed information than is provided by TOEFL scores, (2) because we want specific information about how the students will fit into our particular language program (in terms of their level of ability in each of the skill areas), and (3) because we are also interested in getting information that is more recent than their TOEFL scores (which can be as much as two years old). Placement procedures are particularly important in programs, like our ELI, that have different tracks and levels (refer back to Figure 4.2). Recall that we have four tracks, each of which is focused on one skill (reading, writing, listening, or speaking). Within these tracks there are up to three levels. So the placement decisions (and hence the tests) must be focused on the skills involved.

The ELIPT is a three-hour test battery consisting of six subtests: Academic Listening Test (ALT), Dictation (DCT), Reading Comprehension Test (RCT), Cloze Procedure (CLZ), Writing Sample (WTS), and Academic Writing Test (AWT). The Academic Listening Test and Dictation are used to place students into our listening skill courses (see vertical arrows to the left of the listening courses in Figure 4.2). The Reading Comprehension Test and Cloze Procedure are used for the reading skill courses (represented by the vertical arrows to the left of the reading courses in Figure 4.2). The Academic Writing Test and Writing Sample are employed for placing students into the proper writing skill level (see vertical arrows to the left of the writing courses in Figure 4.2). Notice that we use two test scores for placement into each of the three primary skill areas that we teach. (The Speaking course is presently only available for international teaching assistants. The testing for this course is therefore handled separately from the mainstream program.) In each skill area, one of the subtests is *discrete-point*, that is, it tests the discrete bits and pieces of the language, and one is *integrative*, that is, it requires the student to integrate and use a variety of different language skills. (See Oller 1979 for a more elaborate description of the difference between these two types of test.) This arrangement serves us well by providing two different views of each student's abilities within each skill area.

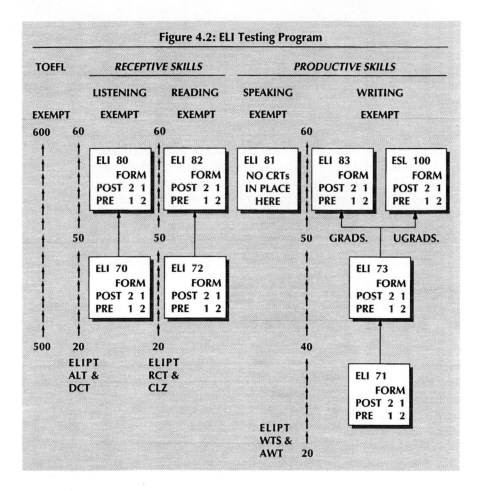

Figure 4.2: ELI Testing Program

Notice that all the ELIPT subtest scores shown in Figure 4.2 are on the same standardized scoring scale with scores of 20–49 being placed into the "70-level courses," scores of 50–59 indicating the upper "80-level" courses, and scores of 60 or higher showing that the student should be exempted. (These scores are standardized as *T* scores—see Brown [forthcoming].) Standardizing in this way makes interpretation of the scores easier when the teachers make actual placement decisions.

However, placement decisions are not based solely on the students' test scores. The actual placement of each student occurs during an individual conference with an ELI faculty member. The instructor has the student's file and test scores in front of him or her at the time of the interview and is trained to base his or her placement decision for each skill area not only on the two subtest scores for that skill but also on the other information in the student's records and any details gained by talking to the student. In cases where the instructor is unsure of the appropriate level for a student or in cases where the student contests the placement decision, the ELI director or assistant director interviews the student and makes a final decision. The students then register for the appropriate courses and classes begin.

We feel that the interview procedure allows us to place students very accurately because the placement decisions are based on many sources of information considered together. The ELIPT subtest scores (both integrative and discrete-point) are considered very important, but we also take into account the length of time that the students have studied English, how long ago they studied it, their TOEFL subtest scores, their spoken language ability during the interview, their academic records, and any other information available at the time. All of this information helps us not only to place students but also to do so in a way that treats them as human beings—individuals who are important to the University of Hawaii at Manoa. However, even so, the process of determining whether or not a student has been properly placed does not stop.

First-Week Assessment Procedures

During the first week of instruction, all ELI teachers administer a criterion-referenced test designed specifically to test the objectives of their courses. The teachers are also asked to keep a close watch on their students to see if any have been misplaced. When teachers find students who seem to be in the wrong level, they consult with the ELI director. Interviews with the students are conducted to find out what they want to do, and they are advised about what we think should happen. In most cases, students who are found to be misplaced are encouraged to switch up or down into a more appropriate course and the process of moving them is set in motion.

Achievement Procedures

At the end of each semester, evaluation report forms are filled out by the teachers about the performance of every student. Teachers are asked specifically what ELI course level the students should take during the next semester. On the basis of classroom performance and the student's score on the criterion-referenced final achievement test, the teachers can suggest that students skip one level or be exempted from any further study in that particular skill area. Again, interviews with the ELI director are arranged, and the students are advised on the course of action that we think would be most appropriate. Copies of these reports are then sent to the students' academic departments so that their advisers will know about the new ELI requirements. In this way, students who have learned more than their peers can be identified and adjustments in their subsequent placement can be made.

Criterion-Referenced Diagnostic and Achievement Procedures

As I mentioned above, there are also tests within each of the courses in the ELI courses that are designed to test the specific objectives of that course. Unlike the criterion-referenced tests developed for the GELC program, the tests in the ELI only exist in two forms. These tests were jointly developed for every course by the teachers in the courses over a period of two years. The tests are reviewed annually to ensure that they match the objectives of the courses as they are taught at the time.

The two forms of each test are used in a counterbalanced design for the course pretest (for diagnosis) and posttest (for final achievement), as Figure 4.2 reveals. These tests, like those at GELC, have proven useful for giving information to the students and their teachers, as well as for assessing the accuracy of our perceptions of students needs and the appropriateness of the course goals and objectives. They also help guide our materials selection and creation efforts. Perhaps most important, the development and maintenance of these tests have provided a set of unifying activities that bind the various teachers of each course into a single unit and the assorted courses into an institution.

This whole system of tests, including proficiency, placement, diagnosis, and achievement, is made relatively efficient by instituting the role of lead teacher for a teacher who is given 50 percent release time to develop, analyze, revise, score, and report the results of ELI tests. During placement tests this lead teacher takes responsibility for administering the tests, while the director is responsible for scoring and analyzing the results as each part is completed. In our present situation, it is useful that the director is a language testing specialist and that the lead teacher for testing is typically a graduate assistant who excelled in our language testing course.

For the criterion-referenced diagnostic and achievement tests, the lead teacher has proven essential in rallying the teachers to review and revise each of the forms for each course and getting the tests to the teachers on time for use in class. In addition, it has proven important that this lead teacher do the scoring and get the results back to the teachers within 24 hours. Such promptness has made the results particularly useful and helped in garnering teachers' support for the entire testing program.

ELI Testing Program

We sincerely hope that the vast majority of the students who are served by the procedures discussed above are correctly classified, placed, diagnosed, and promoted. However, decisions are made by human beings, and even when they are based on seemingly scientific information in the form of test scores, human judgments can be wrong. Incorrect decisions can cost a student a great deal in the form of extra tuition paid or extra and unnecessary time spent studying ESL.

Thus any decisions that we make about students' lives must be based on the best available information—information from a variety of different sources.

Certainly, all of this takes a little more effort on the part of the administrators and teachers, but the benefits gained from effective and humane testing procedures accrue to all: students, teachers, and administrators alike. Note that the strategies that we find so useful can easily be generalized and adapted to other language programs.

One particularly useful side effect of having a complete testing system, or program, is that information gained from one type of test can sometimes be utilized to improve the other types. For instance, information gained from the CRT achievement tests can prove useful in revising the placement procedures so that they more closely match that which is being taught in the classrooms. Brown (1989b) describes one such process. In that study, the RCT subtest of the ELIPT was made to more closely match the kinds of approach, syllabus, techniques, and exercises that actually go on in the reading courses. The procedures and statistics involved in the process are explained step-by-step in the article cited above.

SUMMARY

In this chapter, the discussion has centered on setting up a testing program that can help decision makers match the correct test (and other information sources) to each of the decisions that must be made about students. The distinction between criterion-referenced and norm-referenced tests was shown to be crucial to the process of adopting, developing, or adapting tests that can help with proficiency, placement, diagnostic, and achievement decisions. Strategies for matching decision and test types were discussed (see Table 4.2), as were the characteristics of good tests (see Table 4.3). The elements of a successful testing program were outlined (see Table 4.4) and the chapter ended with descriptions of the rather elaborate testing programs at GELC (Figure 4.1) and in the ELI (Figure 4.2). The overall message of this chapter was that there are a variety of different test types that can help in making responsible decisions about students' lives. In addition, a comprehensive testing system provides valuable information for the revision and development of the other elements of the curriculum, that is, the needs analysis, goals and objectives, materials, teaching, and program evaluation.

■ ■ ■ *CHECKLIST*

The purpose of this checklist is to ensure that you are using the correct tests for different types of decisions.

□ Have you decided about the referencing of the test? (see Table 4.1)
- □ Criterion-referenced?
- □ Norm-referenced?

□ Have you identified the type of decision you must make with the test scores?
- □ Proficiency?
- □ Placement?
- □ Achievement?
- □ Diagnosis?

□ Does your test match your decision type? (see Table 4.2)

□ Have you checked the quality of the test? (see Table 4.3)

□ Are you adequately prepared to create an environment that makes the testing successful? (see Table 4.4)

■ ■ ■ TERMS

achievement decisions	counterbalanced design
diagnostic decisions	criterion-referenced test (CRT)
discrete-point tests	diagnostic testing
norm-referenced test (NRT)	integrative tests
percentile	percentage
placement testing	placement decisions
proficiency decisions	practice effect
testing program	proficiency testing
achievement testing	test items

■ ■ ■ REVIEW QUESTIONS

1. For which type of test (NRT or CRT) would you expect the interpretation to be absolute? And, which type would be relative?
2. For which type of test (NRT or CRT) would you expect the scores to spread students out along a continuum of general abilities or proficiencies?
3. For which type of test (NRT or CRT) would you expect all of the students to be able to score 100 percent if they knew all of what was taught?
4. For which type of decision (proficiency, placement, diagnostic, or achievement) would you use a test that is designed to find each student's appropriate level within a particular program?

5. For which type of decision (proficiency, placement, diagnostic, or achievement) would you use a test that is designed to inform students and teachers of objectives needing more work.

6. For which type of decision (proficiency, placement, diagnostic, or achievement) would you use a test that is designed to determine the degree of learning (with respect to the program objectives) that had taken place by the end of a course?

7. For which type of decision (proficiency, placement, diagnostic, or achievement) would you use a test that is designed to compare individual's overall performance with that of groups or individuals at other institutions?

8. Do you think that the concepts behind CRTs and NRTs can be mixed into one test? If so, how and why?

9. What are the factors you must consider in looking at the quality of a test? Which do you think are the most important?

10. What are the factors you must consider in successfully putting tests in place? Which factors do you think are the most important?

■ ■ ■ APPLICATIONS

A1. Look back at the "Example Testing Programs" section and choose either the GELC or the ELI program description. List the different types of decisions and tests that were described. Next, jot down the purpose of each test (proficiency, placement, diagnosis, or achievement). Finally, enumerate at least three characteristics that you would look for in each of these tests. Would they be NRTs or CRTs?

A2. In the example program that you chose, what other sources of information (in addition to test scores) were also used in making the decisions? What additional sources can you think of that should have been used?

B1. Think of one or two different types of decisions that you have to make in your language program (or will have to make when you become a teacher). Decide what type of decision each one is (proficiency, placement, diagnostic, or achievement) and describe at least three characteristics of the test that you might use to help you make each decision.

B2. Look at some form of decision making that exists in your language program and decide which type of test you would use to make it and what it should be like in terms of overall characteristics, as well as the skills tested, level of difficulty, length, administration time, scoring, and the type of report given to teachers and students.

B3. Match a real test that you know about to a real decision in your language program. How would you administer, score, interpret, and report the results of the test? How would you help others make the appropriate decisions so that they minimize any potential negative affects on the students' lives?

Chapter 5

MATERIALS

INTRODUCTION

Working from the general parameters of the program design, as defined by the needs analysis, goals and objectives, and tests, curriculum developers are in an excellent position to begin materials development. *Materials* will be defined here as any systematic description of the techniques and exercises to be used in classroom teaching. Such a definition is broad enough to encompass lesson plans and yet can accommodate books, packets of audiovisual aids, games, or any of the other myriad types of activities that go on in the language classroom. The key in developing sound materials is to ensure that they are described and organized well enough so that teachers can use them with no confusion and with a minimum of preparation time. The surest test of the viability of a set of materials is for a teacher to be able to implement them without any aid from their original creator. If that teacher is successful, the chances are that the materials are systematically and clearly described.

Before beginning any materials project, it may be useful to stop and take stock of what has been learned about the program thus far. If steps similar to those outlined in the previous four chapters have been followed, the curriculum developers should have a clear understanding of the program's theoretical positions (the approaches and syllabuses), as well as its more practical orientations (techniques and exercises).

I will begin by explaining how the theoretical and practical elements of the curriculum framework can work together with what has been learned in the needs analysis, goals and objectives, and testing stages of curriculum development to form a materials blueprint. Such blueprints will be examined from a number of perspectives, including how blueprints can present the units of analysis, and the scope and sequence of the materials. In addition, I will briefly explore the possibility of using Gantt diagrams to keep the materials development project on track.

I will then turn to the question of where materials come from. Three strategies will be discussed: adopting, developing, and adapting materials. Adopting materials involves deciding on the types of materials that are needed, locating as many different sets of those types as possible, evaluating the materials, putting them to use, and reviewing them on an ongoing basis. Developing materials will be discussed in terms of three phases: developing, teaching (field testing), and evaluating the materials. Adapting materials includes all of the steps necessary in adopting them, but must additionally incorporate phases that allow for analyzing what is worth keeping in the materials, classifying that remaining material, filling gaps from other sources, and reorganizing all of this to fit the program in question. I end by discussing materials development projects at GELC and in the ELI. These examples demonstrate a number of ways that materials development projects can be managed and enhanced.

FRAMEWORK FOR MATERIALS DESIGN

Before actually adopting, developing, or adapting materials, the language program's overall orientation must be considered in terms of approaches and syllabuses, as well as in terms of how that orientation will influence the choices that must be made in the development and implementation of materials. As I just mentioned, materials can be adopted, developed, or adapted, or some combination of the three. However, the choice of overall strategy will depend on the program's overall orientation. Hence the overall strategy must be considered before becoming too involved in actual materials development processes. My discussion of this issue will be organized around the main teaching activities described in Chapter 1: approach, syllabuses, techniques, and exercises.

□ APPROACH

The one point about which most language curriculum developers would probably agree is that there must be some sort of theoretical motivation underlying any curriculum development (for instance, see Anthony 1963; Richards & Rogers 1982; McKay 1978; and Chapter One). In this book, such motivations have been labeled *approaches* and interpreted as ways of defining what the students need to learn based on assumptions and theoretical positions drawn from disciplines as diverse as linguistics, psychology, and education. Chapter One reviewed some of these approaches including the classical approach, the grammar-translation approach, the direct approach, the audiolingual approach, and the communicative approach. Though these approaches can be viewed as historical developments that happened roughly in the order listed, all of these approaches continue in use in classrooms throughout the world today. Moreover, this list is incomplete because the approaches I have named represent only those around which considerable consensus developed, and because other approaches will no doubt surface in the coming years.

Running Example: Approaches

In order to exemplify how approaches, syllabuses, techniques, and exercises fit together, let's use one approach, the communicative approach, as the basis for discussion. I have chosen this approach because a strong consensus has built up worldwide in recent decades in support of this approach. This running example will serve as a model to illustrate the process of fitting syllabuses, techniques, and exercises to any approach, or combination of approaches. In other words, though the example approach is communicative, similar connections can and should be made with any approaches that are pervasive in a particular program.

Let's begin with a communicative approach that takes the position that students should be able to express their intentions and the meanings important in their lives. Let's further suppose that the students are at the intermediate level, ranging from about 450 to 500 on the TOEFL test, and that this approach will be applied to two courses, one for speaking and one for writing. In short, this running example will include two contrasting skill area courses, speaking and writing, that the students need to take in order to learn to express those meanings which are most important to them. Once such a theoretical position is established, curriculum developers will have a basis for beginning to make choices as to how to organize, present, and practice the language in question. Thus the next logical step will be to consider the syllabuses that should be used to organize all other teaching activities.

□ SYLLABUSES

As defined here, the teaching activities called *syllabuses* are predominantly concerned with the choices necessary to organize the language content of a course or program. The procedures involved in developing a syllabus should eventually include examining instructional objectives, arranging them in terms of priorities, and then determining what kinds of techniques and exercises are required in order to attain those objectives. The information gathered in the course of conducting a language needs analysis will help to determine the direction that a particular syllabus planning project will go since the same units of analysis used in the needs analysis will tend to be used in the objectives that result. Thus a program's approach affects the units of analysis in the needs analysis, and—at least in part—predetermines the shape that the objectives will eventually take. For example, if the needs analysts favor the communicative approach, the units of analysis will tend to be the speech acts, functions, interactional moves, and turns familiar to practitioners of discourse and text analysis. Moreover, the needs that are perceived will quite naturally tend to be shaped into these units, which in turn will be used as elements of the objectives. However, as I indicated in Chapters Two and Three, the process of getting from perceived needs to objectives is not easy, nor can we expect a one-to-one correspondence between units of analysis and the objectives that eventually surface.

As I pointed out in Chapter One, a number of different kinds of syllabuses are commonly found in current ESL courses and materials. To review briefly, the seven listed in Chapter One were as follows:

1.   Structural (organized around grammatical structures)

2.   Situational (organized around various settings in which the learners are likely to use the language, such as at the bank, at the supermarket, at a restaurant, and so forth)

3.   Topical (organized around themes or topics, such as health, food, clothing, and so forth)

4.   Functional (organized around communicative functions, such as identifying, reporting, correcting, describing, and so forth)

5.   Notional (organized around conceptual categories, such as duration, quantity, location, and so forth)

6.   Skills (organized around skills, such as listening for gist, listening for specific information, listening for inferences, and so forth)

7.   Task- or activity-based (organized around activities, such as drawing maps, following directions, following instructions, and so forth)

Unfortunately, despite the extensive literature on syllabuses, there is little empirical evidence that any particular type of syllabus works better than any other. In practice, many good teachers probably use a combination of syllabus types since many would agree with Johnson's (1981, p. 34) comment:

> A syllabus is essentially a job specification, and as such it should set out clearly and precisely what is to be done, and the standards or criteria to be met by those who do it. If seen in this light, arguments as to the relative merits of different types of syllabuses: structural, functional, notional, situational, topic based, etc. are no more sensible than arguments as to whether the specifications in a construction contract should cover the foundations, or the steel framework or the concrete or the glass or the interior design etc. The obvious answer is that all of these must be covered.

The degree of detail that will be furnished in a given syllabus design is another important issue. As I noted in the first two chapters, decisions concerning what kind of syllabus and its degree of detail will be determined in part by practical matters in the instructional situation. For instance, in an institution where the teachers are well trained and hold similar views on which approaches are appropriate, detailed specification of syllabus content may not be necessary. The teachers may prefer to work directly from the program objectives, selecting content themselves from the variety of sources made available to them by the program administration. In other situations, because of political or administrative requirements, a detailed syllabus may be necessary to ensure that the desired content for the course or program is covered in a standard sequence. As Johnson (1978, p. 46) has stated:

> A language teaching experience must obviously entail the use of target language forms, but if it is to be a learning experience in any real sense, these forms must be used meaningfully, in situations where they are appropriate, and functionally in that they serve a purpose for the teacher or writer.

If the materials writer fails consistently in any of these particulars, it is necessary for the teacher to compensate, and by intervening in this way a good teacher can often rescue and use effectively even grossly deficient teaching materials. However, if the necessary decisions have been made and carried out explicitly by the syllabus writers, and if the criteria laid down are met by materials writers, then grossly inadequate or irrelevant materials can be eliminated from the classroom, and the professional expertise of teachers can be employed more constructively.

Running Example: Syllabuses

The example courses in speaking and writing, both of which are based on the communicative approach, might at first seem to require organization around a functional syllabus. However, as I already pointed out, there are seven alternative organizing principles that could be employed: structural, situational, topical, functional, notional, skill, and task. These alternatives should all be considered as potentially useful ways to organize the materials. However, let's assume that, based on the needs analysis and the objectives that resulted, the curriculum designers in consultation with the teachers have decided that the communicative curriculum for the example speaking course will be organized around functions. Let's further assume that those functions listed in Table 3.1 were chosen. Recall that the functions listed in Table 3.1 included identifying, reporting (including describing and narrating), correcting, asking, and so forth.

Using the same processes but working with different teachers, the curriculum designers decided that the curriculum for the writing course will be organized around the two types of syllabuses shown in Table 3.9. In this case, the syllabus is ordered partially on the basis of functions (for example, defining, comparing, paraphrasing, and exemplifying) and partially around tasks (for instance, writing an academic note or writing an academic letter). Please refer back to the tables in Chapter Three and have a look at how those two syllabuses were outlined.

□ TECHNIQUES

Once the syllabuses are in place, the category of teaching activities called *techniques* comes into play. In Chapter One, this set of activities was defined as ways of presenting language points to the students. I discussed a number of such techniques, and listed some of the possibilities in Table 1.5. Language can be presented to students in many ways, but presentation typically includes various combinations of interactions between teacher and student, student and student, cassette player and student, and so forth. The teacher selects and uses these learning experiences to help bring about learning. Materials developers must make decisions early in the process about the principal kinds of activities and learning experiences that the program will use and the criteria that will be employed for selecting those activities and experiences. How much weight will be assigned to each activity type per lesson? And what configurations of teacher and learner will activities involve? These are questions that materials developers will have to answer within any program before deciding on detailed specifications for the activities that will go on in the daily classes.

Running Example: Techniques

Assuming that the example program has decided that the organization for the speaking and writing courses will be provided by the syllabuses shown in Tables 3.1 and 3.9, respectively, the decision has been made that the teachers will be left alone to plan the techniques that they feel will be most effective in helping their students to meet those objectives. As a result, one teacher's class period in the speaking course might center around the first part of the second function, reporting (by describing), that was listed in the syllabus and might include the following teaching activities:

1. Review on blackboard of the specific vocabulary needed in describing an object with focus on shapes, sizes, and textures (teacher to learners)
2. Example video tape showing a native speaker describing various commonly encountered objects (video to learners)
3. Lecture on the exponents (grammatical forms and phrases) that are useful for describing objects (teacher to learners).

Clearly, the criteria for selecting activities for this speaking class are related to the idea that it is useful to provide examples of the native speaker using the describing function as a model, as well as the vocabulary and grammatical tools necessary to perform the function. Obviously, on other days, the activities might be entirely different depending on which objectives are being addressed. As I will show in the "Exercises" section, these techniques can then be reinforced by exercises that encourage the students to practice what they have observed, that is, to actually speak instead of just listen.

One writing class on the same day might involve entirely different activities:

1. Demonstration of an example text (teacher to learners)
2. Analysis of models of good writing (learner to group)
3. Blackboard writing (five learners at a time to class) and discussion (teacher to learners).

In this case, the criteria for selecting techniques are related to the idea that it is useful to provide opportunities for students to develop their writing skills in contexts and on the basis of models of teacher and student writing. Again, these activities could vary from day to day because of the variety of objectives that will typically be addressed in such a course.

□ EXERCISES

Once the approaches, syllabuses, and techniques have been tentatively set, the category of teaching activities called *exercises* must be considered. In Chapter One, I defined this set of activities as ways of having the students practice the language points they have been presented. A number of possible exercise types were listed in Table 1.6. Language can be practiced in many ways, but typically such practice centers on the student using the language in some interaction such as learner to learner, learner to self, learner to teacher, learner to group, learner to cassette player, learner to class, and so forth. These learning experiences are selected and facilitated by the teacher to help bring about practice that will reinforce learning. Materials developers must make early decisions about the principal kinds of exercises that will be most appropriate for the program in question, as well as decisions about the criteria that will be used for selecting exercises. The primary questions concern the weight that will be assigned to each activity per lesson or unit and the configurations of teacher/learner/group/class that will be used. These issues must be addressed within the program before deciding on detailed specifications for the exercises that will go on in the daily classes.

Running Example: Exercises

The teaching techniques I described in the running example in the previous section might best be reinforced by selecting exercises that afford the students opportunities to practice what they had learned. The line between techniques and exercises is becoming increasingly blurred because, in communicative approach, teaching techniques often consist of setting up opportunities for students to practice using the language.

For instance, in the example speaking course, the teacher might want to set up practice opportunities for conversational interaction and draw on some or all of the following exercises:

1. Dialogue work (learner to learner)
2. Teacher–student interaction (The teacher circulates around the room to each student, identifying objects that she has in mind without naming them. The students must guess the object.) (teacher to student)
3. Peer feedback sessions (learner to group)
4. Pair work (learner to learner)
5. Free conversation (teacher to learners/learner to learner).

In the writing course, reinforcement exercises might include the following activities:

1. Brainstorming (learner to group)
2. Quick writing (learner to self)
3. Group writing (learner to group)
4. Free composition activities (learner to self).

MATERIALS BLUEPRINT

It is not as difficult as it might seem to keep track of teachers' preferences for approaches and syllabuses in a given program, nor is their influence on the choices of techniques and exercises likely to be a mystery. Once it becomes clear that these categories are useful for purposes of discussing curriculum issues, the categories are likely to pop up in every teachers' meeting, and the point of view of the various teachers is likely to surface rather quickly.

The trick is to channel these various points of view into a set of guidelines that represent a consensus reached among all of the members of the program administration and faculty. To this end, the curriculum developers, whoever they may be, would be well advised to formulate a materials blueprint that represents the kind of language program that they are proposing based on all the information obtained in the needs analysis, objectives setting, and testing stages of program development. This blueprint might at first be very unclear and tentative, yet as time passes and even more information becomes available, its outlines will become increasingly discernable and precise. Such a blueprint might eventually form part of a teacher's manual that can be used to describe the program and its curriculum or to orient new teachers to the program in question. As I will argue in the next chapter, such a teacher's manual can also contain information that will support instructors in their teaching efforts. An example outline of such a materials blueprint (from CAL 1981) is presented in Table 5.1. Notice the types of information included in the Center for Applied Linguistics outline and how useful some of them would be to materials developers.

Whatever form such a materials blueprint eventually takes, it should account for all the relevant information learned in the initial curriculum development stages and include all factors judged to be potentially important influences on the program and its future curriculum. To review briefly, situation factors might include implications from the broader political, social, and educational contexts in which the program will operate, as well as the particular circumstances relating to the kind of institution or setting in which the curriculum will be carried out. Other important factors might include the characteristics of the teachers, learners, and administrators; the resources found in the particular situation; and, of course, the language needs of the students.

Table 5.1   Example of Materials Blueprint (CAL 1981)

DEFINITION: ESL SURVIVAL provides the language necessary for minimum functioning in the specific community in which the refugee is settled.

CLIENTS TO BE SERVED: ESL/SURVIVAL can be used with all clients.

DELIVERY: Any of the delivery settings outlined (non-formal, single multi-level class, center, on-job site) may be used, but the system chosen should be suited to the number of clients to be served and their geographical distribution.

INTENSITY:

* Recommended 6 to 15 hours per week, no fewer than 3 days per week.
* Best offered on a 5 day per week basis with a maximum of 3 hours per day.

CONTENT: ESL/SURVIVAL may include but not be limited to simple statements, questions, and vocabulary concerning:

* Consumer/environmental skills, such as personal information, money/credit, housing, health, communications, shopping (food/clothing, non-essentials), community resources, insurance, taxes, emergency measures
* American systems, such as social customs and manners, classroom procedures, adjusting to American life

OUTCOME: Clients who complete ESL/SURVIVAL should be able to:

* Ask and answers questions related to daily living and other subjects familiar to the client.
* Understand simple statements and questions addressed to them within their limited language scope and be able to ask for clarification where necessary.
* Be understood by native speakers paying close attention after repetition and clarification, since errors in pronunciation and grammar will probably be frequent.
* Possess vocabulary adequate for daily living needs, but probably inadequate for complex situations or ideas.
* Read essential forms, numbers, labels, signs, and simple written survival information.
* Fill out essential forms and write name, address, phone number and make emergency requests.

SPECIAL CONSIDERATIONS:

* ESL/SURVIVAL is the most generally applicable of all frameworks.
* ESL/SURVIVAL overlaps all the other frameworks.
* The use of native language aides is highly recommended.

The instructional blueprint should probably include many of the topics covered in the checklist given in Table 5.2. However, decisions about the blueprint's content should naturally be left entirely up to those responsible for materials development because the relevance of these topics will differ from curriculum to curriculum. Nonetheless, it cannot hurt to begin by considering those topics presented in Table 5.2, then to subtract or to add to the list as the materials development process progresses.

To begin with, any document describing the instructional blueprint should probably include a brief section detailing whatever background information the teachers should know. At a minimum, this background probably should include an overall introductory description of the program and of any umbrella institutions of which it is a part, as well as a short history of the program and associated institutions.

After the background section, an overall curriculum description would be appropriate. This should probably include discussion of the overall syllabuses that serve to organize the curriculum (for instance, into skills areas, functional units, structures, and so forth), as well as a review of the dominant approaches in the program.

The next logical step might be a description of the program's needs presented in terms of its teachers and students. To begin, it might prove useful to describe the typical teacher in terms of background, training, or other interesting characteristics. Next, it might make sense to list the situation and language needs of the learners as determined in the needs analysis (see Chapter Two). A description of the situation needs might be as simple as a table showing the students' ages, number, and other characteristics, or it might be a quite detailed prose description. The explanation of students' language needs might be as modest as an overview of the units of analysis used in the needs analysis and summary of the findings, or it might be a detailed list of language needs that naturally lead to the objectives that follow in the next section.

At some point, a description of the goals and objectives of the program (as shown in Chapter Three) will be useful. This description might include the general type of language program (for instance, whether it is an ESP program, a vocational ESL program, a survival English program, or an individual tutoring program) or a simple statement of the program's general goals. Statements of the program's objectives can be explicitly listed or appended to the document. Teachers will benefit from being able to refer to these for purposes of writing materials, planning techniques and exercises, as well as for suggesting modifications and improvements in the program.

Naturally, these objectives will be considerably stronger if they have been verified as being appropriate on the basis of norm–referenced and criterion–referenced tests (see Chapter Four): norm–referenced tests for proficiency and placement, and criterion-referenced tests for diagnosis and achievement. A description of the testing program can help teachers to understand how the students are admitted and placed, and thereby help them get an accurate fix on the

Table 5.2   Checklist for a Materials Development Blueprint

A. Background
   1. Introductory overall description of the program and any institutions of which it is a part
   2. History of the program and associated institutions

B. Overall curriculum description
   1. The organization of the curriculum
   2. Discussion of approaches

C. Needs (Review Chapter Two)
   1. The teachers (qualifications, skills, numbers)
   2. The learners (their age, number, characteristics)

D. Goals and objectives (Review Chapter Three)
   1. The overall goals of the program
      a. The type of language program
      b. The general purposes and goals of the program
   2. The objectives the program will seek to achieve

E. Tests (Review Chapter Four)
   1. Norm-referenced tests for proficiency and placement
   2. Criterion-referenced tests for diagnosis and achievement

F. Materials (all elements of this chapter as well as Chapter Six)
   1. Describe the instructional materials
   2. Describe the materials in terms of units of analysis
   3. Describe the materials in terms of scope and sequence
   4. Detail further development plans, perhaps in a Gantt diagram

G. Teaching (see Chapter Six)
   1. Describe dominant techniques
   2. Describe dominant exercises

H. Program evaluation (see Chapter Seven)
   1. Detail plans for studying effectiveness of the materials
   2. Discuss processes that will be instituted to constantly revise and upgrade materials

general level of the students, as well as understand how learning problems are diagnosed and how achievement is assessed at the end of the term.

With all of the needs, objectives, and testing information in hand, at least a tentative program framework is in place, and the materials that result can most likely be based on the information outlined in these broad brush strokes. Conversely, if no objectives and tests have been developed, the directions that materials might take must be guessed at and developed from scratch.

The next logical step in a blueprint for the systematic development of materials is some sort of description of the types of instructional materials (for instance, textbooks, readers, and workbooks) that are envisioned. The materials can then be described in terms of units of analysis that were used in developing the syllabuses involved, as well as in terms of the scope and sequence of any resulting units. In addition, detail about the various stages involved in materials development may prove useful. Such scheduling details can be presented very efficiently in the form of a Gantt diagram (see discussion below).

With regard to teaching, such a blueprint might include a discussion of the dominant techniques that are likely to be employed in presenting the language to the students (based on whatever consensus has been reached among the teachers on approaches and syllabuses). In addition, information about the different types of exercises that will likely be used to help the students practice the language may also prove useful. The point of discussing techniques and exercises should not be to limit the number and types of each, but rather to serve as a guide to how they are related to each other and as an indication of the general form they might follow. Other ideas for techniques and exercises, regardless of the sources, should always be welcomed and considered.

Finally, an effective blueprint for materials development must include some form of evaluation component (see Chapter Seven for more on evaluation). This component might take the form of detailed plans for studying the effectiveness of the materials, or discussion processes that will be instituted to constantly revise and upgrade materials, or both. Some form of regular evaluation of materials is essential because no set of materials is perfect and because the conditions within a program and the needs of the students may change, thus eventually making the materials inappropriate or ineffective.

In short, the checklist for a materials development blueprint that is provided in Table 5.2 can serve as a framework for thinking through all the essential parts of such a project so that needless expenditure of effort can be avoided and so that the energies involved can be focused on efficiently producing materials that maximally fit and serve the program involved. The next three sections will present more detailed information about three of the elements listed in Table 5.2: units of analysis, scope and sequence charts, and Gantt diagrams, all of which can be very useful tools in materials development projects.

□ UNITS OF ANALYSIS

Syllabus design theory has been an active area of investigation within applied linguistics for a number of years (Wilkins 1976; Yalden 1983, 1987; Nunan 1985, 1988, 1991; Clark 1987; Dubin & Olshtain 1986; White 1988). As I explained in Chapter One, conceptions of the nature of a syllabus are related to the approaches to language and language learning processes to which the curriculum designers and program participants subscribe. Under the influence of prescriptive, grammar-based approaches to language learning, syllabuses are traditionally expressed in terms of grammar, sentence patterns, and vocabulary. As a result of the more recent movement toward communicative theories of language and language learning, syllabuses have tended to be expressed in more communicative terms. For example, in the Council of Europe's *Threshold Level* (van Ek & Alexander 1980, pp. 17–117), the following components of a syllabus are specified:

1. The situations in which the foreign language will be used, including the topics that will be dealt with
2. The language activities in which the learner will engage
3. The language functions that the learner will fulfill
4. What the learner will be able to do with respect to each topic
5. The general notions that the learner will be able to handle
6. The specific (topic-related) notions that the learner will be able to handle
7. The language forms that the learner will be able to use when the course is completed
8. The degree of skill with which the learner will be able to perform.

These syllabus components include both objectives and content, and clearly assume a communicative approach. Notice how this relatively comprehensive list suggests areas in which units of analysis might be found—units that would be of interest in doing a needs assessment or in developing materials in any language curriculum (in this case, topics, activities, functions, general notions, and specific notions). While it may be true that not all of these potential units of analysis will prove necessary and useful in a particular situation, they should, at minimum, be considered.

□ SCOPE AND SEQUENCE CHARTS

Closely related to syllabus design is the question of deciding what kind of organizational framework to adopt for developing materials. Given a certain time frame (often expressed in terms of the number of hours of instruction), the syllabus should be thought out in terms of units of analysis and then in terms of curriculum scope and sequence. The syllabus itself is not a learning program, but it can be turned into one. For example, a syllabus for a beginning conversation course might specify that greetings and introductions are among the functions to be covered. Will they be taught together or separately? How much time will be spent on these two items as opposed to other items in the syllabus? How often will they appear in the course?

Now consider how different a reading course might be. Let's say the purpose of the reading course is to teach a variety of reading skills, including skimming, scanning, reading for meaning, reading for learning, vocabulary building, and use of the dictionary. How will each of these be reflected in the course structure?

One way to express a course structure is to delineate the scope and sequence in a chart. For example, an intermediate–level general course might follow a scope and sequence chart like that shown in Table 5.3. Table 5.3 lays out each of the first three units of *Time for English* (Vincent, Foll, & Cripwell 1985) with the subactivities involved in each unit.

Table 5.3 Example Scope and Sequence Chart (adapted from Vincent, Foll, & Cripwell, 1985)

Unit 1. Lesson 1.

Functional category:	Greetings and introductions.
Functions:	Greetings and leave-taking; asking about, and giving personal identification; making introductions
Syntax:	'be' 3rd person singular; affirmative and interrogative
	Examples:
	This is . . .
	My name's . . .
	What's . . .?
	Demonstrative pronoun: this
	Possessive adjectives: my and yours
Lexis:	Cardinal numbers 1–10
	Alphabet: A, B, C
	English names
	Greetings
Phonology:	/ei/ /ai/ /i/

Unit 1. Lesson 2.

Functional category:	Asking about
Functions:	Asking about the identity of others: numbers
Syntax:	Imperative
	Possessive adjectives: his and her
Lexis:	Vocabulary for the classroom and classroom activities
	Alphabet: D, E, G, I, P, T, V, Y.
Phonology:	/ei/ /ai/ /e/ /i/

Unit 1. Lesson 3.

Functional category:	People and places
Language use:	Greeting friends, asking about, and confirming the identity of place
Syntax:	'be' 1st and 2nd person singular;
	there is/there are;
	Personal pronoun: I, you, and it;
	Is it . . .? questions
Lexis:	Traffic and city buildings
Phonology:	Rhythm practice (including practice of initial /b/ and /t/ and end position /k/)
	/i:/ /e/ /ae/ /o/

A somewhat clearer representation of the same information is provided in the adaptation shown in Table 5.4. This *scope and sequence* chart turns out to be more transparent and easier to interpret because it captures and delineates the repetitive elements of the curriculum in an efficient manner that minimizes redundancy.

Eventually, some overall curriculum plan that specifies the techniques that will be used should be developed. Otherwise, the teachers will have to fill this gap. Such plans can take a variety of forms, ranging from very detailed to relatively informal. For instance, a detailed curriculum might provide day-by-day "teacher-proof" lesson plans, while an informal curriculum might take the form of a list of activities that the teacher jots down each day on the way to meeting with the students. In either case, some sort of plan must be made with regard to the techniques and exercises that will be used in the classroom. The more consistently sequenced and integrated they are, the more cogent the resulting curriculum is likely to be. However, like everything else in curriculum development, a cogent plan may not be the best plan if it becomes too permanent.

Thus, once again, planners face a set of trade-offs. A formalized lock-step curriculum complete with lesson plans that detail every minute of classroom time may be highly cogent in the sense of being carefully sequenced, integrated, and logical. Unfortunately, such a curriculum may be viewed as stifling by the teachers, and if that curriculum is viewed as a finished product, it may become difficult to revise and change it (even in small ways). This, in turn, may mean that the curriculum will eventually become inflexible and unable to meet changes in students' needs or modifications in program conditions. On the other hand, a teacher who plans his or her classroom activities on the spur of the moment, while maximally positioned to be flexible and respond to needs for change, may be presenting instruction that lacks any sense of sequencing, integration, and logic. The best position to take is probably a compromise position somewhere between these two extreme ways of doing curriculum.

□ GANTT DIAGRAMS

One useful technique for representing the different steps involved in large-scale materials development and implementation projects is the Gantt diagram. A *Gantt diagram* is a two-axis figure with time divisions labeled across the horizontal axis and task divisions down the vertical axis.

Consider the list of curriculum activities shown in Table 5.5. These are taken from a project designed to develop a new program within the New Intensive Course of English (NICE) at the University of Hawaii at Manoa. The first six week stage (during summer 1989) included only needs analysis and objectives setting, and is given in considerable detail. The second stage (fall 1989) included further development of the objectives, as well as test and materials development. The third stage (winter 1990) was set for implementation of the new program.

Table 5.4 Scope and Sequence Chart for Table 5.3 Curriculum (adapted from Vincent, Foll & Cripwell 1985)

UNIT	FUNCTIONAL CATAEGORY	FUNCTIONS	SYNTAX	LEXIS	PHONOLOGY
1.1	Greetings and introductions	Greetings; Leave-taking; Asking about; Giving personal identification; Making introductions	'be' 3rd person singular; affirmative and interrogative (e.g., *This is . . .; My name's...; What's . . .*); Demonstrative pronoun *this*; Possessive adjs. *my and yours*	Cardinal #s 1–10; Alphabet: A, B, C; English names; Greetings	/ei/ /ai/ /i/
1.2	Asking about	Asking about the identity of others; Numbers	Imperative; Possessive adjs. (*his and her*);	Vocabulary for the classroom and class-room activities; Alphabet: D, E, G, I, P, T, V, Y	/ei/ /ai/ /e/ /i/
1.3	People and places	Greeting friends; Asking about and confirming; Identifying places	'be' 1st and 2nd person singular; *there is/there are*; Personal pronouns *I, you* and *it*; *Is it . . .?* questions	Traffic and city buildings	Rhythm practice (including initial /b/ /t/ and end /k/); /i:/ /e/ /ae/ /o/

The same information is given in the Gantt diagram shown in Figure 5.1. Notice how much easier it is to simultaneously grasp all the dimensions of the project in this visual format. (However, you will also notice that some of the detail included in Table 5.5 has necessarily been condensed.) A Gantt diagram

Table 5.5   Needs Analysis and Objectives Setting in the New Intensive Course of English (NICE) at the University of Hawaii at Manoa (NICE 1990)

DATE	ACTIVITY
6/30/89	Preassessment considerations identified (process and procedures developed)
7/ 3/89	Results of records survey compiled
7/ 6/89	Initial task delegation assigned and distributed for curriculum developers
7/17/89	Interview with NICE coordinators completed and results recorded
7/18/89	Class observations completed
7/21/89	NICE target student interviews completed and results recorded (by one group of curriculum developers)
7/21/89	NICE instructors and administrators interview completed and results recorded (by other group of curriculum developers)
7/28/89	Needs assessment questionnaire for NICE students completed and duplicated
8/2/89	Needs assessment questionnaire administered to NICE students
8/10/89	Analysis of needs assessments completed and reported to NICE administration with tentative outline of curriculum direction and design considerations for program policy procedures
9/1/89	Tentative goals and objectives completed and distributed to all concerned parties
9/15/89	Achievement tests in two forms designed and piloted
10/1/89	Materials blueprint constructed from all of the above information
10/15/89	Tentative materials for weeks 1 and 2 developed
11/1/89	Tentative materials for weeks 3 and 4 developed
11/15/89	Tentative materials for weeks 5 and 6 developed
12/1/89	Tentative materials for weeks 7 and 8 developed
12/15/89	Tentative materials for weeks 1 through 8 reviewed and revised
3/21/90	Field testing of curriculum completed
5/1/90	Evaluation of curriculum and evaluation document presented to the NICE administration
5/30/90	Revision of needs, objectives, tests, and materials completed and all curriculum documents compiled and presented to the NICE administration

Figure 5.1: Gantt Diagram of the Information Shown in Table 5.5 (NICE 1990)

NICE CURRICULUM DEVELOPMENT PROJECT

ACTIVITIES	June	July	August	September	October	November	December	January	February	March	April	May
Preassessment Activities	—·—											
Records survey	—·—											
Initial task delegation		¦										
Coordinator interviews		¦										
Class observations	—·—											
Student interviews		- - -										
Staff interviews		- - -										
Student questionnaire developed	—·—·—											
Student questionnaire administered		¦										
Needs assessment document	—·—·—											
Goals and objectives		—·—·—										
Achievment tests		—·—·—·—										
Materials blueprint		—·—·—·—										
Weeks 1 and 2 materials				- - -								
Weeks 3 and 4 materials					- - -							
Weeks 5 and 6 materials						- - -						
Weeks 7 and 8 materials							- - -					
Materials review and revision							- - -					
Field testing								—·—·—·—				
Evaluation document										—·—·—		
Revision										—·—·—·—		
Curriculum documents compiled										—·—·—·—		

is useful for providing an overview that can be understood at a glance. It shows all the tasks involved and the time frames in which each task must be begun and completed. Not only can such a diagram be a useful tool for explaining a curriculum development project to outsiders, but it also can help to keep the insiders on schedule.

WHERE DO MATERIALS COME FROM?

In one way, it is easiest for a teacher to simply adopt a textbook, open to page one and begin teaching systematically through the prepared materials. Using this strategy, a teacher need not invest too much thought or effort in the process. On the other hand, the teachers that I have known almost always say that they cannot find a textbook that really matches their classroom needs. This section will suggest ways that materials can be put into place that do match the materials blueprint and therefore are likely to meet the needs of the students. Three strategies will be suggested: adopting, developing, or adapting. One or all of these strategies should help in settling on materials for any language program.

Working from program goals and objectives, the teacher must address the essential questions of what the content will be and how it will be sequenced. The needs analysis, objectives, and tests should provide information that will suffice for answering the first of these questions. Adopting, developing, or adapting materials that match that content is the next logical step. The sequencing of that content should also be addressed in the process, but will probably shape up as the materials development progresses.

□ ADOPTING MATERIALS

Adopting materials in a rational manner is not as easy as it might at first appear. First, it is necessary to decide what types of materials are desirable. Second, all available materials of these types should be located just in case they might prove useful. Third, some form of review/evaluation procedures must be set up to pare this list down to only those materials that should be seriously considered so that final choices can be made. Fourth, some strategy for the regular review of these adopted materials must be set up to make sure that they do not become irrelevant to the needs of the students and the changing conditions in the program.

Deciding on Types of Materials

The broad definition of materials I provided at the beginning of this chapter indicates that they can come in many different forms. Materials can also be based on many different approaches and can be organized around a number of different syllabuses.

Materials can also be presented on a number of media and take many physical forms on any one of those media. Thus, many options must be considered long before any decisions can be made as to what specific materials to adopt. The following list of possible media for materials may help with these deliberations:

books	teachers books
workbooks	magazines
journals	pictures
maps	charts/graphs/diagrams
realia (erector sets, models, vocabulary items)	cassette tapes computer software
video tapes (language, authentic, genuine)	videodisc/computer combinations

Notice that the further down the list a medium is, the more equipment and technology is involved. Since technology is generally expensive, making choices regarding items on this list may create a tension between what teachers would like to use and what the program can afford. Remember also that complex equipment may entail providing teachers with special training before they can effectively use that equipment, another expensive process.

Locating Materials

Three sources of information immediately spring to mind that can help in finding existing materials that might be suitable: publishers' catalogs, "Books Received" sections of journals, and teachers' shelves.

Publishers' catalogs are usually free for the asking. Addresses for some of the most prominent publishers of ESL materials are listed in the appendix. Many of these publishers also produce materials for other languages, so this list should provide at least a starting point for any language teacher looking for published materials. Naturally, these organizations will be happy to send a catalog upon request. Such catalogs are usually very well organized, including at least lists of relevant publications and brief descriptions of each one with its price. An order form is usually provided to facilitate ordering.

To make even a short list of candidates for materials that might be adopted, hands–on examination is necessary. Most publishers are happy to send teachers *desk copies* of their materials. A desk copy is a textbook, manual, workbook, or other form of material sent free of charge for consideration by teachers who might adopt the material in their courses. The teacher may usually keep a desk copy even if student copies are not subsequently ordered. Since each publisher has a different policy toward desk copies, it will be necessary to examine each catalog for the description of that policy. Typically, publishers who send desk copies will only send them to bona fide teachers who make requests on official institutional letterhead stationery. Publishers may require a brief description of the course for which the materials are being considered, a description of the current materials being used for that course, and the number of students who normally enroll in the course. Increasingly, publishers offer examination copies instead of desk copies.

Examination copies, also called *review copies,* are also sent so that they can be considered for adoption in courses. However, examination copies are only free of charge if the teacher subsequently orders the material(s) for his or her students within a certain number of days (usually 60 or 90 days). Otherwise, the teacher must either send the materials back to the publisher or pay for them. (This less liberal policy has no doubt saved some publishers money on desk copies, but it has probably also cost them dearly in terms of good will and number of adoptions.) Remember that publishers' catalogs are designed to sell language teaching materials. Hence they will best be used as a source list of available materials, not as the definitive word on the quality of those materials.

Another source of relatively up-to-date information on language materials is the *"Books Received"* section that is found in many of the prominent language teaching journals. Since publishers find it to their advantage to have their books reviewed—after all, a positive review is a form of free advertising—they generally send copies to the appropriate journals for that purpose. These "Books Received" are usually listed near the back of a journal. Such listings are usually fairly current. However, since such lists include only the author, title, and publisher, sending for desk or review copies will still be necessary.

One last source of information about materials should not be overlooked. The *teachers' shelves* within the program may be full of materials that could prove interesting and useful. More to the point, teachers are more likely to have experience with materials they already own. Such materials are readily located, are available for immediate inspection, and can be commented on by teachers who are known to all the other teachers in the program. This sounds like a good argument for publishers making sure that desk copies be made readily available to teachers. Even if they are not adopted in the first round of ordering, the very fact that they are physically present in a program may enhance the probability that they will eventually be ordered.

Evaluating Materials

Whether materials are found in publishers' catalogs, "Books Received" sections of journals, or teachers' shelves, firsthand examination will eventually be necessary to determine the suitability of the materials for a particular program. This process might safely be called *materials evaluation.* If teachers individually select the materials that are to be adopted and ordered for their courses, they should be given as much information as possible to draw on in making those decisions. If all the faculty teaching a given course make collective decisions, they will also need information upon which to base their decisions. In both cases, consider looking at reviews by competent professionals in the field in addition to doing a firsthand review.

The *reviews* in professional journals and newsletters typically reflect only the views of one individual. If possible, seek out two or three reviews of a book or other materials. One review can be helpful, but a number of reviews will offer a more comprehensive picture of the book or materials under consideration. It is also a good idea to establish a file of reviews that might be of interest to program faculty and administrators. They should be encouraged to examine the file regularly, and to add to it copies of any interesting reviews they discover in the course of their reading.

Firsthand review of materials is clearly the most personal and thorough method for evaluating them. Stevick (1971) suggested that materials should be evaluated in terms of qualities, dimensions, and components as follows:

Three qualities:	Strength, lightness, transparency (as opposed to weakness, heaviness, opacity)
Three dimensions:	Linguistic, social, topical
Four components:	Occasions for use, sample of language use, lexical exploration, exploration of structural relationships.

The checklist provided in Table 5.6 may prove more useful than Stevick's list simply because the checklist contains more detail. Notice that Table 5.6 considers materials from five perspectives: background, fit to curriculum, physical characteristics, logistical characteristics, and teachability. All of these judgments can be made only with the materials physically in hand. However, if some program teachers have previously used them, judgments related to teachability may be enhanced.

In the checklist in Table 5.6 *materials background* refers to information about the author's and the publisher's credentials. Naturally, this includes more than whether the author has significant formal education, perhaps in the form of a Ph.D. degree. Consider also the amounts and types of experience the author has had in teaching and administration, as well as in curriculum and materials development. The author may have a reputation for producing innovative materials, or no previous standing in the field. In addition, consider the publisher's reputation. Some publishers have a reputation for producing better products. However, all of these factors should probably carry less weight than personal observation of the degree to which a particular set of materials relates to a given program.

The degree of relationship between a set of materials and a particular program can best be determined by considering the degree to which the materials *fit to the curriculum*. To begin with, consider the extent to which each set of materials agrees with the overall approach and syllabus (or combination of approaches and syllabuses). Next, focus on the degree to which the materials

Table 5.6 Checklist for Adopting Textbooks

A. Materials background
   1. Author's credentials (education and experience)
   2. Publisher's reputation
B. Fit to curriculum
   1. Approach
   2. Syllabus
   3. Needs
      a. General language needs
      b. Situation needs
   4. Goals and objectives
      a. Percentage of match
      b. Order
   5. Content
      a. Consistent with techniques used in program
      b. Consistent with exercises used in program
C. Physical characteristics
   1. Layout
      a. Space
      b. Pictures and text
      c. Highlighting
   2. Organization
      a. Table of contents
      b. Index
      c. Answer keys
      d. Glossary
      e. Reference potential
   3. Editorial qualities
      a. Content is accurate and edited in a manner consistent with your style
      b. Directions clear and easy to follow
      c. Examples clear
   4. Material quality
      a. Paper
      b. Binding
      c. Tear-out pages
D. Logistical characteristics
   1. Price
   2. Auxiliary parts
      a. Audiovisual aids
      b. Workbooks
      c. Software
      d. Unit tests
   3. Availability
E. Teachability
   1. Teachers edition
      a. Answer key
      b. Annotations to help teachers explain, plan activities, and the like
   2. Reviews
   3. Acceptability among teachers

match the language needs of the students in a general way. Early in the process, the materials should also be examined for overall level of proficiency so that materials that do not match the program in this global sense can immediately be eliminated. Likewise, many materials that do not match the situational needs of the program (based on realities like the resources available and cultural appropriateness) can immediately be eliminated.

This general elimination process should result in a gradual winnowing of materials. Next, the specific language and situation needs of the students should be considered. The match of the materials to these needs can best be assessed by comparing the materials to the detailed information that was obtained in the needs-analysis and objectives-setting phases. Even if a fairly close match is found with the program's objectives, consider the degree to which the materials are ordered appropriately and the degree to which they use techniques and exercises that are acceptable to the teachers in the program. The teachers are, of course, the best people to help with this type of judgment.

Next, examine any materials that are still in the running for adoption in terms of their physical characteristics. *Physical characteristics* may take the form of layout considerations such as the amount of free space on each page, the relative quantities and qualities of pictures and text, the effectiveness of highlighting, and so forth.

Other physical characteristics might include organizational issues like the existence and quality of a table of contents, index, answer key, and glossary, as well as the general reference potential of the book after the course is finished. Editorial characteristics like the following should be considered: the accuracy of the content, the degree to which the material is edited in a manner consistent with the program's style, the degree to which the directions are clear and easy to follow, and the clarity of the examples. Also consider the quality of the physical materials used. For instance, if the materials are in the form of a textbook, consider the paper quality, the binding, whether or not there are tear–out pages that may fall apart, and so forth. If the materials are cassette tapes, the quality of the tape, the case, and the labeling may be important, as well as the clarity of the recording on the tape. Any other types of materials should also be examined for physical characteristics as appropriate.

Logistical characteristics might include such mundane (but important) issues as the price and number of auxiliary parts (that is, audiovisual aids, workbooks, software, unit tests, and so forth) that are required, as well as the availability of the materials, time that it will take to ship them, and the like.

Finally, the *teachability* of the materials should be appraised. This decision may hinge on whether there is a teacher's edition, an answer key, annotations to help teachers explain and plan activities, unit reviews, and so forth. It is also important to ask the teachers if they think the set of materials will work and is otherwise acceptable to them.

This teachability issue reemphasizes the degree to which all of these decisions are probably best made as a team effort. If all the teachers are involved in the decisions about which materials to select and have input into that process, they will probably be much more willing to use the chosen materials even if they did not fully agree that the selected materials were the best of all possibilities. Moreover, evaluating materials, like much else in curriculum development, should call on the teachers' expertise because teachers represent a relatively large labor pool to help in the selection process and because they represent a potent political force within the program.

Ongoing Review of Materials

Even after a set of materials is in place for each course, the materials evaluation process must continue while they are being used, as well as after each implementation period. Teachers can keep notes on their reactions to the materials as they use them. Such notes can be as simple as scribblings in the margins of the teacher's edition, or as formal as typed reviews of the materials in question. Once the term or year is finished, time should be set aside for a comprehensive review of all materials. After all, teachers change, as do students' needs, so periodic review of the materials seems advisable and necessary. This review might take the form of a yearly straw count of how many teachers want to continue using the same texts, or a more involved series of meetings during which all program texts (and potential alternatives) are evaluated using either Stevick's guidelines (listed above) or the checklist shown in Table 5.6. The important point is that materials must be reviewed periodically so that they do not become stale with regard to the particular curriculum involved.

□ DEVELOPING MATERIALS

The primary thrust of this book has been the systematic design of curriculum. Within that framework, needs assessment, goals and objectives, and tests have already been discussed at great length. If the tentative needs, objectives, and tests do indeed describe a program, and if all efforts to adopt materials for purposes of teaching those objectives fail to uncover suitable materials, it may be necessary to consider developing them from scratch. I treat this option as a second option not because it is an undesirable alternative, but because it represents a tremendous amount of work. Nevertheless, with the help and ideas of a number of people within a program, especially the teachers, materials can be developed that will create the best possible match between materials and the curriculum in question. Table 5.7 outlines one set of steps for creating materials from scratch.

Notice that the checklist shown in Table 5.7 begins with overall curriculum issues including deciding on the theoretical bases of the program in terms of approaches and organizational principles in terms of syllabuses. The checklist

Table 5.7   Checklist for Developing Materials from Scratch

A. Overall curriculum
    1. Approach
        a. Theoretical bases
        b. Revise
    2. Syllabus
        a. Organizational principles
        b. Revise

B. Needs
    1. Define
    2. Revise

C. Goals and objectives
    1. Define
    2. Revise

D. Tests
    1. Proficiency or placement—Get a fix on overall level
    2. Diagnostic or achievement—Get a fix on appropriateness of objectives

E. Creating
    1. Find teachers willing to work as materials developers
    2. Ensure that all materials developers have copies of relevant documents (program description, goals and objectives, materials blueprint, scope-and-sequence chart, Gantt diagram, or whatever)
    3. Divide the labor
    4. Work individually or in teams to create the materials
    5. Establish a resource file
    6. Consider working modularly in materials packets

F. Teaching
    1. Pilot materials
    2. Discuss their effectiveness
    3. Revise

G. Evaluating
    1. Evaluate your own materials (see Table 5.6)
    2. Revise materials
    3. Produce materials in a relatively durable format
    4. Consider publishing the materials
    5. Remember that materials are never finished—that is, consider ongoing materials development particularly in terms of how well all materials are meeting the needs of your students

also suggests looking at the students' needs, defining the goals and objectives, and using the tests to get a fix on the students' overall levels in terms of proficiency or placement and the appropriateness of the objectives in terms of diagnosis or achievement testing. Notice also that each of these must be defined and perhaps revised before it makes much sense to proceed with the creation of materials.

The central steps involved in materials development are presented in Table 5.7's points E through G (creating, teaching, and evaluating). During the *creating phase,* the first step is to find teachers who are willing to work on materials. Teachers are much more likely to be willing participants in a materials development project if they see something in it for themselves, that is, if they are paid for their efforts, or get release time, or, at the very least, if they expect to have an easier job with the new materials in hand. Once a pool of materials developers has been identified, make sure that all of them are provided with copies of all relevant documents. Such documents may include a program description, a copy of the goals and objectives for the course in question, a version of the materials blueprint, or other important documents. Next, divide the labor so that all the materials developers are pulling their own weight in the project. Such division of labor often requires getting commitments from individuals to take responsibility for a certain prescribed task or amount of work and to finish that work by specific dates. My experience is that the chances of the work actually being done on time will be increased if the completion dates coincide with review meetings at which individuals or teams will present their product to the group as a whole for comments and suggestions. Peer pressure can be a wonderful curriculum tool. Using this strategy facilitates task completion individually or by teams, yet enables the group as a whole to have some say in the development of the different sets of materials during the review meetings. This type of working arrangement can be enhanced by using a modular system in which the overall set of materials consists of a collection of materials modules developed separately by different groups, but fit together into a single cogent pattern as established by a scope-and-sequence chart.

The *teaching phase* listed in Table 5.7 can be viewed as an opportunity to field–test the materials. Preferably, more than one teacher will be involved in this effort. It seems most useful if the original developers can be involved in the field testing along with at least one other teacher who was not involved in the original development process. The materials can then be tried out and discussed in terms of their effectiveness, and suggestions can be made for improving them. Revisions should be made, as necessary, with input from all teachers who may ultimately use the materials because their ideas may prove useful and because these teachers may be more willing to use the materials if they had some say in their development.

During the *evaluating phase,* the materials developers should be just as critical of the program's materials as they would be of commercially prepared materials (see Table 5.6). When revisions shift from significant to minor matters, it may be time to consider producing the new program materials in a relatively durable format so they can be used in an ongoing manner. In fact, at this point it might be worthwhile to consider sending the materials to a publisher. After all, if they are good enough for one program and serve the needs of its students, other programs might find them useful.

However, remember that materials are never finished so provisions should be made for ongoing materials development, particularly in terms of reviewing

Table 5.8   Steps for Adapting Materials

A. Finding and evaluating (see Table 5.6)

B. Analyzing
    1. Matches to current objectives
    2. Mismatches to current objectives
    3. Percent of objectives that need to be supplemented from outside these materials
    4. Percent of existing matches that will require revision
    5. Decide which set(s) of materials to adapt

C. Classifying
    1. Use any logical classes of objectives to help you group them for analysis
    2. List places in materials where each objective is addressed
    3. Leave blanks where supplemental materials are needed

D. Fill in the gaps
    1. From other materials
    2. From created materials
    3. Teachers as resources
    4. Resource file

E. Reorganizing
    1. Complete the list
    2. Reorganize

how well all materials are matching the needs of the students, the goals and objectives, the tests, and so forth.

□ ADAPTING MATERIALS

Conventional wisdom in language teaching suggests that there is no such thing as a perfect textbook. This is likely to be true whether the materials in question were commercially produced or created within a given program. Moreover, the task of completely reinventing the materials for all the courses in a program on a continuous basis is a staggering undertaking. One viable solution to both these problems is to use what is of value in an existing set of materials, while adapting it to the needs, or changing needs, of the program. This process of adapting involves all of the steps listed above for finding and evaluating materials plus several distinctive features. These new features include analyzing, classifying, filling the gaps, and reorganizing (as shown in Table 5.8).

The first stage in adapting materials is to find and evaluate materials that might serve at least some of the students' needs and help to meet at least some of the course objectives. This process is virtually the same as the one described in the previous section for adopting materials. However, as the materials are being evaluated, teachers should also analyze the degree to which each set of existing materials matches the course objectives, as well as the degree of mismatch. In this case, the ultimate goal of the analysis is to decide which of the potential sets of materials contains the highest percentage of matches. This will, in turn, determine the percentage of objectives that will need to be supplemented from outside these materials. In the end, a decision must be made as to which set, or sets, of materials will be adapted.

Once usable/revisable materials have been identified, it may prove useful to think of grouping the useful elements of the materials in a way that is different from how they were grouped in the original so that the resulting adaptation will more closely match the groupings and orderings in the course objectives. For future reference, while doing this, a list should be compiled of all of the places in the materials where each of the objectives is addressed. In any such list, be sure to also list and group those objectives that are not covered by the materials. Obviously, these blanks will indicate areas in which supplemental materials will be needed.

Next, fill in the gaps that have been identified. Other materials that have been spotted during the review process may serve this purpose. Certainly, teachers in the program may know from their own experience existing materials that may help to fill the gaps. Or materials creation may be necessary for some of the missing elements. A materials resource file may prove useful in this process of filling the gaps. This file should have folders for each of the missing objectives. If each teacher is expected to contribute to this file and can then draw on it, such a resource file strategy (see fuller explanation below under "ELI Example Materials") can help substantially to fill gaps while leaving the teachers with maximum freedom to pick and choose what they wish to use.

Once decisions have been made about which objectives are covered by which materials and which can be covered by supplementary materials, this list can be further analyzed so that the materials can be reorganized to better match the existing objectives and syllabus. Such a reorganization may entail changing the list so that it progresses objective by objective through the syllabus, or it might mean that each objective will be covered in turn and then recycled systematically at a higher level of complexity or difficulty. There are a number of ways that this process of reordering materials can be done to make sense of the materials in a particular syllabus. The point I wish to make is that reordering should be considered as an option in the materials adaptation process. Students are often uncomfortable about skipping around in materials unless they understand the purpose. Therefore, an explanation to the students about why and how the materials have been reorganized may head off criticisms from them on this issue.

EXAMPLE MATERIALS DEVELOPMENT PROJECTS

☐ GUANGZHOU ENGLISH LANGUAGE CENTER, ZHONGSHAN UNIVERSITY

All three materials strategies were applied in the ESP program that we set up in China: sometimes materials were adopted, sometimes they were developed, and sometimes they were adapted. In the initial materials reviews, during the summer of 1980, we tried to evaluate and select all necessary materials (in fact, much more than we anticipated actually needing) so that we could take them with us. A vast number and variety of ESP materials were reviewed by dividing up the labor and meeting often to discuss relevant issues. Once we had received desk copies (or otherwise found sets of all of the materials that we thought might be potentially useful), we divided them up and did evaluations both individually and in teams using an evaluation checklist that has long since disappeared (similar to the checklist shown in Table 5.6, but not nearly so detailed). We then met together and made final decisions, thrashing out our differences on the spot. Because of our particular situation, we felt that it would be far better once we arrived in China to have too many types of materials with us than to end up with too few. Once selected, the materials were ordered, packaged, and shipped.

Only after teaching had begun did we realize the degree to which some of the materials failed to match the courses for which they had been selected. We found that some were partially suitable while others were such bad mismatches that we had to abandon them entirely in favor of materials created on the spot. Thus, for the most part, we ended up with materials that were either adapted to our courses or created specifically for them.

Consider the speaking courses. In the lowest level speaking course (Speaking Level A in Figure 1.3), we ended up relying fairly heavily on Bates and Dudley-Evans's (1976) text; however, we had to be very selective and also to heavily adapt much of the material to the speaking needs of our science students. In particular, such adaptation meant supplementing the book with many techniques and exercises that were devised by us as appropriate for our approaches and syllabuses. For Speaking Level B, we relied primarily on the *Gambits* books by Keller and Warner (1979a, 1979b, and 1979c), but again we found that selectivity and adaptation were essential in order to tailor the materials to the special needs of our Chinese scholars. In Speaking Level C, we found absolutely nothing that was suitable for advanced speaking skills, and we therefore ended up creating our own materials from scratch based largely on public speaking courses that various teachers remembered taking in their undergraduate years. Similar processes went on in the other four skill areas.

Clearly, the materials adoption, development, and adaptation activities that went on in GELC required a prodigious amount of energy. It was only due to the amount of institutional support built into the program that efforts on this scale were possible at all. To begin with, we were all employed full-time with a maximum teaching load of three contact hours per day. This left time for about three hours of paper correction and preparation per day, as well as plenty of time for meetings, curriculum development, and research. In short, most of us on the teaching staff felt that we were being paid to do curriculum development, which naturally included materials. Still, many of us found ourselves putting in 12 to 16 hours per day. (One theory, popular at the time, was that these long hours were only made possible by the superior quality of Tsingtao pijou, a Chinese beer.) In addition, the American teachers were living together in the same "Foreign Experts" compound, and our Chinese colleagues lived on campus at Zhongda within easy walking distance. In short, we all had ready access to each other and to our common meeting rooms.

Moreover, the program was set up from its very inception to provide logistical support for curriculum development. Resources devoted to this purpose included a materials library, typewriters, duplication and copying machines, access to the university print shop, work space, Chinese secretaries and typists, and so forth. With all of these factors designed to support our curriculum development efforts, along with a systematic curriculum development framework much like the one described in this book, there was at least a good chance that we would be able to adopt, develop, or adapt all of the materials that we would ever need. Nevertheless, we had to work very hard.

Throughout the first two years, when I was directly involved in the program, teamwork was a key issue on many of our projects, and this need to work together (while living very closely together) created some interesting personal problems which we also had to manage. Initially, teams were established for each skill and level course. This meant, for instance, that the three teachers teaching the three sections of Level B Speaking would meet on a weekly basis to share ideas and work together on developing materials (as well as other elements of the curriculum). These groupings were encouraged to stay with the same courses for several of the 10-week sessions so that continuity would occur in the development process for each course. While we all enjoyed teaching a variety of courses, these groupings gradually led to most of us thinking of ourselves as specialized in two or three of the courses. In my case, for instance, I found myself most interested in the speaking courses at all levels.

Once each of the courses became fairly well designed on its own, it was a natural progression for us to think in terms of integrating our objectives, tests, and materials across levels within each skill area. We did this by holding additional skill area meetings in which we dealt with such issues. Later, we also held regular meetings to help us create some degree of integration across the skill areas within each level. Due to these efforts, a student might find herself doing extensive reading in her scientific field (in the reading course) that would be applied to a term project that she was writing (for the writing course) and to the final speech that she was giving in front of a video camera (for the speaking course). Our goal was never to totally integrate the courses across levels or skills, but rather to integrate them only in ways that we felt were appropriate and useful.

The teachers at GELC attended a large number of meetings. For instance, I often attended Speaking B and C meetings, as well as occasional Speaking skill area meetings and level integration meetings. Lest this seem like cruel and unusual punishment, remember that these meetings were all held within working hours and were not considered optional. In addition, I always felt that I was benefiting directly from them in terms of materials that made my job easier and improved my teaching. These feelings were not universal among the teachers, but they were the arguments that were used to convince, coax, or cajole the teachers into attending.

To focus this example even further, let's consider the whole materials development process for one particular course: Speaking B. In our initial meetings, wherein we were very interested in sharing our ideas for what should be going on in the Speaking B course, a number of us (Candy Mocko, Celeste Scholz, and myself, and later Ann Hilferty) decided that we would use a common lesson plan, or activity format, in describing any speaking activities that we wanted to share. The format that we decided to use had three parts for each lesson:

1.   *Description* of the activity and its relationship with other lessons
2.   *Materials* that would be needed
3.   *Procedures* that should be followed in organizing the activity.

An example lesson is shown in Table 5.9.

We later decided to keep the disposable materials as one set called the *Activities Book,* which would be copied afresh each term for each teacher. The lesson plans themselves were meant to be more durable and were passed from teacher to teacher. Later, the disposable materials were packaged as *Student Books* which were given to the students at the beginning of every Speaking B course. So the initial lesson plans, which were designed only to help us share ideas, went through many metamorphoses. Eventually, they formed the core of a set of materials that had the rather tortured title of $E = MC^2$: *English Modern Conversation Course.* I am told that these materials were later combined with the materials for Speaking C, heavily edited, and printed up so that they could be used at other centers in China. Thus these speaking materials evolved from shared notes and lesson plans to a published version.

Table 5.10 gives an overview of the Speaking B course that evolved. This list of interaction types and subjects also served as a scope-and-sequence chart at various stages of course development. Giving this overview to the students on the first day of class also proved useful so that they would know where the course was headed.

In sum, the materials in the GELC program were either heavily adapted from those that had originally been adopted, or were created by us for our specific students. All in all, I think that most of the teachers felt that the process of doing all this was exhilarating, productive, and exhausting.

Table 5.9   Format for Sharing Speaking B Activities* (GELC 1982)

SITUATION 3.5 PHYSICS PROBLEM GROUP WORK

DESCRIPTION: In this activity, students seek and provide explanations for everyday phenomena. The activity goes well with gambits for Seeking Information (see Activities Book) and a review of gambits for Generalization Links (Gambits II, 52), Giving a Reason (Gambits II, 9), Explaining a Result (Gambits II, 10), and Cause and Effect in these materials (2.2)

MATERIALS: A copy of a different everyday physics problem** for each group (cut the Activities Book pages into strips) and the problem solutions for the teachers reference in later discussion.

PROCEDURES: (Time: 30-35 minutes, 15 minutes for group problem solving, and 20 minutes for presentations of solutions to class.)

1. Divide the class into four groups of five or six with discussion leaders appointed. The discussion leader's function is to start discussion, take notes, and report back to the class. Make sure that there is at least one physicist or student of advanced physics in each group. Explain that the assignment is to provide a simple though scientific answer that can be explained in five minutes or less. If the group is not sure of the answer, they should propose a possible solution.

2. Give each group one of the physics problems and have them plan a five-minute explanation.

3. Have the discussion leader from each group present the problem and solution. Help students keep within the five-minute range.

4. Encourage students to address questions to the presenter if they disagree with, or do not understand, his explanations.

* An accompanying set of materials that we called the Activities Book (which had all of the disposable materials in it) contained two sheets of 15 physics problems (from Walker 1977), three sheets that contained the answers to those problems, and a list of supplementary gambits that the students might find particularly useful in doing this task.

** EXAMPLE PHYSICS PROBLEM: Squeaking Chalk—Why does a piece of chalk produce a hideous squeal if you hold it incorrectly? Why does the orientation of the chalk matter? What determines the pitch you hear? (Walker 1977)

□ ENGLISH LANGUAGE INSTITUTE, UNIVERSITY OF HAWAII AT MANOA

Within the ELI the overall strategies have been a bit more orderly, and include all of the following steps: setting up a blueprint, finding ways to support materials and other curriculum development, learning to work together on curriculum projects, doing regular materials reviews, and setting up materials resources files.

	Table 5.10 First-day Handout for Speaking Level B (GELC 1982)		

COURSE PLAN

To develop speaking ability in free conversation in pairs, small groups, large groups, and with professional colleagues, and in general to develop conversational strategies leading to formal discussion.

DESCRIPTION

Week	Type of Interaction	Subject	Evaluation
1	Exchanging personal information	Personal relationships	Test I
2	Exchange of opinion	Social problems	
3	Addressing a problem	Environmental problems	
4	Agreeing and disagreeing	Consumerism	
5	Giving advice	Problems of modern life I	Test II
6	Social planning	Problems of modern life II	
7	Informing	Science and the occult	
8	Argument	Presentation and discussion	
9	Suasion	Presentation and discussion	Test III

TEXTBOOK—*E = MC²: English Modern Conversation Course* (Student Book)

EVALUATION

There will be three oral interview tests during the quarter. All three tests are similar. The first two serve as practice for the third, which is the final exam.

Materials Blueprint

The document that currently serves the purpose of a materials blueprint in the ELI is entitled *Teacher's Handbook for Graduate Assistants and Lecturers.* Among other useful information, this handbook discusses most of the categories listed in Table 5.2 and is the first exposure that some of the teachers have ever had to systematic curriculum development. The 36–page (single-spaced) handbook is revised yearly and given to the teachers at the orientation meeting held before fall semester begins. With this document in hand, as well as a set of the objectives and existing materials for each course, teachers are in a fairly good position to perform the materials portion of their jobs. The handbook also provides a systematic framework to which the teachers can always refer.

Support for Materials Development

The teacher's handbook outlines the structure of the ELI, which has recently been altered to support teachers in all aspects of curriculum development (see Chapter Six for more on ELI structure). During the orientation meeting held each semester, we stress the importance of the teachers' constructive input on the ELI curriculum. We also stress the fact that there is more to the job than just teaching. All of the teachers are paid for 20 hours of work per week and the maximum teaching load is seven contact hours per week. Given that seven additional hours are allowed for class preparation and two are expected to be used as office hours, there remain four hours per week that the teachers are expected to devote to meetings and curriculum development. We emphasize the point that the teachers are also being paid for these curriculum activities, and that such activities are part of each teacher's professional responsibilities. In addition, we remind the teachers that four hours per week for fifteen weeks amounts to sixty hours and that an educated person can accomplish much in sixty hours. Finally, we reemphasize the degree to which we desperately need their help and professional experience and point out that in any case the activities are not optional.

Logistical support (for such mundane things as paper clips and such major items as computer services, duplication, and studio taping) are viewed as the responsibility of the administration. In other words, within reason, the administration should provide the teachers with all the tools they will need to meet the program's materials development (and other curriculum) requirements. Naturally, there are limits. But insofar as possible, the teachers should not have to worry about finding necessary supplies and services; instead, they should put their best efforts into creating the curriculum from which all the teachers and students will benefit.

Working Together

As in the GELC program, cooperative efforts among teachers are crucial to materials development in the ELI. We offer as many as five or six sections of some courses during our heavy season in the fall semester. Clearly, if we can get these five or six teachers to put their heads together on any project, the results should be superior to the efforts of any one individual. In addition, the amount of work that any individual must put into the project is relatively small in relation to the magnitude of the final product from which that individual will benefit. Equally important from a political point of view, any project to which all teachers have contributed is much more likely to be accepted and to succeed.

Another administrative innovation that has helped get curriculum done in the ELI was the creation of the job of "lead teacher." One lead teacher for each skill area is given release time (that is, the teacher is released from teaching one full course) to coordinate and foster curriculum development among the teachers in that skill area. A "faculty resource" person from the Graduate Faculty in the Department of English as a Second Language is also assigned to each skill area. These two individuals work together to meet with teachers in the particular skill area and work on the curriculum. It is through these weekly meetings that most materials development has occurred in the ELI. (See Chapter Six for discussion concerning the effectiveness of this lead teacher strategy.)

Cooperation among teachers is not always guaranteed. One stance that has helped us to smooth out problems and avoid ruffling feathers concerns the nature of criticisms that are acceptable in the ELI. Any criticism that proposes a viable solution is welcomed—particularly if the person proposing the change is willing to contribute to the work involved in accomplishing that solution. Negative criticism that offers no alternative or suggests no means for finding a solution is discouraged. This system reduces gratuitous negativism and prompts people to think about what they are criticizing in practical terms. At the same time, all of us are encouraged to think in terms of problem solving, rather than simply tearing down existing curriculum elements. If teachers must "put their money where their mouth is," they are much more likely to be thoughtful in their criticisms because they will not want to waste their own time and energy on unproductive curriculum change. Given these criteria, we find that a great deal is accomplished in our meetings with regard to materials adoption, development, and adaptation.

Annual Materials Review

An example of how this attitude toward curriculum criticism can be applied occurs each year in our materials review process. Each spring semester, before the textbook order date, the teachers from each skill area meet together to decide on the materials that will be used for the next 12 months. Criticisms of the existing materials are welcomed, but the issuer of the criticism must be willing to contribute to the search for alternative materials. Typically, all available materials for potential review are sought out in publishers catalogs, in "Books Received" sections of journals, and from our teachers' shelves. These materials are sorted through and considered in contrast to the existing materials in terms of the characteristics shown in Table 5.6, as well as in terms of the relative percentage of each text that would be directly useful or adaptable to our purposes. Sometimes, this process results in the adoption of new textbooks for the ensuing 12-month period; sometimes, the materials remain the same; in most cases, however, the discussion generates useful spin–off ideas on ways that the materials can be adapted or supplemented from other sources (or from newly created materials).

Materials Resources

Individual teachers themselves are another constant source of creative ideas. In the ELI, teachers can make unlimited copies for their classes. In return, they are asked to make one extra copy of any handouts or classroom materials they duplicate, to jot down the name of the course for which they are intended, and to drop the copy into a special box next to the duplicating machine. Periodically, these handouts are sorted into the materials resource files. These files are organized according to skill area drawers and course levels by various topics that have evolved over the years. The files also include copies of all of the more formally developed modules and units that have been put together in teachers' meetings and developed individually or in groups. In fact, any resources that the teachers might find useful are put in these files. Every teacher has access to these materials with the proviso that anything borrowed be quickly copied and returned to the file.

In addition, a major effort has recently been made to reorganize and supplement the audiovisual aids used in the ELI. These have been cataloged and sorted so that the teachers will have ready access to them. The files and audiovisual aids are housed in a self–access room (only teachers have the number combination that opens the lock) that also contains the audiovisual equipment they may need.

In sum, the materials development in the ELI has been somewhat more systematic than it was in the GELC program. A blueprint was provided. Clear means were found for supporting materials development and other curriculum development. We had specific strategies for fostering cooperation among teachers on materials projects. Regular materials reviews were institutionalized, and we created useful materials resources files, as well as accessible audiovisual materials and equipment.

SUMMARY

This chapter claimed that given a sound framework for materials design (including clearly defined approaches, syllabuses, techniques, and exercises), materials blueprints can be developed (including the items shown in Table 5.2, as well as description of the units of analysis, scope and sequence charts, and Gantt diagrams) that will help with the adoption, development, and adaptation of materials.

In adopting materials, decisions have to be made about the types of materials that would be appropriate, and then those materials have to be located (through publishers' catalogs, "Books Received" lists, or on fellow teachers' shelves). The materials can then be evaluated using the checklist in Table 5.6. However, even after materials have been adopted, some sort of regular materials evaluation should be institutionalized so that the materials do not become stale with regard to the particular curriculum in question. In developing materials, three phases—creating, teaching, and evaluating—were suggested and elaborated upon in Table 5.7. In adapting materials, it was suggested that procedures similar to those for adoption be followed with the addition of analyzing, classifying, gap filling, and reorganizing, as described in Table 5.8.

The example materials development projects from GELC and the ELI provided instances of how much can be accomplished by determined groups of teachers who have adequate institutional support and who work together for the common good in adopting, developing, and adapting materials.

■ ■ ■ *CHECKLIST*

The following checklist is provided to ensure that those elements of materials development discussed in this chapter will all be included in the overall curriculum development process (as appropriate).

- ☐ Framework for materials design
  - ☐ Approaches clear?
  - ☐ Syllabuses well outlined?
  - ☐ Techniques considered?
  - ☐ Exercises considered?

- ☐ Materials blueprint (Used checklist in Table 5.2?)

- ☐ Where do materials come from?
  - ☐ Adopting materials?
    - ☐ Decided on types of materials?
    - ☐ Located materials?
      - ☐ Publishers' catalogs?
      - ☐ Reviews?
      - ☐ Teachers' shelves?
    - ☐ Evaluated materials (Used checklist in Table 5.6?)
    - ☐ Actually adopted materials?
    - ☐ Set up ongoing review processes for materials?

  - ☐ Developing materials (see items in checklist in Table 5.7)?
    - ☐ Gone through a materials creating phase?
    - ☐ Used a teaching phase?
    - ☐ Included an evaluating phase?

  - ☐ Adapting materials (see checklist in Table 5.8)?
    - ☐ Used checklist in Table 5.6?
    - ☐ Analyzed the useful material that matches the objectives?
    - ☐ Classified that material?
    - ☐ Filled the gaps that remain?
    - ☐ Reorganized the materials to match your objectives and syllabus?

■ ■ ■ TERMS

approaches
examination copies
fit to the curriculum
logistical characteristics
materials background
physical characteristics
reviews
syllabus design
teachability
techniques

desk copies
exercises
Gantt diagram
materials
materials evaluation
review copies
scope-and-sequence chart
syllabuses
teachers' shelves

■ ■ ■ REVIEW QUESTIONS

1. What are the four categories of teaching activities discussed in this chapter in terms of forming a framework for materials design? Do you recall from Chapter One how each of these categories is defined?

2. Why should a materials blueprint be considered before starting to develop materials? What are some of the potential units of analysis that should be considered in developing materials?

3. What is a scope-and-sequence chart? A Gantt diagram? Why might these tools prove useful in the materials development stage of curriculum development? Could they prove equally useful at other stages of curriculum development?

4. Where do materials come from? In other words, what are the three strategies that can be used to put materials in place in a curriculum?

5. What steps should be taken in adopting materials? Why do you think that a regular materials review process is stressed so much in this chapter?

6. Do you think that there is any set of materials in the entire world that would be 100 percent acceptable to three language instructors teaching the same course? Why or why not?

7. What steps should be taken in adapting materials? Should there also be a regular review process set up for adapted materials?

8. What are the three phases presented in this chapter for creating materials?

9. How are the three phases for creating materials related to the elements of curriculum (needs, goals and objectives, tests, materials, teaching, and evaluation) discussed in this book as a whole? (Hint: see Table 5.7)

10. Can all three strategies be combined in the same language program? Do you think that such combinations are necessary and useful? Why?

■ ■ ■ APPLICATIONS

A1. Examine the description given for either the GELC program or the ELI at UHM (in the "Example Materials Development Projects" section). Briefly jot down the approaches, syllabuses, techniques, and exercises that you think would be included in the framework for the program that you have chosen.

A2. Next, decide whether the materials for the program were adopted, developed, or adapted, or some combination of the three.

A3. Look back at the steps followed and strategies used by the program in materials development and decide if important elements were left out. How might they have been included?

B1. Consider some language program that you are now involved in or know about. Which of the strategies for materials development (adopt, develop, or adapt) is best matched to the financial resources available and to the skills/abilities of teachers in the program? If existing materials are going to be used (for example, commercially published textbooks), what kind of preparation will teachers need in order to use them effectively? If materials are to be specially written for the program, who will be involved in preparing the materials and under what circumstances? Will adequate provisions be made for development, review, and revision of the materials?

B2. Outline a materials blueprint for your program (see Table 5.2). What will you include? What information is superfluous?

B3. Apply the checklist given in Table 5.6 to a set of materials with which you are familiar. You will probably find that you must do so with a particular course and program in mind. What percentage of the materials do you think is appropriate for that course given the setting?

Chapter 6

Teaching

INTRODUCTION

So far, I have covered four of the six curriculum development elements that are central to the well-being of any curriculum. In this chapter I will examine how the needs analysis information, objectives, tests, and materials can be implemented in the teaching phase of curriculum development. The focus of the teaching phase is on the kinds of instruction that will characterize the program, that is, on the kinds of teaching that will be required to achieve the goals of the program.

Teaching is a complex and controversial profession, and the education literature is full of teaching models that present varied conceptualizations of the nature of teaching. I will treat language teaching as the relatively limited set of activities involved in implementing a language curriculum at the classroom level. For my purposes, teaching consists of those activities directly related to delivery of instruction. One could argue that all the activities I have described in this book are part of teaching, and one would be correct. However, when I refer to teaching as a distinct activity within the systematic curriculum model, I will be using a narrow definition of *teaching* that includes only those activities (techniques and exercises) rationally selected by the teacher to help students achieve learning. To be rational, these activities must be justified according to the kinds of objectives that the program has developed and the teachers have set out to accomplish, but also must be related to the overall approaches and syllabuses that motivate and organize the curriculum.

I have argued repeatedly in this book that one purpose of all the elements of curriculum design is to support teachers and help them to do what they do best: teach. In this chapter I will discuss four ways that a language program, through its curriculum, can directly help teachers to do their job: orienting teachers to the new curriculum, supporting their teaching efforts, monitoring instruction, and providing ways for teachers to revitalize themselves.

ORIENTING AND INVOLVING TEACHERS IN THE CURRICULUM

Chapters One and Two emphasized the importance of teachers in the curriculum and the necessity for meeting their needs, as well as the needs of the students in an institution. In this section, I will not dwell on those suggestions; instead, my discussion will center on ways to put initial information in various forms into the hands of teachers, especially those who are new to the program. Generally, the purpose of such information dissemination is to anticipate the kinds of questions that all instructors will have so that each teacher individually will not have to waste time seeking out the answers.

□   INITIAL INFORMATION

The impressions and facts that teachers receive in the first few weeks or months of their stay in a language program may well shape their views and actions within that program for years to come. Hence the initial information that teachers get is an important part of the teaching element of curriculum development. Such initial information can take the form of an orientation meeting during which the basic information needed to perform adequately can be conveyed to teachers, or be delivered in the form of a written teacher's guide, or both.

Orientation

Preferably before the instruction period begins, but certainly as soon as possible, new teachers should be oriented to the language program in which they are working. Instructors who have already been teaching in the program for a while may also benefit from periodic reorientation—especially if the program has a dynamic, rapidly evolving curriculum. Such a meeting may take many forms. An *orientation* meeting might consist of nothing more than a one hour get-together during which the teachers are given the basic information they will need to accomplish their jobs. A half-day series of workshops complete with tours of relevant buildings and facilities might be more effective. Another alternative would be a retreat to some attractive site where teachers can not only be provided with vital information, but can also get to know each other and other program personnel. The form that such a meeting takes will depend on the amount of information that must be conveyed, as well as on the personalities of the people involved in planning and carrying out this type of activity. Regardless of the type of get-together that emerges, curriculum planners must provide some mechanism for communicating information to new teachers, as well as for periodically disseminating information to all continuing staff.

   In order to involve both new and old instructors in the process, curriculum planners would be wise to include the continuing staff members in some sort of buddy system as informants, as leaders of certain sessions, as agents of orientation to certain courses or skill areas, and/or as providers of information about the needs, goals and objectives, tests, materials, teaching, and evaluation in the program. If they feel they are contributing to the orientation process, veterans are less likely to object to attending the orientation meeting, and they may even find that they benefit from what goes on there. After all, the program may have changed since they themselves were oriented, they may have forgotten some of that initial information, or they may now see some aspect of the program in a new light. The truth of the matter is that there is only a certain amount of information that any human being can absorb in an orientation, so multiple orientations cannot hurt anyone.

Teacher's Guide

Unfortunately, it is impossible to predict which bits of information will be retained by which individuals, so it is a good idea for planners or administrators to prepare a handy guide or handbook containing all vital program information so that teachers can refer to it when they have questions. This guide should contain as much information as possible. In the next section, I suggest many options concerning what teachers need to know. Only some of the issues I discuss will apply to any particular program; conversely, other important issues I do not discuss might well apply to a specific curriculum or program. A teacher's guide has the added benefit of saving administrators, curriculum developers, and secretarial staff from being asked numbingly repetitious questions by the new teachers.

Reference Documents

Other types of documents may serve as useful references for new teachers. For instance, in addition to the teacher's guide, copies of any needs analysis documents might prove interesting to the teachers, particularly those documents that apply to the same course or skill area to which they have been assigned. Teachers should also receive copies of the relevant course objectives and any first day handouts that have been used in the past to describe the courses. (These handouts are traditionally called "syllabuses" in classrooms in the United States. I have carefully avoided this use of the term in this book to avert confusion with the broader definition given in the first chapter.)

Naturally, the teachers should also have copies of all the materials that will be used in their classes. If a resource file and audiovisual equipment are part of the program's materials, new teachers should be provided with pertinent lists of resources and equipment. New teachers might also be loaned such supplementary materials as packets/modules that can be used in their courses, reference dictionaries, grammars, and the like. Edited collections of relevant, up-to-date professional articles may also prove useful. If possible, a language program should have its own professional library of books, journals, and other materials.

□   TYPES OF INFORMATION TEACHERS NEED

Whether through orientation meetings, a teacher's guide, and/or resource documents, certain information must be conveyed to new teachers. The administrators or planners must carefully consider what kinds of information to convey to new staff because it will have an impact on the entire curriculum in the form of how teachers initially feel about and carry out their work. I will classify and list some of the possible types of questions that teachers might need to have answered. These questions will be arranged into categories about the context of the program, the learners, the teachers, the administrative processes, and the instruction itself.

Context of the Program

If the curriculum is large-scale and for use in a public school setting, information might usefully be supplied about the national, state, or school district language policies, as well as their impact on teachers and teaching practices, parental attitudes and support, the school system and its operation vis-à-vis language programs, the examination system, and materials (as well as how they are put into place and used). For all language programs, useful information might include a description of the institution itself, its resources, and the administrators, teachers, and learners involved. Additional information might be provided on the curriculum development stages that have already taken place. This kind of information is fundamental since no program can be planned or taught in a vacuum.

For example, curriculum developers might consider providing teachers with answers to questions about the program such as the following:

1.   To what extent is the program consistent with federal, state, and local government policies?
2.   Is there a generally felt need for this kind of program, or is it being imposed on teachers and learners from above?
3.   Can the school curriculum support changes in student behavior of the kind that are expected?
4.   Will opportunities be arranged for articulating the theoretical approach of the program to education officials, teacher trainers, teachers, learners, parents, and other interested parties?
5.   What kinds of external tests and examinations are teachers required to administer or learners required to take? How do these tests affect the curriculum?
6.   What kind of support will innovations be likely to receive from teacher organizations, educational leaders, and administrators at various levels?
7.   What kind of community support is probable for the program, if any?

Learners

New teachers will quite naturally be curious about the learners they will be teaching. Since groups of students can vary widely, curriculum designers should provide teachers with information that focuses on ways in which the students' characteristics are related to the design of the program and directly to the teaching. In other words, curriculum designers must determine from the possible range of learner variables those that are most likely to influence the delivery of instruction and the outcome of the program.

A program designed for very young children, for example, will necessarily require a different approach from one designed for adults. Or, for another example, learners coming from an educational background in which the teacher's role is authoritarian may react unfavorably to a teaching approach that requires learners to take responsibility for their own learning by working with their fellow students. Hence any language program must take into account learner considerations such as the following:

1. Who will the program serve?
2. How many learners will the program serve?
3. What is their educational and cultural background?
4. What are their previous language learning experiences?
5. What circumstances have led them to enter the program?
6. Are there any positive or negative side effects resulting from how they have entered the program?
7. How are learners expected to learn within the program?
8. What are the learner's responsibilities within the program?
9. What expectations are learners likely to have concerning the techniques and exercises, as well as the approaches and syllabuses?
10. Do teachers and students have conflicting sets of expectations? What are they?
11. How are learners likely to feel about the success of their own learning? Do student views differ from teachers' views?

Answers to such questions will provide information about the degree to which the learners form a heterogenous or homogeneous group, the kinds of problems that curriculum planners and teachers are likely to face, and some notion of the learner's expectations.

Teachers

Teachers are also interested in fellow teachers. The curriculum planners will have gathered important information about the kinds of teachers the program depends on. Teachers may differ in their individual teaching skills, in their attitudes toward teaching, in how they teach, in the demands that can be made on them, and so forth. Because all these factors and more may play a crucial role in determining the effectiveness and dynamics of the curriculum, teachers might beneficially be described to themselves. For instance, their educational and cultural background may have a great influence on how a program will be implemented. Teachers who have had little or no teacher training may do little more than present the material in the textbook. Trained teachers, on the other hand, may prefer to adapt the book and create their own supplementary materials. One teacher may see herself primarily as a motivator, while another sees his role in the classroom as an organizer of communicative activities.

A related problem is that curriculums often make culture-bound assumptions about the teachers who will use them. In the Western tradition, for example, teaching is sometimes presented as a democratic process in which learners and teachers are collaboratively involved. The teacher presents herself as a friend and counselor. In another culture, the teacher may be viewed as an authority figure who is expected to provide and direct learning.

The following are examples of questions about teachers that teachers might need answered:

1. What teaching skills do the teachers have?
2. Are the teachers native speakers of the language that they are teaching? If not, what is their proficiency level?
3. What expectations are teachers likely to have concerning the approaches, syllabuses, techniques, and exercises?
4. Are there any conflicting sets of expectations among teachers?
5. What is the place of the teacher in the classroom? Should teachers view themselves as counselors, facilitators, directors, or all three?
6. Where do teachers fit into the program as a whole? Are they needs analysts, objectives setters, test developers, materials creators, and program evaluators, as well as classroom teachers?
7. How are they expected to teach in the program?
8. What would be regarded as good teaching?

Administrative Processes

Teachers will also need information about the administration of the program. Employee issues, or issues of how various personnel interact in the program, might be included under this category. Any constraints concerning how decisions are made and implemented should be described. Institutional requirements should also be covered, for instance, whether teachers are required to submit formal lesson plans or serve on curriculum committees, and whether teachers are assigned to or choose their own teaching responsibilities. Still other considerations may be related to resources and budget. In short, information on the administrative processes can be very complex, so those in charge of introducing new teachers to a program need to provide information about these processes to help new teachers avoid, or at least minimize, mistakes later.

The following are examples of the types of questions that might usefully be answered about administration:

1. How many teachers are needed to staff the program? What kinds of teachers are selected? How many different kinds of teachers are required?
2. What other kinds of personnel are involved (for example, administrative, secretarial, and so on)?
3. What provisions are made for teacher training or retraining?
4. What provisions are made for teachers to develop curriculum and materials?
5. How are teachers monitored and evaluated?
6. What channels of communication exist between the teachers and the administrators involved in the program?
7. How are conflicts resolved within the program and its administrative support system?
8. How do learners enter and exit from the program or move from one level to another?
9. How are teachers assigned duties and responsibilities?
10. How are equipment and materials acquired, checked out, and used?
11. How are budgets established and spent?
12. How is the effectiveness of the program monitored, evaluated, and defended?
13. What provisions are made for curriculum revision?

Instruction

Another category of information that may prove useful will describe the types of instruction that have been adopted in the program, and how best to implement them. Here, the kinds of questions to be answered are of the following types:

1. What overall approach has been adopted? How can this overall approach be characterized?
2. Does the program have a particular emphasis? Is the program a special-purposes program, a vocational program, an academic program, a competency-based program, or one based on a set of general proficiency guidelines?
3. What were the units of analysis in the needs analysis? In what form are the program goals and objectives stated? What kinds of learning outcomes are expected?
4. Under what circumstances is the program being taught? Is instruction to be in a school, at a job site, or where? Are classrooms comfortable, air-conditioned, and so forth?
5. What is the duration and intensity of the program?
6. How many learners are there in each class?
7. What kind of syllabus is being used (structural, situational, topical, functional, notional, skills specific, task-based, or some combination of these)?

8. What kinds of learner exercises and teaching techniques are recommended?

9. What kinds of testing and evaluation procedures are used? When and how are these developed and administered?

10. What are the instructional materials in the program? Are teachers required to teach from a textbook, select their own materials, adapt those materials, or create their own materials?

11. Are learners given materials or do they have to purchase them?

12. To what degree is there control over the content and form of instruction? Are teachers given a choice about approaches and materials to be used? To what degree is a uniform theoretical approach followed?

13. What kinds of classroom equipment are necessary to deliver instruction (for example, tape recorders, video equipment, or a language laboratory)?

SUPPORTING TEACHERS

The various types of orientation information I have described will help teachers to get their feet on the ground. However, a successful curriculum will provide much more in teacher support. Such support may take the form of helping the teachers to understand their place in the curriculum vis-à-vis the students, helping them to think about their own teaching, providing a framework of administrative and curricular support, or providing means for dealing with the inevitable politics that will emerge in any language program.

□ THE TEACHER'S AND STUDENT'S PLACE IN THE CURRICULUM

Teaching is usually regarded as something that teachers do in order to bring about changes in learners. A central component of teaching is how teachers view their place in this process. What is a teacher? What teaching styles are desirable? What kinds of teacher-learner interactions work well? And what is a good atmosphere to create in the classroom? The following are some of the roles that teachers may assume in the classroom:

1. Needs analyst
2. Provider of student input
3. Motivator
4. Organizer and controller of student behavior
5. Demonstrator of accurate language production

6. Materials developer
7. Monitor of students' learning
8. Counselor and friend

These self-imposed roles may provide the basis from which some teachers develop personal views of what a good teacher is.

An equally important set of issues for teachers concerns the question of how the learners view their place in the learning process? How do they expect to learn? Do they see themselves as passive recipients of knowledge from an educational system that is imposed on them, or do they view themselves as active participants responsible for their own learning? To what extent are students consulted concerning the kinds of learning and learning activities that will go on in the classroom? Is there any conflict between the students' views and those of the teachers? In general, the place of learners in the curriculum will relate to their preferences with regard to concepts like the following:

1. Learning approaches
2. Attitudes toward learning
3. Learning styles
4. Strategies used in learning
5. Learning activities
6. Patterns of interaction
7. Degree of learner control over their own learning
8. What constitutes effective teaching
9. The nature of effective learning

Where conflicts are identified between how learners and teachers view such things as learning styles, the role of the teacher, or preferred learning activities, discussion with the students about the reasons for doing things as they are done may: (1) help to convince the students of the efficacy of these strategies, (2) help teachers to see the students' points of view, and (3) help both groups move toward a compromise on these issues.

□ HELPING TEACHERS TO TEACH

On the basis of their background, training, and experience, teachers will determine what techniques and exercises to use in setting up the learning experiences that they believe will best help bring about learning. Teachers should continually think about and discuss teaching issues so that the assumptions that guide their teaching will always be clear to them. Willing (1985) suggests a number of exercises that enable teachers to explore these issues. For example, teachers may discuss questions such as:

1. Suppose a total stranger walked in and observed one of your classes. What aspects of your teaching style would give that person clues as to your basic personality?
2. What aspects of your teaching style might mislead that same person about your true personality?
3. Who does best in your classes? How would you describe a typical "excellent learner" for the sort of teaching you do?
4. Have you ever gone through a major change of teaching style? (Willing 1985, p. 14)

Ultimately, all that a curriculum can do in terms of helping the instructors to teach is to ensure that they have everything they need in the way of resources and support because the ultimate responsibility for what occurs in the classroom will rest on their shoulders. In the previous section I listed a number of variables as factors that can affect the ways teachers and students view their respective places in the curriculum. Quick consideration of these factors will reveal that students might vary considerably among themselves concerning their attitudes about their place in the classroom. Only the teacher who is in daily contact with these individuals will have any hope of creating an atmosphere in the classroom and selecting techniques and exercises that will maximize learning among these diverse individuals. Since teachers can vary just as much as students, the way a particular teacher chooses to handle the myriad student variables will also differ from individual to individual as a function of the teacher's personality and teaching styles.

□ PROVIDING A FRAMEWORK OF SUPPORT

Is there any doubt that teachers need as much help as they can get? I have repeatedly argued in this book that a systematic curriculum provides teachers with the kinds of support they need. What I have not yet clarified is the fact that such support can come in the form of administrative support or curricular support.

Administrative Support

Teachers who feel isolated may spend a disproportionate amount of their time planning and preparing for class. Alternatively, a curriculum in which the administrators view their job as supporting the teachers will be a curriculum in which the teachers are in a better position to do a good job of teaching. In turn, these administrators can help most by providing the teachers with buffers between them and negative aspects of the world outside the program, by eliminating all unnecessary paperwork, and by ensuring that all required resources are available for the teachers to deliver instruction and to continue developing themselves professionally.

In a sense, providing buffers means protecting the teacher from external influences that might interfere with job performance. This responsibility typically falls on the program administrator to perform, but may also be a committee function. "Protecting teachers" may refer to activities as simple as making sure that teachers are not disturbed in their classrooms by needless interruptions. Such buffers can also be considerably more complex, including issues like (1) making sure that the teachers are supported against arbitrary bureaucratic change at higher levels; (2) fighting for adequate salaries, full-time employment, or daycare for teachers' children; or (3) securing an adequate budget to support instruction. My experience as an administrator indicates that there will be no lack of battles to fight on behalf of a program's teachers. Thus I must emphasize that curriculum should make provision for specific administrators, or faculty committees, or both, to take responsibility for such eventualities.

One part of every teacher's job deserves special attention, that is, the area of paperwork. Curriculum development, indeed much of what has been written in this book, will generate paperwork for the teachers. This is not good. The teacher's job is to teach, but classroom activities by themselves generate large amounts of record keeping and paperwork. Teachers do not need gratuitous paperwork to keep them busy. Still, curriculum development will necessitate compiling and sharing information, and that will probably be done on paper. (It has been widely noted that the advent of personal computers, printers, and copying machines has increased, not decreased, the amounts of paper in our lives.) Since much of what I advocate in this book encourages more paperwork, I am duty-bound to mention the problem and to beg curriculum planners to make every effort to reduce the teachers' paperwork load to the absolute minimum necessary to do their jobs and help with the curriculum development.

The last but most important type of administrative support involves ensuring that all reasonable resources be provided to the teachers. In today's world, that means everything from paper clips to computers and software, from duplication paper to a professional reference library. Provision should be made in the curriculum for mechanisms to determine what resources are needed and to oversee their acquisition and maintenance. Like many other logistical aspects of a language program, this may be an administrative responsibility, or it may be handled by a committee of teachers.

Curricular Support

Teachers should not have to develop all the curriculum elements for their courses in isolation. As I have pointed out repeatedly, needs assessment, goals and objectives, testing, materials, teaching, and program evaluation can all be supported by sound curriculum development processes that are designed to make the individual teacher's job easier. The more these processes draw on the combined energies of the entire staff, teachers and administrators alike, the more effective, and indeed supportive, the processes will be.

□ DEALING WITH POLITICS

The idea that politics impacts language programs is denied by some language teachers who apparently feel that they should be above such petty concerns. The truth (and there are very few such truths in our field) is that language teachers can be just as petty and political as any other group of people. If one takes the view that politics is one of the important means by which curriculum is implemented, politics can be viewed positively and handled in such a way that the overall curriculum will benefit.

Curriculum Implementation

Every situation will vary in terms of how politics must be handled. After all, the dynamics of a program will largely be a function of the personalities and problems interacting at a particular point in time. Therefore, it would be irresponsible for me to prescribe political solutions for each and every situation. However, I can suggest some general guidelines so that curriculum developers can increase their chances of avoiding resistance and calamitous problems in implementing a program:

1. Involve all the participants in the process of curriculum development at least to the point of consulting with each interest group and seeking their views.
2. Avoid taking the position of an omniscient "expert" who knows what is good for the program.
3. Make only reasonable demands on the time and energy of the people involved.
4. Remember that any group of people may be entrenched and resistant to change.
5. Avoid making people feel threatened or defensive.
6. Remember that the teachers may have been absolutely independent and all-powerful in their classrooms until the curriculum started changing around them.
7. Try not to threaten the "turf" staked out by administrators.
8. Remember that much more can be accomplished through discussion and compromise than through dictated policy decisions and inflexibility.

I believe that the systematic approach to curriculum—including all of the elements discussed in this book—can facilitate political processes, but will never replace them. Only through cooperation and compromise can curriculum be implemented. If this is properly done, the politics of ongoing program management, discussed next, will be considerably easier.

Program Management

The position I take in this book is that curriculum development processes are never finished: they are perpetually ongoing and evolving. Hence everything said in the previous section would apply here too. However, at some point, it would be very nice from the administrator's point of view to have a system of management that could help in maintaining equilibrium in the program. Pennington (1983, pp. 30-31) has pointed to the following as program characteristics that administrators should foster:

1. To provide good quality instruction (an objective shared with ESL teachers)
   a. Maintain high standards
   b. Have well-defined, testable objectives
   c. Have systematic and consistent placement and advancement of students.
2. To have everything run smoothly
   a. Avoid frequent major changes
   b. Devise a curriculum which is easy to implement
   c. Please supervisor, teachers, students, themselves.

MONITORING TEACHERS

Though it is often seen by teachers as something other than support, monitoring teachers' performance in the classroom can be a way of bolstering their efforts. Many teachers are defensive about monitoring of their teaching because such supervision smacks of accountability. In most professions, accountability is accepted, even expected. However, in the language classroom, the teacher has often been in total control inside of the classroom, answering to nobody. Accountability threatens this sovereignty. Yet regularly scheduled monitoring, as part of the curriculum can help both the program staff as a group and teachers as individuals to think about what good teaching is and improve in-class performance. However, whether it be in the form of administrator or peer observations or student evaluations, such monitoring should be structured to minimize the defensiveness that teachers may naturally feel about the process.

□ WHAT IS GOOD TEACHING?

Pennington and Brown (1991) include three indicators of excellence in all aspects of a language program: consistency, efficiency, and effectiveness. Similar to these categories, but with specific reference to classroom instruction alone, I will offer my own three categories to describe good teaching: consistent instruction, relevant instruction, and efficient instruction. These three categories are very similar to those discussed in Chapter Four as characteristics of good tests: reliability, validity, and usability.

Consistent instruction is the first of the qualities important to sound language teaching. The results of the learning process in a program should be consistent over time and between sections of the same course. Imagine, for instance, a program wherein the instruction was very effective, but only some of the time; or a pair of sections of the same course that are supposedly alike, but that have teachers who deliver completely different results. Students, who naturally talk among themselves, may join into open rebellion if they feel that a teacher is providing sound instruction only part of the time, or if they sense that they are not getting the same quality instruction as their friends in other sections. In addition, a program that is not delivering consistent instruction can hardly claim to be producing 100 percent relevant instruction because inconsistent instruction cannot be said to be relevant, except perhaps for part of the time.

Thus *relevant instruction* is the second crucial characteristic of sound instruction. The relevancy of a program's instruction can be defined as the degree to which a program delivers what it claims to be offering, as well as the degree to which what it is producing reflects sound language teaching practice. For example, consider a course designed to teach conversational English for social purposes. If monitoring reveals that the instruction is focused on grammatical structures, the monitor might legitimately question the relevancy of the curriculum because the course does not appear to be delivering on its stated purpose. However, even if the course design indicates a more general focus on verbal communication for social purposes, instructional emphasis on grammatical structures rather than communication skills indicates that course goals and actual instruction are out of phase. The question remains as to whether the students' needs are reflected in the stated purpose of the program. For instance, a group of Chinese nuclear engineers heading for lengthy stays at British universities might have needs that include social conversation, but also a number of other types of language. The program above might indeed be delivering what it claims, but would not be sufficiently relevant to the needs of this group of engineers. Hence the relevancy of a language program must be assessed in terms of the specific learners being served.

The last important characteristic that should be fostered by a program's curriculum is *efficient instruction.* The concern here is that a program be practical. Clearly, if given an infinite amount of time and unlimited resources, any program could teach students to a level of almost-native proficiency in any language. In the real world, however, language programs do not have unlimited time or resources, so efficiency must be considered an important characteristic of teaching.

This quality of efficiency can be broken down into two subcategories: program efficiency and instructional efficiency. I will define *program efficiency* as the degree to which a program is efficient in the sense of not being wasteful of the funding, resources, and energy of those individuals who make it work. For instance, some programs might demand so much paperwork from teachers on a daily basis that the teachers have little time for class preparation. Such a state of affairs would not be efficient and might lead to inconsistent results, which in turn would bring into question the relevancy of the entire program. Obviously, the curriculum of such a program would be greatly enhanced by limiting the amount of unnecessary paperwork.

I will define *instructional efficiency* as the degree to which teaching is efficient in the sense of not wasting the students' money, time, or energy. Students usually pay for their instruction in one way or another, whether it be in the form of tuition charges, their parents' taxes, or simply through spending valuable time in the classroom. Thus they have a right to expect that instruction will be fairly efficient in terms of not wasting their energy, time, or money.

In sum, the essential questions which must be addressed in working out the teaching part of the curriculum design is whether the instruction is consistent and relevant, as well as reasonably efficient for the learners. These three issues might seem to be fairly straightforward, but remember: good management of a curriculum demands that all points of view be considered in making decisions that will foster these three characteristics.

□ OBSERVATIONS

Now that I have discussed some of the parameters of what can be considered good teaching, I will turn to the topic of classroom observations as a means of supporting teachers. A *classroom observation* is any situation in which the teacher is being observed for whatever reasons in the act of teaching. The observation may be for purposes of helping teachers grow, for needs analysis, for research, or for teacher performance evaluation. This last category worries teachers the most because a performance evaluation can have serious consequences in terms of pay raises, promotions, continued employment, or termination. Personal financial issues like these arouse strong passions even in people who may not be prone to such emotions. Hence the purpose of any classroom observation should be clearly explained before it happens. Moreover, the visitor, whatever his or her purpose, should probably notify the teacher (and any other pertinent administrators) before the visit so that the teacher is not taken by surprise.

The most common types of observations in the institutions with which I have been associated are administrative observations, peer observations, and self-observations in the form of videotapes. I will discuss each of these types of observations, and also comment on the importance of feedback.

Administrator Observations

Most competent teachers that I know welcome classroom observations of their work as long as they are warned in advance about when the visit will occur and who will be doing the observing. If such observations are regularly scheduled and built into the curriculum, teachers will seldom refuse to participate.

In doing observations, administrators must recognize that the teacher is probably nervous because of the professional importance of the observations. As a result, the teacher may have prepared a "special" lesson that is not representative of that teacher's normal classes. Administrators must also realize that the students may be nervous during an observation because of the presence in the classroom of an extraordinary person—one who may be an authority figure to them. Such nervousness may cause the students to become quiet and uncommunicative, which will make the teacher's job more difficult, or it may result in them trying to "help" the teacher by being overly verbal. In either case, unusual student behavior may throw the teacher off-balance. In short, the administrator should recognize that the class period being observed may not be exactly like the regular classes. Nonetheless, such an observation does provide some idea of the general classroom atmosphere, as well as evidence of how the teacher reacts under pressure.

In order to be an effective observer a responsible administrator must give the teacher feedback. Indeed, feedback will often be demanded by the teacher. To understand this point of view, consider how the teacher would feel if someone observed a class for an hour and then left with an empty "thank you" and nothing else. Most teachers want to improve their teaching and will solicit the observer's comments for that reason. Others might simply want to know how their teaching struck the observer.

Peer Observations

Peers are another effective resource for helping to monitor teachers in a way that contributes to the professional development of both the observer and the teacher. If each teacher is required to observe at least two other instructors who are teaching the same or similar courses (or even different ones, for that matter), they are bound to learn something of use in terms of teaching content, style, organization, atmosphere, attitudes, or any number of other classroom characteristics. However, once again, feedback in some form should be provided so that the observed teacher does not feel left out of the process. One real danger that must be considered in setting up peer observations stems from the territoriality and resulting insecurity that some teachers have with regard to their classrooms and teaching. In peer observations, the feedback must be channeled such that it is constructive and useful, not destructive and negative. I advocate creating an evaluation sheet designed to channel each peer observer's attention into positive and beneficial comments.

Self-Observation

Another effective alternative to traditional classroom observation practices is to conduct observations via video camera rather than in the person of an administrator or a peer. The resulting tape can be viewed by the teacher alone or can be reviewed by the teacher in the company of his or her immediate supervisor. I advocate this latter strategy because it allows the teacher to make observations, allows the administrator to observe and explain what is on his or her mind, promotes discussion of teaching issues, and—perhaps most importantly—ensures that the administrator will spend a certain amount of time talking with each teacher. This private time together may have a better effect on teacher morale and performance than all the other face-to-face contacts throughout the semester put together.

Feedback

Feedback is probably the single-most-important influence on the quality of any observation experience whether it be an administrative observation, a peer observation, or a self-observation. The entire observation experience can be colored for both the teacher and the observer by the amount and nature of the feedback that the observer provides the teacher. Feedback may take many forms, from an informal discussion over coffee afterwards to a more formal set of comments on a standard evaluation form. The choices of format for feedback will typically hinge on the purpose of the observations and on the personalities involved.

Classroom observation feedback forms come in a variety of configurations. For instance, an observation feedback form can be friendly, open-ended, and positive, or it can be detailed and negative in nature. I prefer an open-ended format like that shown in Figure 6.1. This example is very open-ended and purposely designed to channel all comments into either "Positive Aspects" or "Suggestions/Ideas." Thus the feedback is channeled into affirmative directions that generally make the observation process a positive one. One problem, at least from an administrator's point of view, is that this form does not work very well for teachers who have serious teaching deficiencies because it does not allow for enough negative (constructive) feedback. Notice also that the form in Figure 6.1 is so open-ended that the observer might have trouble thinking of comments to make. However, I always take the list shown in Table 6.1 with me into the classroom to help me remember options in the different categories. Such a list can never be 100 percent comprehensive and clearly represents a particular point of view. Therefore, this list must be viewed simply as an aid to help the observer focus on some of the important aspects of classroom teaching. To be fair, the observer should consider giving this list to the teacher prior to the observation to inform him or her about what types of things will be considered important during the observation.

Figure 6.1   Observation Form for Administrative Visits to the ELI
(Brown unpublished ms)

English Language Institute
DEPARTMENT OF ENGLISH AS A SECOND LANGUAGE
UNIVERSITY OF HAWAII AT MANOA
1890 East-West Road, Room 570, Moore Hall
Honolulu, Hawaii 96822 USA

CLASSROOM OBSERVATION

Teacher _____ Observer _____

Class _____ Date _____ Time _____

Nature of Lesson _____

_____

CATEGORY	POSITIVE ASPECTS	SUGGESTIONS/IDEAS
Pace of Lesson		
Teacher Presentation		
Class Management		
Teaching Aids		
Student Production		

Overall Impression

_____
                                                           Signed

**Table 6.1 Descriptors to Help ELI Classroom Observers
(Brown unpublished ms)**

Any or all of the points listed below may be commented on while observing classes. However, this list should be viewed as a resource rather than a constraint on your comments. Please feel free to add anything that you find pertinent.

A. PACE OF CLASS
- teacher's enthusiasm for
  lesson/ students' learning
- good eye contact with students
- active body language
- moved about the room well
- adequately loud voice
- presentation at appropriate
  speed
- teacher in control of learning
  processes
- variety of different techniques
  & exercises used during class

B. TEACHER PRESENTATION
- previous lesson reviewed
- lesson well-organized
- objective(s) clear
- lesson related to previous
  lesson, knowledge, or interests
- examples, demonstrations, &
  illustrations meaningful
- used learner-centered activities
  (individual, pair, or group work)
- provided opportunities for
  language practice
- summarized main points of lesson

C. CLASSROOM MANAGEMENT
- instructions simple and clear
- mechanics of roll, announcements,
  etc., short and to the point
- interruptions minimally disruptive
- class time utilized efficiently
- pleasant seating order
- comfortable atmosphere in class

D. TEACHING AIDS
- audio-visual aids used
- audio-visual aids handy & ready
- audio-visual interesting & useful
- effective use of blackboard
- handouts clear & meaningful
- realia used

E. STUDENT CHARACTERISTICS
- seemed highly motivated
- actively involved in lesson
  (Some Ss? All Ss?)
- actively involved in learner-
  centered portions of lesson
- error correction effective

The observation form shown in Figure 6.2 is considerably more detailed. Some might find this form more negative and threatening than that in Figure 6.1. The form in Figure 6.2 clearly emphasizes tallying teacher performances in terms of both negative and positive aspects of teaching. From an administrator's point of view, the form in Figure 6.2 would be easier to use for the purpose of giving negative feedback to teachers (as well as for building a case for dismissing a teacher).

Even more detailed and threatening forms do exist. Consider a form that I once encountered in a Middle Eastern company's language program, called a "Company Recertification Profile." This form began with categories like the following: the teacher describes the objective of the language program; processes company forms; describes the proper line of communication to the director; identifies differences among assigned, special-assigned, voluntary, in-policy, and out-of-policy students; and so forth. The almost military air of these categories

**Figure 6.2: A Portion of the State of Florida Observation Form
(adopted from Florida State Department of Education 1983)**

SUMMATIVE OBSERVATION INSTRUMENT

DOMAIN	EFFECTIVE INDICATORS	
3.0 INSTRUCTIONAL ORGANIZATION AND DEVELOPMENT	1. Begins instruction promptly	
	2. Handles materials in an orderly manner	
	3. Orients students to classwork/maintains academic focus	
	4. Conducts beginning/ending review	
	5. Questions academic comprehension/lesson development	asks single factual (Dom. 5.0)
		requires analysis/reasons
	6. Recognizes response/amplifies/gives corrective feedback	
	7. Gives specific academic praise	
	8. Provides for practice	
	9. Gives directions/assigns/checks comprehension of homework, seatwork assignment/gives feedback	
	10. Circulates and assists students	
4.0 PRESENTATION OF SUBJECT MATTER	11. Treats concept definition/attributes/examples/non-examples	
	12. Discusses cause-effect/uses linking words/applies law or principle	
	13. States and applies academic rule	
	14. Develops criteria and evidence for value judgment	
5.0 COMMUNICATION: VERBAL AND NONVERBAL	15. Emphasizes important points	
	16. Expresses enthusiasm, verbally challenges students	
	17.	
	18.	
2.0 MGT OF STD CONDUCT	19. Uses body behavior that shows interest—smiles, gestures	
	20. Stops misconduct	

(Figure 6.2 continued on page 201)

Figure 6.2: A portion of the State of Florida Observation Form (continued)

Frequency	Competency	Frequency	INEFFECTIVE INDICATORS
	15.17		Delays
	15.17		Does not organize or handle materials systematically
	1.12,13.15		Allows talk/activity unrelated to subject
	1.9.11		
	1.6/19,11		Poses multiple questions asked as one, unison response
	6/19,11.15		Poses non-academic questions/non-academic procedural questions
	1.3,6/19 12.20.21,22		Ignores student or response/expresses sarcasm, disgust, harshness
	6/19,12 21.22		Uses general, non-specific praise
	11		Extends discourse, changes topic with no practice
	6/19,11.13 16		Gives inadequate directions/no homework/ no feedback
	6/19.12		Remains at desk/circulates inadequately
	1.6/19.11		Gives definition or examples only
	1.6/19		Discusses either cause or effect only/uses no linking word(s)
			Does not state or does not apply academic rule
	6/19 22.23		States value judgment with no criteria or evidence
	1,9		
	6/19,17.17 21.22		
	1.9.13		Uses vague/scrambled discourse
	1.17		Uses loud grating, high pitched, monotone, inaudible talk
	6/19 17.17 21.22		Frowns deadpan or lethargic
	6/19 15.16 17.21.27		Delays desist/doesn't stop misconduct/desists punitively

provides an extreme example of the most rigid and threatening type of observation feedback. Remember that hundreds, if not thousands, of our fellow language teachers are living with this kind of feedback on a regular basis.

The degree to which an entirely positive, or half-positive and half-negative, form should be used in a curriculum is an important decision because of the impact it can have on teachers' morale. The degree to which such forms will be open-ended or relatively circumscribed in format will be equally important because of the relative freedom that is given to the observer by the various formats.

□ STUDENTS' EVALUATIONS

As an administrator who has conducted hundreds of classroom observations (always announced in advance), I cannot help but wonder how it is possible that virtually all the lessons I see are so innovative and interesting. Are the teachers (and students) performing in some special and self-conscious way because "the boss" is coming to observe? Of course, they are.

One excellent source of information for monitoring the classroom performance of teachers on a day-to-day basis is provided by the teachers' students. The information thus obtained probably offers a closer reflection of the normal operations in the classroom than information obtained during a formal observation. However, such information must be weighed carefully, for it presents the point of view of a biased group: the students. In general, if carefully obtained and balanced with information gained by classroom observation, data on students' attitudes and feelings about various aspects of their teacher's performance can be useful. After all, since the students are the ultimate clients in this business of language teaching, their attitudes and feelings should be taken into account when monitoring the quality of the service that is being provided. Student input into the monitoring of teaching is typically obtained in three ways: through course evaluation forms, through individual interviews, and through student representative meetings.

Course Evaluation Forms

Course evaluation forms, usually done as questionnaires, are probably the most efficient and common way of obtaining student feedback on courses and teaching. However, a number of dangers must be guarded against when such questionnaires are used: (1) evaluating too many different courses with one form, (2) addressing too many issues on one questionnaire, and (3) attempting to be too empirical.

The first of these problems, *evaluating too many different courses with one form,* is common in large institutions like universities, where a standard student evaluation form is used for all the courses taught. This type of questionnaire usually has the distinct advantage of being provided by the institution, being machine scorable, and therefore being easily summarized by computer so that the teacher can get immediate feedback. While this type of information may prove useful for making cross-campus or interschool comparisons, it often turns out to be too general to be of much use to the individual classroom teacher. In addition, students are less likely to be candid when they know that the information is being gathered on a large scale and could adversely affect their teacher's job.

Because I advocate using all types of information, I have used institutional forms, but I supplement them with questionnaires that are directed toward the particular course involved. It may also be useful to ensure, as a matter of curriculum policy, that these supplementary forms are to be strictly confidential in the sense that students need not sign their names on the forms and in the sense that only program administrators and the teacher involved in the evaluation will see the forms (and even he or she will not see it until after he or she has turned in grades). Consider the questionnaire shown in Figure 6.3. Notice it is geared to a specific course and to that course alone.

Second, even when they are designed for the specific course in question, student evaluation questionnaires may promote another problem, *addressing too many issues on one questionnaire.* This problem occurs when the questionnaire lacks focus; for example, it may ask questions about the teaching of the course, questions about course design, or questions about the placement test, and questions about dormitory accommodations. While all of these separate issues may be of interest to program administrators, the focus of a student evaluation questionnaire should be clear and concise so that it does not become too long and confusing. If the quality of teaching is the issue, the questions should focus on various aspects of that issue. If the quality of the curriculum is another important issue, then another set of questions on the curriculum can be included in a separate section. Notice how the questionnaire shown in Figure 6.3 addresses this problem by having two clearly distinct types of questions: some Likert-scale questions that ask about the curriculum (actually, about the objectives of the course in this case), and other very open-ended questions that address the issues of student self-evaluation and teaching quality.

Third, for reasons that remain unclear to me, questionnaires of this sort often fall into the trap of *attempting to be too empirical.* The *Likert scale* type of questions (that is, those with the "Very useful 1 2 3 4 5 6 7 Not very useful" structure) in the first part of Figure 6.3 exemplify this problem. In some cases, this type of information may be fine, depending on the purposes of the questionnaire. Such question formats clearly have the advantage of being easily scored and formatted; but they also have the distinct disadvantage of restricting the range of responses, with the potential result that the questionnaire actually prompts the kinds of answers students can give. In other words, the students may not be able to express what they are really feeling because the questionnaire asks questions from a teacher's or administrator's point of view. The solution to this problem (a solution adopted in the questionnaire shown in Figure 6.3) is to

Figure 6.3   Student Evaluation Form for ELI 72 (ELI 1991)

ENGLISH LANGUAGE INSTITUTE   ELI 72 Sec.
University of Hawaii at Manoa   SP SSI SSII FA 19 _____

EVALUATION FORM

Teacher's Name _____
                    (Family Name)   (Other Names)

To the student: As you complete the evaluation below, please remember that your HONEST and THOUGHTFUL answers will be used to improve ELI courses and teaching for the benefit of future students.

1. How much do you feel that your OVERALL ABILITY as an English reader has improved as a result of taking this course?
   Very useful   1   2   3   4   5   6   7   Not very useful

2. How much has your ability to read in your UNIVERSITY CONTENT COURSES improved as a result of taking this course?
   Very useful   1   2   3   4   5   6   7   Not very useful

3. How much do you think your VOCABULARY has increased as a result of taking this course?
   Very useful   1   2   3   4   5   6   7   Not very useful

4. How much do you think your SKIMMING and SCANNING ABILITIES have increased as a result of taking this course?
   Very useful   1   2   3   4   5   6   7   Not very useful

5. How much has your SPEED in reading increased as a result of taking this course?
   Very useful   1   2   3   4   5   6   7   Not very useful

6. How much has your ability to UNDERSTAND THE MAIN IDEAS increased as a result of taking this course?
   Very useful   1   2   3   4   5   6   7   Not very useful

7. How much has your ability to STUDY MORE EFFICIENTLY improved as a result of taking this course?
   Very useful   1   2   3   4   5   6   7   Not very useful

8. How helpful was the VOCABULARY TEXTBOOK used in this course?
   Very useful   1   2   3   4   5   6   7   Not very useful

9. How helpful was the COURSE TEXTBOOK used in this course?
Very useful   1   2   3   4   5   6   7   Not very useful

(Figure 6.3 continued on page 205)

include some open-ended questions in the second part so that the students also have greater freedom to answer as they want to. Of course, such responses may be harder to summarize, but they may well prove more meaningful.

The questionnaire in Figure 6.3 was developed by teachers in the ELI at

---

Figure 6.3   Student Evaluation Form for ELI 72 (continued)

---

10. How helpful were the SUPPLEMENTARY MATERIALS used in this course?

    Very useful   1   2   3   4   5   6   7   Not very useful

11. How effective were the SKIMMING exercises in improving your reading ability?

    Very useful   1   2   3   4   5   6   7   Not very useful

12. How effective were the SCANNING exercises in improving your reading ability?

    Very useful   1   2   3   4   5   6   7   Not very useful

13. How effective were the SPEED READING exercises in improving your reading ability?

    Very useful   1   2   3   4   5   6   7   Not very useful

14. How helpful was the GROUP DISCUSSION of reading materials and exercises?

    Very useful   1   2   3   4   5   6   7   Not very useful

15. Were written exercises used in this class? [ ] Yes [ ] No
    If yes, then answer Question 16.

16. How useful were the WRITTEN EXERCISES on reading materials in helping you understand the main ideas or the organization of reading passages?

    Very useful   1   2   3   4   5   6   7   Not very useful

17. How much effort did you put into this course? Did you put a lot of effort into it or did you just do enough work to pass the course? Why? (List *any* reasons—too many other courses, working at a job, laziness, disinterest, etc.)

18. Write a short paragraph to explain your overall evaluation of the strengths and weaknesses of the instructor.

UHM for the purposes of separately assessing the quality of the existing course objectives, as well as gathering information about student self-assessment and the teacher's performance. A consensus evolved while the questionnaire was being discussed: we wanted to be able to assess the quality of the objectives in a Likert format, but we also felt that open-ended questions would provide more information about the quality of teaching and would be more interesting to the teachers. The form that resulted was the work of a group of teachers who knew that they were being monitored by the administration: in the sense that the completed forms would be reviewed by the director and would then become part of the teacher's file.

Interviews

Teaching can also be monitored through formal or informal interviews. To do this, there would probably have to be some individual teacher or administrator, or a committee, that has responsibility for fielding student complaints and suggestions that arise in this manner. Regardless of who is in charge of such interviews, they are generally unplanned and relatively spontaneous. Either the student stops the person in the hall or comes to the office for discussion of some problem with a given teacher. Unfortunately, students rarely take the trouble to set up such a meeting if everything is going fine and the teacher is appreciated. In other words, the information so gathered tends to be negative in nature and should be viewed as just what it is: a complaint about a teacher's performance or about the course. Since such complaints may be due to unavoidable personality differences rather than to real problems with classroom practices, careful interpretation is called for—perhaps, ultimately in consultation with the teacher, or the teacher and the student. However, if a pattern of complaints begins to emerge against a particular teacher, then the person in charge may be forced to take action. Appropriate actions might include investigating the charge by observing the class, interviewing other students from the class, and talking to the teacher. Since such problems do arise, contingency plans for dealing with them should be built into the curriculum so that the program does not find itself reacting to them in an ad hoc manner and improvising a response.

Student Representative Meetings

Another source of information on the quality of the teaching in a program is student representative meetings. In this system, a student representative from each class is elected by fellow students to represent them in regular meetings held with program adminstrators. At these meetings, administrators can get a general sense of student satisfaction with the instruction going on in the institution. Information gathered face to face like this allows those in charge of the process to ask any questions that might help clarify what they are hearing and help them to interpret the general mood. Information gathered in this fashion is much more likely to be positive than information gathered through interviews. If teachers are not present during the meetings, the students may be more candid than they would be on a questionnaire—either in the meeting itself or afterward in the kind of personal discussions that often arise from such meetings. In any case, student representative meetings provide administrators with a direct line of communication with students and also help to release tension within a program. This type of meeting also enables administrators a chance to find out what is on the students' minds and to informally assess what their expectations are with regard to the teaching and learning processes. Moreover, the students may have good ideas about how to improve instruction, facilities, funding, or other aspects of the program. They are, after all, living, breathing, creative human beings who are only temporarily playing the role of students.

REVITALIZING TEACHERS

Teachers are also rumored to be living, breathing, creative human beings. Since they are human beings, they often have problems that may interfere with their work. Consequently, some provision should be made for helping teachers to feel upbeat and positive about what they are doing. I firmly believe that a teacher who is not improving and expanding professionally is probably sliding backward. For that reason alone, plans should be made within the curriculum for teacher self-improvement in various forms.

□ TEACHER BURNOUT

Because teachers are human beings, they do not have infinite reserves of stamina; in fact, they may sometimes get tired and run down. Such a state of affairs can be symptomatic of what Grasse (1982: p. 4) describes as *burnout,* which she defines as "the exhaustion that results from excessive drain on a person's energy and resources because of overwhelming problems. Victims of burnout feel frustrated and cynical about their work and gradually lose their effectiveness on the job." She identifies three main causes for burnout: stress, frustration, and low status. Of course, these may be common problems for all teachers, not just for language teachers (at least in the United States). A survey of the membership of the TESOL Organization revealed that many ESL/EFL teachers worried particulary about low status and lack of respect (see Brown 1992b & 1992c).

Another inescapable problem is that the average teacher is an *average* teacher, and as such may feel threatened when confronted by the excellent teaching of an outstanding colleague. I believe that any and all language teachers can improve in terms of their presentation of classroom techniques and facilitation of exercises, and so I believe that instructors should be supported beyond the walls of their classrooms so that they will become better teachers. Only through change and growth can their interest level in their profession be kept at a high level. Then stress, frustration, and feelings of low status will be minimized by the fact that the teachers will no longer feel helpless. If teachers are learning and growing, they are trying to do something about their problems. The importance of this aspect of the curriculum cannot be overestimated. In the same way that a curriculum that is not changing and growing is actually dying, a teacher who is not growing professionally is probably burning out.

□ GROWING AS A TEACHER

As a remedy for the burnout problem, Grasse (1982, p. 5) suggests that teachers must adopt positive attitudes toward their subject matter, their students, their colleagues, the program, and themselves. She suggests that developing a positive attitude toward the subject matter may be accomplished by varying what I call techniques and exercises in this book, as well as the materials and courses taught. She also recommends exchanging ideas with fellow teachers, setting realistic goals, and developing professionally. To promote a positive attitude toward students, she advises getting to know them individually as people, showing interest in them, and developing sensitivity for their personal needs and reasons for studying the language. Positive attitudes toward fellow teachers and the program can be fostered by being supportive of fellow teachers, keeping channels of communication open through positive suggestions, and showing pride in working with fellow teachers and in the program. Finally, to reinforce positive attitudes toward self, teachers should have confidence in their abilities, keep the magnitude of problems in perspective, and face problems realistically while seeking workable solutions. However, shaping attitudes, as useful as it may be, is only part of the solution (Grasse 1982, p. 5). In short, there must be means for teachers to continue growing if they are to continue to do a reasonable job of delivering instruction.

Helping teachers to expand their potential, better themselves, and grow professionally can be accomplished in a number of ways. A program can send a few of its teachers to attend a national or regional language teaching conference each year. Teachers can be encouraged to attend locally available workshops or workshops that are sponsored by the language program itself (in this case, the workshops are brought directly to the teachers). Conceivably, teachers can also be encouraged through promotion and salary incentives to further their education at nearby colleges or universities. A professional resources library can be set up for the teachers so that they have ready access to an array of relevant professional books, materials, journals, and newsletters in a comfortable setting conducive to private thought and congenial discussion with fellow teachers. Finally, teachers can be encouraged to develop professionally simply by getting them excited about the curriculum development processes that are described throughout this book. Involving teachers in systematic curriculum development may be the single best way to keep their professionalism vital and their interest in teaching alive.

EXAMPLE TEACHING COMPONENTS

□ GUANGZHOU ENGLISH LANGUAGE CENTER, ZHONGSHAN UNIVERSITY

During the first year of the GELC program, there was little problem with orienting and involving teachers in the curriculum because we were all new to the program and we were being paid, in part, to develop the curriculum as a group. In the second year, several new Chinese teachers and three new Americans joined the faculty. However, since we lived together and took most of our meals together, information beyond just the initial orientation to places and resources was easily shared on an ad hoc basis. A number of different reference documents did evolve, mostly in the form of the yearly report (discussed in Chapter Seven) sent to all responsible parties. These could serve as a source of information on the context of the program, the learners and their characteristics, the teachers and what was expected of them, the administrative processes and the curriculum processes, including student needs, objectives, tests, materials, teaching, and evaluation.

From its very outset, the program was designed to support the teachers. The fact that the Chinese director was a talented and respected woman, working with an American chief-of-party and two American senior scholars, provided an administrative framework that put several buffers in place. The Chinese director was in a position to protect the American teachers from the Chinese bureaucracy, to represent Chinese points of view, and to mediate between the Chinese and the American teachers. The American chief-of-party was in a position to represent the interests of the American teachers, as well as to help mediate between the American and the Chinese teachers. The two senior scholars were available to help in coordinating curriculum and research efforts. Hence the other two administrators were free to concentrate on their relatively political tasks.

Teachers were also supported in the sense that ample resources were provided: some hard currency resources, especially items not available in the PRC, were provided by the University of California, while other soft currency, locally available items were provided by the Chinese government through Zhongshan University. Since these resources included all our living and working necessities, the process was very complex. The most essential support provided for the teachers was curricular, which took the form of providing Chinese and American teachers help when they needed it through direct access to UCLA, through the efforts of the senior scholars, and through combining the energies of all teachers, as I reported in Chapter Five.

Perhaps the trickiest of the support problems faced in this program were the mechanisms involved in dealing with the politics of curriculum implementation and program management. The support problems were made even more complex than the normal problems I discussed in this chapter because the teaching staff was binational. Intercultural problems arose because the Americans were initially off-balance and sometimes somewhat unstable due to the effects of the culture shock of living in a very unfamiliar environment.

One drawback to the curriculum at GELC was the lack of any systematic plan for monitoring teachers' performance. Very few, if any, classroom observations were made and no efforts were made to do peer or self-observations. Perhaps this was due to insecurity on the part of the administration or just to the fact that no such observations were built into the curriculum from the start (including no teaching feedback mechanisms). Students' evaluations in the form of evaluation questionnaires, interviews, and student representative meetings were in place and were taken seriously, but they were usually focused on revising curriculum elements other than teaching.

Burnout was often a topic of discussion, for our workdays were long and work continued for many weeks without a break. However, week-long breaks were built into the schedule every 10 weeks so that we could vacation in Hong Kong or elsewhere in China to recharge our energy levels. In addition, the change and professional growth that were fostered within the program helped to revitalize most of the teachers.

Certainly, the program encouraged conference presentations. Any teacher whose paper was accepted by a conference received release time to attend that conference. We also held our own conference at Zhongda to which teachers from all over Guangdong province were invited. Workshops were a standard part of our weekly work schedule with one meeting per week for research issues and another for ESP (English for specific purposes) issues. Professional resources were also available to us, insofar as they could be reasonably expected. Our main meeting room had shelves that held a number of otherwise unavailable resources including pertinent books, journals, and other materials.

Since part of our job was to get excited about curriculum development and to get involved in the systematic development of curriculum, the professional interests of most of the teachers remained high, perhaps higher than at any other time in their careers, before or since. However, one teacher chose to resist getting involved in the curriculum, so this teacher's one-year stay at Zhongda must have been boring and seemingly interminable.

□ ENGLISH LANGUAGE INSTITUTE, UNIVERSITY OF HAWAII AT MANOA

In the ELI, the processes of orienting and involving teachers in the curriculum are far more formal. There is a high turnover in the teaching staff almost every year because the bulk of the instructors are graduate assistants and lecturers hired on a semester-by-semester basis, primarily from among the graduate stu-

Table 6.2 Table of Contents for *Teacher's Handbook for Graduate Assistants and Lecturers* (Brown et al. 1989)

dents in ESL doing M.A. or Ph.D. degrees. The orientation consists of a three-hour meeting during which the new teachers are oriented toward the program (and old teachers reoriented), mostly on topics that are also covered in a reference document that we call the *Teacher's Handbook* (Brown et al. 1989). The topics covered in both the meeting and the reference document are displayed in the table of contents given in Table 6.2. These topics are discussed with all teachers, veteran and novice alike, present, so that the veteran teachers can contribute ideas and hints. The testing program is heavily stressed because the teachers are almost immediately involved in all aspects of the testing program and need orientation concerning all the steps in the ELIPT battery for place-ment, as well as the procedures necessary for administering the course criterion-referenced tests.

At the end of the formal meeting, textbooks and other supplementary and reference materials are checked out to the teachers. The group is then divided up by skill areas for further meetings with the lead teachers for each skill. The lead teachers take responsibility for showing the teachers the ropes in the partic-ular courses to which they have been assigned. During this time, course objec-tives are discussed, sample first-day handouts are distributed, the textbooks are reviewed (as are the supplementary texts and reference materials) and the mate-rials resource file is shown to the newcomers. These sessions go on until the teachers are comfortable with what they need to know. The lead teacher and the faculty resource person continue to serve as people to whom teachers can turn throughout the semester. In addition, during these skill-area orientations, the new teachers have an opportunity to get to know the more experienced teachers who will be teaching in the same skill area.

Many aspects of the jobs of the director and assistant director of the ELI are designed to protect the teachers from outside political and bureaucratic influ-ences, as well as to provide ever-expanding (or at least not diminishing) resources and information. Yet, the most important support that teachers get may well come from the lead teachers, who conduct meetings and are in charge of drawing the teachers into all the curriculum development activities generated by the Curriculum Committee. This Curriculum Committee consists of the five lead teachers, five resource faculty, the assistant director, and the director as Fig-ure 6.4 demonstrates. The Curriculum Committee is charged with the task of overseeing the general thrust of curriculum development. The lead teachers hold weekly meetings with the teachers to get their ideas and input, as well as to get them working on projects that feed into the overall plan. These teachers' meetings also serve as forums in which to periodically review and revise various aspects of the curriculum, including objectives, tests, materials, teacher observa-tion strategies, and so forth. Thus the collective energies of the teachers are mar-shalled to improve the curriculum in each course they teach, but those energies are also marshalled in such a way that the teachers have some input into the gen-eral curriculum processes. From time to time, meetings of all ELI staff members are held during which policy and curriculum matters can be discussed more directly, but these meetings are kept to a minimum because they tend to be less focused and less productive.

Each teacher's performance is monitored on a regular basis in a number of ways. One constant is the administrator observation, which occurs at least once per teacher during each semester of the academic year. This is done using the form shown in Figure 6.1 and the descriptors shown in Table 6.1. At least one other form of classroom observation takes place during each academic semester. Some semesters, peer observations are used; in alternate semesters, self-observa-tion procedures (through use of video cameras) are employed. This pattern has

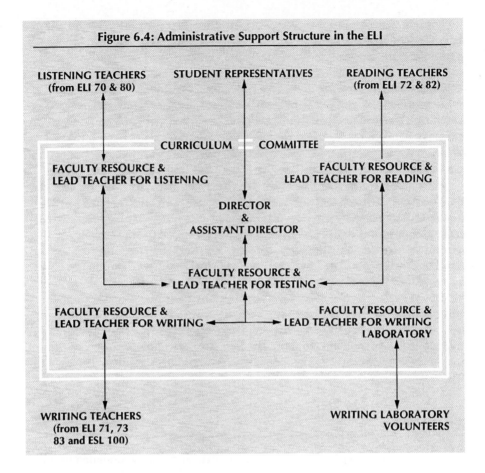

Figure 6.4: Administrative Support Structure in the ELI

evolved because we feel that teachers benefit from experiencing a variety of observation techniques over the course of an academic year.

Student evaluations are also an important source of information for our program. Evaluation forms like the one shown in Figure 6.3 have been developed for each course; they cover issues that are specific to that one course and its present state of development in the program. At the present time, the teachers in all the courses have opted for open-ended assessment of their teaching and more structured responses about the curriculum involved in the course. These forms are distributed during the last week of classes and are delivered directly to the secretaries, who give them to the director of the ELI for safekeeping until grades have been turned in. At that time, the teachers may come to the director to read their evaluation forms and discuss them. These forms are then reviewed by the director and added to the teacher's departmental employment file.

212 □ THE ELEMENTS OF LANGUAGE CURRICULUM

Student representative meetings are another source of information about the quality of ELI instruction. In addition to serving as a valuable source of communication between lead teachers, the director, and the students, these meetings enable students to convey subtle messages about their teachers that are sometimes worth following up with more concrete methods of investigation. If severe problems in teacher performance surface, the problems are always discussed with the teacher involved. In addition, the teachers have a set of clear-cut grievance procedures they can follow if they feel they have been mistreated. While, to my knowledge, no teacher has ever used these procedures, it is still comforting that they are in place to protect the teachers.

Revitalizing teachers is also a high priority in the ELI. After all, these teachers, who work 20 hours per week, are also graduate students taking a full load of courses. Moreover, they also have personal lives that make still other demands on them. Burnout is a very real issue, one circumscribed to some degree by the importance placed on professional growth. Teachers are encouraged to relate projects for their graduate courses to the ELI curriculum development, which in turn is directly related to their teaching; they are encouraged to experiment and do research; they are encouraged to present papers and workshops at conferences (indeed, their expenses are partially covered); they are all furthering their educations as language teachers; and very often, they get quite excited and involved in the curriculum. In short, the ELI is a perfect place for professional development, particularly for a student who is attending a graduate program in language teaching.

SUMMARY

This chapter explored a variety of ways that curriculum can be designed to promote sound teaching practices within a program by properly orienting the teachers, giving them support as needed, monitoring the quality of instruction, and institutionalizing strategies for revitalizing teachers.

It was argued that the purpose of orientation is to provide initial information to the teachers, especially when they are new to the program, and that orientation can take the form of a series of meetings or of a teachers' guide (and other reference documents), with the combination of the two being most effective. In addition, examples were given of questions that teachers might want answered. These were presented in five categories: questions about the context of the program, about learners, about teachers, about administrative processes, and about instruction itself.

A number of strategies were also suggested for supporting teachers. One way that this can be accomplished is by helping teachers to understand their place and the place of their students in the curriculum. Since one goal of the teaching component is to help the teachers teach, a number of alternative forms of administrative and curricular support were also suggested. Administrative support may prove most valuable if it helps to buffer teachers from negative influences of various types and ensures that the teachers have all the resources they need in order to do their jobs. Curricular support may be most useful to teachers if it provides them with help in the form of information, tests, materials, ideas, and feedback when they need it and helps them to work together with colleagues so that they can all benefit from their combined energies. Finally, some of the issues involved in dealing with politics were discussed, with particular reference to curriculum implementation and program management.

The monitoring of teachers can also be seen as a means for supporting them—if it is handled wisely. Monitoring through observations was discussed in terms of administrator, peer, and self-observations, and the importance of feedback was stressed. Student evaluations were also covered, including evaluation forms, interviews, and student representative meetings as effective ways of finding out the students' views of teacher effectiveness.

Since teacher burnout can become a very real problem in language programs, revitalization strategies were considered. The importance of change and growth was stressed. Hence, the discussion was organized around three facets of becoming a better teacher: changing various sets of teachers' attitudes (toward work, colleagues, and so forth), growing as a teacher (through attending conferences, workshops, and so forth), and teachers getting involved in systematic curriculum development.

The central point of this chapter was that all too often teachers are left to fend for themselves. Entirely on their own, they have to determine the needs of their students, plan their objectives, design tests and materials, teach, and (in their spare time) evaluate the effectiveness of what they are doing. These tasks are impossible for any human being to accomplish well. Hence, it was argued that teaching should draw on all the other curriculum elements and form an important component of the curriculum in its own right, one that will help teachers to escape the isolation that may be a root cause of burnout.

■ ■ ■ CHECKLIST

The following checklist is provided to help you remember to include in your curriculum those elements of the teaching component that you feel are important.

- □ Orientation
  - □ Format
    - □ Orientation meeting
    - □ Orientation document(s)
  - □ Types of information
    - □ Context of the program

- □ Learners
- □ Teachers
- □ Administrative processes
- □ Instruction
- □ Supporting teachers
  - □ The teacher's and the student's places in the curriculum
  - □ Helping teachers to teach
  - □ Providing a framework of support
    - □ Administrative support
      - □ Providing buffers
      - □ Providing resources
    - □ Curricular support
      - □ Providing help when needed
      - □ Using the combined energies of all teachers
  - □ Dealing with politics
    - □ Curriculum implementation
    - □ Program management

- □ Monitoring teachers
  - □ Consider what good teaching is
  - □ Observations
    - □ Administrator
    - □ Peer
    - □ Self (video)
    - □ Feedback
  - □ Students' evaluations
    - □ Evaluation forms
    - □ Interviews
    - □ Student representative meetings

- □ Revitalizing teachers
  - □ Burnout
    - □ The average teacher is average
    - □ Any teacher can do better
    - □ The importance of change and growth

□ Facets of becoming a better teacher
  □ Attitudes
  □ Growing as a teacher
    □ Conferences
    □ Workshops
    □ Continuing education
    □ Professional resources

□ Get teachers excited about curriculum development

■ ■ ■ TERMS

administrator observations
classroom observation
efficient instruction
instructional efficiency
orientation
program efficiency
self-observation
efficient instruction

burnout
consistent instruction
feedback
Likert scale
peer observations
relevant instruction
teaching

■ ■ ■ REVIEW QUESTIONS

1. What are the purposes of orienting new teachers? How are orientation meetings and orientation documents different in what they have to offer the new teacher?

2. What five types of initial information are important to include in either an orientation meeting or a teacher's guide?

3. What types of other reference documents might also usefully be supplied to new teachers?

4. What duties do teachers commonly see as their responsibility? What roles do students commonly assign themselves? How might differences occur in these two viewpoints during the teaching and learning processes? How might these differences be resolved?

5. What are two major ways that administrators can support teachers? What are two major ways that curricular support can be provided for teachers?

6. Dealing with politics can often be difficult. Problems most often arise with reference to curriculum implementation or program management. What strategies can be used to effectively contain political issues and channel those energies in constructive directions?

7. How do classroom observations and student evaluations differ in terms of the type of information obtained? What are three forms that observations can take? How do the three differ in terms of the types of feedback that will typically result? Why is feedback so important?

8. What are three forms that student evaluation can take? How can constructive feedback on students' views be given to teachers?

9. What is teacher burnout? Why is change and growth so important to avoiding burnout?

10. What are some of the curriculum strategies that are suggested for avoiding teacher burnout and revitalizing the teachers?

■ ■ ■ APPLICATIONS

A1. Consider both of the descriptions provided in this chapter for the GELC program and the ELI at UHM (in the "Example Teaching Components" section above). Briefly describe the differences and similarities in the teacher orientation strategies that the two programs used.

A2. Next, list ways that the two programs supported their teachers, and decide if you think that these strategies were adequate. What other strategies would you have used? What strategies were used to avoid teacher burnout? Were they adequate?

A3. Monitoring teachers is often a touchy issue. In the ELI, what strategies were used to perform observations and student evaluations? How were they shaped to be most positive?

B1. Consider some language program that you are now involved in or know about. Take out a piece of paper and jot down ways that you see the teachers being oriented, supported, monitored, and revitalized. Are these tactics adequate?

B2. What changes would you make in the ways that teachers are oriented, supported, monitored, and revitalized? Be sure to focus on ideas that would improve the lot of the teachers in the program and help them to become more effective teachers.

Chapter 7

Program Evaluation

INTRODUCTION

To this point, the primary information gathering and organizational elements of the curriculum have been included in the needs analysis and testing components as represented by the goals and objectives. The insights and information gained from these curriculum activities can be further analyzed and synthesized into what I have labeled the materials and teaching components of the systematic curriculum model that serves as the basis of this book. From the way I present the model, readers might think that needs analysis, goals and objectives, testing, materials, and teaching are five sequential steps that should be instituted chronologically. However, if the reader looks back at my model (shown in Figure 1.2), he or she will see that all the elements are interconnected by bidirectional arrows to each other and to a never–ending process called evaluation. The arrows and the links to evaluation are meant to imply three things.

First, in an ideal situation, curriculum development *would* start with a thorough needs analysis and progress through the steps that I have enumerated. However, such an ideal situation is actually very rare. In the typical, real-world situation, the program is already ongoing, perhaps even fairly well entrenched, when the curriculum process is initiated. Hence, for political or other reasons, the curriculum planners may start the process with some element other than needs analysis. In fact, it is often the case that needs analysis, formulation of goals and objectives, articulation of tests, and delivery of instruction are all going on at the same time.

Second, the process of curriculum development is never finished (unless of course a program is canceled). Thus provisions must always be made for revision of all the curriculum elements with a view to improving them. Indeed, the bi-directionality of the arrows within the model signifies that as focus is placed on any particular element of the curriculum the work on that component may reveal a need for revisions in the preceding (or succeeding) elements.

Third, the ongoing program evaluation on the right side of the model is the glue that connects and holds all the elements together. In the absence of evaluation, the elements lack cohesion; if left in isolation, any one element may become pointless. In short, the heart of the systematic approach to language curriculum design is evaluation: the part of the model that includes, connects, and gives meaning to all the other elements.

Richards et al. (1985, p. 98) define evaluation as "the systematic gathering of information for purposes of making decisions." At first glance, this seems to be a serviceable definition, but reflection reveals that it is too broad and could equally well be used to define other curriculum components such as needs analysis and testing, both of which are ways of systematically collecting information for "purposes of making decisions." In truth, needs analysis and testing information might well be included in an evaluation, but this fact does not strengthen the definition given above.

Another definition was proposed by Popham (1975, p. 8), who noted that "systematic educational evaluation consists of a formal assessment of the worth of educational phenomena." If the Richards et al. definition was too broad, Popham's is too restrictive. Certainly, there should be an element within a program evaluation that focuses on "formal assessment," but there is also room for a number of other more informal activities, as I will explain below. Moreover, many forms of evaluation focus in one way or another on "the worth of educational phenomena." However, there are also forms that focus on improving the curriculum, and they are perhaps the most constructive and useful types. In short, Popham's definition does not seem adequate for my purposes in this book.

A less restrictive alternative offered by Worthen and Sanders (1973, p. 19) might help: "Evaluation is the determination of the worth of a thing. It includes obtaining information for use in judging the worth of a program, product, procedure, or object, or the potential utility of alternative approaches designed to attain specified objectives." This definition is less restrictive in the sense that it includes the notion of "the worth of a program," but it also provides for judging "the potential utility of alternative approaches." Unfortunately, the goal of this view of evaluation is to "attain specified objectives." Again, this may be unnecessarily limiting—implying a goal–oriented approach to the evaluation process, while ignoring the potential of evaluation to affect curriculum improvement.

Clearly, then, a new definition is needed, at least for my purposes in this book. *Evaluation* will be defined here in the same way that it was in Brown (1989a, p. 223) as "the systematic collection and analysis of all relevant information necessary to promote the improvement of a curriculum and assess its effectiveness within the context of the particular institutions involved." This definition requires that information be gathered and analyzed in a systematic manner and that only relevant information should be included, that is, information must necessarily be filtered so that irrelevant information can be ignored. Notice that there are two purposes for the information: the promotion of improvement and the assessment of effectiveness ("worth" in the Popham or Worthen and Sanders definitions). As with so many of the concepts I have discussed, this definition also stresses that evaluation must essentially be site-specific with a clear focus on the particular curriculum that is being examined. In other words, any evaluation is inescapably connected to the institution(s) being evaluated, whether that be one school, all the schools in a school district, or the school system of an entire nation. Once the institution of focus have been defined, the evaluation processes will naturally center on that institution.

"Evaluation" is a term that is used in a number of different ways. In this book, I have taken care to use it differently from the terms "testing" and "measurement." I use the term *testing* only to refer to procedures that are based on tests, whether they be criterion-referenced or norm-referenced in nature (and whether they be for proficiency, placement, diagnosis, or achievement decisions). I employ *measurement* more broadly to include testing, but also other types of measurements that result in quantitative data such as attendance records, questionnaires, teacher ratings of students (or student ratings of teachers), and so forth. The still broader term *evaluation* includes all kinds of testing and measurements, as well as other types of information, some of which may be more qualitative in nature. Such qualitative data–gathering procedures as interviews, case studies, classroom observations, meetings, diaries, or even conversations over coffee, can serve useful purposes—as useful, in fact, as the quantitative information gathered using various measurements. (I will address the distinction between qualitative and quantitative methods in greater detail later in this chapter.)

Now that I have provided the reader with a clear definition of evaluation, as well as a description of how evaluation differs from, but includes, testing and measurement, I will devote the remainder of the chapter to covering three major topics: different approaches that have been developed for the task of program evaluation, the various dimensions that must be considered in making evaluation decisions, and the steps involved in actually performing a curriculum evaluation. The chapter will end as usual with discussion of some of the program evaluation aspects of the example GELC and the ELI programs.

APPROACHES TO PROGRAM EVALUATION

Historically, a number of approaches have been suggested in the educational literature for performing program evaluation. As Brown (1989a) points out, these can all be placed into one of four categories: goal-attainment approaches, static-characteristic approaches, process-oriented approaches, and decision-facilitation approaches. I will discuss each of these approaches briefly, and then make suggestions about how they might best be applied for the purposes of evaluating language curriculum.

□ PRODUCT–ORIENTED APPROACHES

Product–oriented approaches are just what they sound like. When these approaches are used, the focus of the evaluation is on the goals and instructional objectives with the purpose of determining whether they have been achieved. The primary advocates of this approach were scholars like Tyler, Hammond, and Metfessel and Michael.

Tyler (1942) felt that programs should be built on explicitly defined goals, specified in terms of the society, the students, and the subject matter, as well as on measurable behavioral objectives. From his perspective, the purpose of a program evaluation is to determine whether the objectives have been achieved, and whether the goals have been met. To this end, the objectives should be measured at the end of the program with one of two possible outcomes. If the objectives have not been achieved, there has been a failure to attain the goals of the program. If the objectives have been achieved, the program has been successful in meeting its goals. While this seems obvious today, it was not always so. In all fairness, I must point out that Tyler's thinking was considerably more complex than my summary would indicate. For example, the development of goals and objectives was to be based on a number of sources including, but not restricted to, the students, the subject matter, instructional materials, the society at large, philosophy of eduction, learning philosophy, and more (Tyler 1951).

The approach that Hammond (cited in Worthen & Sanders 1973, p. 168) advocated was also product–oriented. His model included five steps to be followed in performing a curriculum evaluation:

1. Identifying precisely what is to be evaluated
2. Defining the descriptive variables
3. Stating objectives in behavioral terms
4. Assessing the behavior described in the objectives
5. Analyzing the results and determining the effectiveness of the program.

Metfessel and Michael (1967) share the product–oriented approach, but they provide more detailed steps, including eight major evaluation phases:

1. Direct and indirect involvement of the total school community
2. Formation of a cohesive model of broad goals and specific objectives
3. Translation of specific objectives into communicable form
4. Instrumentation necessary for furnishing measures allowing inferences about program effectiveness
5. Periodic observations of behaviors
6. Analysis of data given by status and change measures
7. Interpretation of the data relative to specific objectives and broad goals
8. Recommendations culminating in further implementation, modifications, and in revisions of broad goals and specific objectives.

The product that was to result from the evaluation approaches advocated by Tyler, Hammond, and Metfessel and Michael was a set of student behaviors that met the goals and instructional objectives of the curriculum. The success of a program could then be measured in terms of the degree to which those objectives were achieved. This approach may seem cold, clinical, and somewhat behaviorist from today's perspective, but there is some merit to the idea of evaluating a program to determine the degree to which it is accomplishing what it set out to accomplish in the first place, as specified in its goals and objectives. Remember that goals and objectives have been defined rather broadly in this book (see Chapter Three).

□ STATIC-CHARACTERISTIC APPROACHES

One alternative to the product-oriented approaches I just described are the *static-characteristic approaches*. Like product-oriented approaches, static-characteristic evaluation is also performed to determine the effectiveness of a particular program. This type of evaluation is conducted by outside experts who inspect a program by examining various accounting and academic records, as well as such static characteristics as the number of library books, the number and types of degrees held by the faculty, the student-to-teacher ratio, the number and seating capacity of classrooms, the parking facilities, and so forth. Imagine the disruption that would occur as a program organized its records and readied its facilities in anticipation of such inspections. The experts would then formulate a report based on their observations. Such static-characteristic evaluations are used even today for institutional accreditation.

Accreditation is a process whereby an association of institutions sets up criteria and evaluation procedures for the purposes of deciding whether individual institutions should be certified (accredited) as members in good standing of that association. Since various elements of prestige, budget, course transferability, and so forth, may be attached to these accreditation procedures, they are often taken very seriously.

Given the importance of such evaluations, it is a shame that they have often been based solely on the static-characteristic approach. As Popham (1975, p. 25) points out,

> A major reason for the diminishing interest in accreditation conceptions of evaluation is the recognition of their almost total reliance on intrinsic rather than extrinsic factors. Although there is some intuitive support for the proposition that these process factors are associated with the final outcomes of an instructional sequence, the scarcity of empirical evidence to confirm the relationship has created growing dissatisfaction with the accreditation approach among educators.

Such dissatisfaction led to changes in evaluation procedures, at least in some quarters.

☐ PROCESS-ORIENTED APPROACHES

One significant shift was to *process-oriented approaches*. This shift was partially due to the realization that meeting program goals and objectives, while important, was not very helpful in facilitating curriculum revision, change, and improvement. Scriven and Stake were two of the most important advocates of process-oriented approaches.

Scriven's (1967) model contributed a number of principles that have promoted a process–oriented approach to program evaluation. For example, Scriven was the first to distinguish between formative and summative evaluation (discussed below). He also stressed the importance not only of evaluating the degree of attainment of program goals but also questioning the very worth of those goals in the first place. The model he advocated was called *goal–free evaluation,* that is, evaluation in which limits are not set on studying the expected effects of the program vis-à-vis the goals. Instead, he felt that evaluators must remain open to other possibilities, perhaps unexpected outcomes, which, once recognized, could be studied further. Scriven's most important influence on my views has to do with the fact that he deemphasized a focus on products in favor of process–oriented evaluation (that is, formative and goal-free).

Stake's (1967) approach to process evaluation was called the *countenance model.* It consisted of the following basic elements:

1. Begin with a rationale
2. Fix on descriptive operations (intents and observations)
3. End with judgmental operations (standards and judgments) at three different levels: antecedents (prior conditions), transactions (interactions between participants), and outcomes (as in traditional goals but also broader in the sense of transfer of learning to real life).

For me, Stake's contributions are most meaningful because they acknowledge that evaluators engage in descriptive as well as judgmental activities. Stake argued that evaluators must keep the differences between these two types of activities in mind. To accomplish this, he suggested a transaction component to evaluation, one that should be dynamic as opposed to static (in the sense that outcomes are static). This dynamism justifies including his ideas in the discussion of process-oriented approaches.

☐ DECISION-FACILITATION APPROACHES

The last kind of program evaluation discussed here is one that holds that the most important function of evaluation is to help in making decisions. Hence, such evaluation procedures are called *decision-facilitation* approaches. In these approaches, evaluators attempt to avoid making judgments. Instead, they favor gathering information that will help the administrators and faculty in the program make their own judgments and decisions. Examples of this approach are the CIPP, CSE, and Discrepancy models of evaluation.

CIPP, described in Stufflebeam et al. (1971), is an acronym for Context (rationale for objectives), Input (utilization of resources for achieving objectives), Process (periodic feedback to decision makers), and Product (measurement and interpretation of attainments during and at the end of a program). Stufflebeam (1974) lists four key elements that should be remembered in performing program evaluation:

1. Evaluation is performed in the service of *decision making,* hence it should provide information that is useful to decision makers.
2. Evaluation is a cyclic, continuing *process* and therefore must be implemented through a systematic program.
3. The evaluation process includes the three main steps of delineating, obtaining, and providing. These steps provide the basis for a methodology of evaluation.
4. The delineating and providing steps in the evaluation process are *interface* activities requiring collaboration.

The CSE model is named after the acronym for the Center for the Study of Evaluation at UCLA. Similar to the CIPP model, this is an approach designed to help in decision making. Alkin (1969) suggests that evaluations should provide information for five different categories of decisions:

1. Systems assessment (the state of the overall system)
2. Program planning (a priora selection of particular strategies, materials, and so forth)
3. Program implementation (appropriateness of program implementation relative to intentions and audience)
4. Program improvement (changes that might improve the program and help deal with unexpected outcomes)
5. Program certification (the overall value of the program).

The *discrepancy model* as advocated by Provus (1971) was also designed to help with decision making. Provus defined evaluation as follows:

> Program evaluation is the process of (1) defining program standards; (2) determining whether a discrepancy exists between some aspect of program performance and the standards governing that aspect of the program; and (3) using discrepancy information either to change performance or to change program standards.

This definition initially appears to represent a regression to the product-oriented approaches discussed earlier. However, examination of the following five stages suggested by Provus will show that this is actually a process-oriented approach:

1. Program description stage
2. Program installation stage
3. Treatment adjustment stage (process)
4. Goal achievement analysis stage
5. Cost-benefit analysis.

Note that the "treatment adjustment" stage is clearly designed in Provus's work to be a stage in the evaluation during which the processes of revision and improvement take place. In addition, Provus advocated using these five stages to promote sound decision making:

> Successive reappraisals of program operations and of the program standards from which program operations are derived are generally consequences of the decisions made by program staff on the basis of discrepancy information reported in Stages II, III and IV. If a decision is made to reformulate standards rather than to revise program performance, there are immediate implications for the negotiation of all subsequent evaluation stages.

Provus's model shows the degree to which the evolution of evaluation approaches has been a healthy and progressive one. While the development of each approach was a reaction to the shortcomings of other approaches, the strengths of those other approaches were incorporated in their descendants. For example, product-oriented and static-characteristic approaches were improved by the addition of process considerations, and in turn, these three approaches were refined by adding decision-facilitation dimensions. Language program evaluators should learn from the 40 or more years of development that has already occurred in education circles. Certainly, the ideas discussed above should not be dismissed out of hand, but rather should be considered in developing a model for evaluating any particular program—perhaps a model that draws on several or all of the approaches described above.

THREE DIMENSIONS THAT SHAPE POINT OF VIEW ON EVALUATION

In thinking about the similarities and differences among existing approaches to evaluation, the reader should notice that they differ primarily in the points of view taken by the evaluator(s) while studying a program. Among the differences in perspectives, there are certain patterns that emerge. These patterns are only important insofar as they help in deciding on the points of view that are important to include when specially tailoring a set of evaluation procedures for a particular program. The patterns involve at least three dimensions (also discussed in Brown 1989a): formative versus summative, process versus product, and quantitative versus qualitative. I have labeled these seeming dichotomies *dimensions* because there is no clear dichotomy in any of the pairs. In each case, they seem to be points at the ends of a scale along which variation can occur. These dimensions differ from one another in that the first is related to the purposes for gathering the information, the second is associated with the types of information being gathered, and the third is connected with the sorts of data and analyses that will result.

□ PURPOSE OF THE INFORMATION

Typically, *formative evaluation* takes place during the ongoing curriculum development processes. The aim of this type of evaluation is to collect and analyze information that will help in improving the curriculum. The types of decisions that result from formative evaluation are usually numerous and relatively small in scale because such decisions are meant to result in modifications to and fine tuning of an existing curriculum. Alternatively, *summative evaluation* is usually characterized as occurring at the end of a program. The purpose for gathering information in a summative evaluation is to determine the degree to which the program was successful, efficient, and effective. The decisions that result from summative evaluations tend to cause sweeping changes and are fairly large in scale. Examples of such decisions might include the cancellation or continued funding of a program, or moving a program to a much more suitable site.

Although formative and summative evaluation fall along a single dimension, I have deliberately offered definitions that reflect the extreme positions that would be taken in any actual evaluation situation. However, the reader should realize that even in these extreme versions, formative and summative evaluations simply represent two differing purposes for collecting and analyzing the same types of information.

It could be argued that all evaluation should rightfully be called "formative" because it results in information that can be used to revise and improve the objectives, testing, materials, teaching, and indeed the view of what the students need to learn. Any other use of this extensive investment of resources and energy makes little sense unless it also directly benefits the curriculum, and therefore the administrators, the teachers, and the students.

The definition of summative evaluation given above ignores one important reality: most language programs are continuing institutions that do not conveniently come to an end so that a summative evaluation can be performed. Nevertheless, it may prove healthy for the administrators and faculty in a program to occasionally pause and pose the types of questions that are typically addressed in a summative evaluation.

If such an evaluation is performed only when required by outside authorities, it will probably be conducted in a crisis atmosphere. This would be the case, for example, if outside authorities required a program to demonstrate its worth to the funding agency if it wanted to continue to operate. Such crisis-induced evaluation can be quite harmful to clear thinking and to generating the kind of constructive results that help to improve a curriculum.

More benefit for all involved parties would result if both the formative and summative views of evaluation were used together in some combination. Formative evaluation can be built into the curriculum as it is in the model I present in this book. When planners make such evaluation a regular part of the curriculum, they are in the enviable position of constantly being able to gather and analyze information to be used in changing, developing, and upgrading their program. However, from time to time, a summative evaluation may prove useful if it can be viewed as a pause during which focus will be brought to bear on assessing the success, efficiency, and effectiveness of the program—at least to that point in time. Such summative evaluation might take the formal shape of a yearly report to a higher administrative authority, or it might take the relatively informal shape of an internally motivated analysis and revision deadline set by the members of the program.

Either way, a summative evaluation can produce beneficial results. First, a summative evaluation allows for a pause in which to consider some of the larger, more general issues like the success or failure of the program. All too often the focus of evaluation is concentrated on the smaller day-to-day issues directly related to implementing instruction.

Second, a summative evaluation can be important (and sometimes heartening) because it provides an opportunity to stand back and consider what has been achieved in the longer view. Teachers sometimes lose sight of what is being accomplished because they are so involved in the smaller details of teaching and surviving. For instance, imagine the satisfaction that teachers could derive from stopping to examine the program if one result was recognition that the students' language skills have improved significantly. One realization that can result from such findings is that something more than merely coping is being accomplished.

Third, and politically most important, regular formative evaluation procedures and self-induced summative evaluations can put a program and its staff in a strong position for responding to any crises that might be brought on by evaluation from outside the program. If formative and summative evaluation are built into the curriculum and conducted on a regular basis, then up-to-date information will always be readily available and mechanisms will be in place for marshalling and assessing that information. As a result, program staff can meet outside evaluation requirements without feeling intense pressure, which means that the evaluation can be conducted with considerably more thought and care. In short, a program that conducts regular formative evaluations and periodic self-induced summative evaluations will be in a much better position to defend itself against pressures from the outside world.

In other words, both formative and summative evaluation procedures seem to be much more useful if they are built into the curriculum development process from the beginning. The balance that a curriculum will strike between formative and summative approaches will naturally depend on the conditions in the particular program.

□   TYPES OF INFORMATION

The next dimension of interest includes process evaluation at the one end and product evaluation at the other. While the relationship between formative and summative evaluation depends on variations in the purposes for gathering information, the difference between process and product evaluation depends on variations in the types of information that will be used. I define *process evaluation* as any evaluation that focuses on the workings of a program (processes). I define *product evaluation* as that sort of evaluation in which the focus is on whether the goals (products) of the program are being achieved.

This distinction between process and product might at first seem to be directly related to the formative-summative dimension discussed above. In reality, summative evaluations tend to center on products in the form of goal achievement. After all, the purpose of gathering the information is to assess whether the goals of the program have been accomplished. At the same time, formative evaluations tend to examine processes because the purpose for the information is to examine the degree to which the workings of the program are effective. In planning evaluation procedures for a program, consider including both product and process types of information. To that end, both quantitative and qualitative means for gathering and analyzing evaluation information may prove useful.

□   TYPES OF DATA AND ANALYSES

The last dimension I wish to discuss includes quantitative types of data and analysis at one end and qualitative types of data and analysis at the other end. *Quantitative data* are countable bits of information which are usually gathered using measures that produce results in the form of numbers. Examples of such measures include tests, quizzes, grades, student rankings within their class, the number of students in each class, the number of males and females in a program, and so forth.

In contrast, *qualitative data* consist of more holistic information based on observations that may not readily lend themselves to conversion into quantities or numbers. Examples of these types of observations might include student or teacher journal entries, minutes from faculty meetings, classroom observations, or even recollections of key conversations.

□   INTERACTIONS AMONG DIMENSIONS

The discussion in the preceding three sections was intended to help planners in choosing among the available options and tailoring a set of evaluation procedures for a particular program. These decisions will probably entail considering options somewhere between the extremes of the dimensions involved. Once again, note that the stance taken with regard to one dimension will interact with and affect all the other choices program planners make. In other words, like the dimensions discussed in Chapter Two, the point of view that is taken on any one of these dimensions will probably affect the views that are adopted for the other dimensions because they tend to interact. The relationships shown in Figure 7.1 may help planners to decide on a tentative position to be taken while considering all three dimensions simultaneously. For instance, an evaluator who takes a purely quantitative approach to examining the goal achievement (product) in a summative evaluation would best be represented by a single point in the lower right corner at the front of Figure 7.1. Naturally, myriad other positions can be taken with regard to the interaction of these three dimensions.

DOING PROGRAM EVALUATION

The evaluation approaches and dimensions I have discussed so far can help evaluators decide at the outset which combinations of approaches and dimensions will work best in a given situation. However, all these decisions must eventually lead to the actual gathering of evaluation data. I believe that quantitative and qualitative information should be gathered periodically on each of the curriculum components so that each can be revised and improved, but also so that the degree of overall success of the entire program can be assessed.

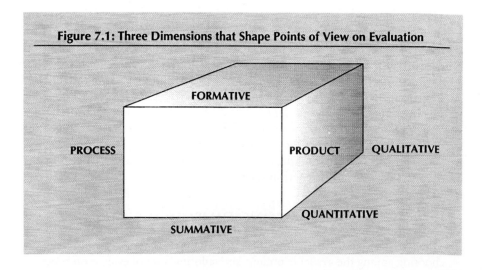

Figure 7.1: Three Dimensions that Shape Points of View on Evaluation

FORMATIVE

PROCESS   PRODUCT   QUALITATIVE

QUANTITATIVE

SUMMATIVE

INSTRUMENTS AND PROCEDURES	QUANTITATIVE	QUALITATIVE
Table 7.1 Procedures Can Be Quantitative, Qualitative or Both (adapted from Tables 2.2 and 2.3)		
Existing Information		
Records analysis	X	X
Systems	X	X
Literature review		X
Letter writing		X
Tests		
Proficiency	X	
Placement	X	
Diagnostic	X	
Achievement	X	
Observations		
Case studies		X
Diary studies		X
Behavior observation		X
Interactional analyses		X
Inventories	X	
Interviews		
Individual	X	X
Group	X	X
Meetings		
Delphi technique		X
Advisory		X
Interest group		X
Review		X
Questionnaires		
Biodata survey	X	
Opinion survey	X	X
Self-ratings	X	
Judgmental ratings	X	
Q sort	X	

□ GATHERING EVALUATION DATA

Once again, the scope of this book prohibits going into details about all of the different types of data that might be of interest in each and every language program evaluation. However, I can give examples that will provide the reader with ideas about how to get the evaluation process started.

Quantitative Evaluation Studies

As I mentioned above, *quantitative data* are those bits of information that are countable and are gathered using measures that produce results in the form of numbers. Table 7.1 recapitulates the listing of instruments and procedures used in needs analysis (as defined and discussed in Chapter Two). For each of these procedures, the table indicates with an "X" in the appropriate column whether the procedure is used primarily to gather quantitative or qualitative information, or both. Notice that nine of the procedures are labeled as being used mostly for quantitative information gathering (proficiency tests, placement tests, diagnostic tests, and achievement tests, inventories, biodata surveys, self-ratings, judgmental ratings, and Q-sorts). In other words, the procedures just listed are predominantly used to collect quantitative data, though in some cases they may be modified to obtain qualitative data.

The importance of using quantitative data is not so much in the collection of those data, but rather in the analysis of the data, which should be carried out in such a way that patterns emerge. With luck these patterns will help to make sense of the results and assess the quality of the program.

Such analyses are most often accomplished using descriptive and/or inferential statistics. These analyses are well beyond the scope of this book; indeed, they form the basis for many books. (For much more on descriptive and inferential statistics in the language teaching field, see Brown 1988; Butler 1985; Hatch & Farhady 1982; Hatch & Lazaraton 1991; Seliger & Shohamy 1989; Woods, Fletcher, & Hughes 1986. For information on statistics in the general social sciences, see Guilford & Fruchter 1973; Shavelson 1981; Tuckman 1978.) A now classic example of the application of quantitative data gathering and analyses applied to foreign language evaluation can be found in Smith (1970), and a review of the use of such methods in bilingual education is located in Tucker and Cziko (1978).

A classic example of what many people think an evaluation study ought to be is a quantitative, statistics-based experimental study designed to investigate the effectiveness of a given program. To help the reader understand how such quantitative studies can be designed for evaluation purposes, I must first define certain key terms. The subjects (usually students) are typically divided (preferably on a random basis) into two groups: an experimental group and a control group. The *experimental group* is the one that receives the treatment, while the *control group* receives no treatment. A *treatment* is something that the experimenter does to the experimental group, or rather an experience through which they go (as in a learning experience). In a medical study, the treatment might be a vaccine; in a language program, the treatment might be the language training itself.

The purpose of giving a treatment to the experimental group and nothing to the control group is to determine whether the treatment has been effective. Therein lies the connection of this discussion to evaluation. After all, the purpose in a product-oriented evaluation is to determine whether the treatment (for example, language training) has been effective. To achieve this purpose, some sort of observation must occur that allows a comparison between the two groups. Such *observations* may take many forms. In a quantitative study, an observation may be a simple tally, a comparison of rankings, test scores, and so forth. The point is that something worthy of being compared, something meaningful that distinguishes the two groups, is observed or measured. Logically, of course, whatever is measured should be related to the treatment. Thus in a language program evaluation language proficiency or achievement test scores might appropriately be the focus of study.

Before I move on, I must point out that such studies (if they involve anything other than a straightforward examination and description of test scores) are generally more difficult to conduct than might initially be expected (see Brown & Hilferty 1986, 1987, for an example of the difficulties that can arise in such a study). Planners face not only the problem of designing an airtight study, which is difficult in any teaching and learning situation, but also the problem of using statistics; indeed, considerable knowledge of statistics is necessary to avoid their misuse—and abuse. This warning is not meant to diminish the importance of this type of study but rather to provide an impetus for evaluators to seek proper help (perhaps from paid consultants) if quantitative data are to be analyzed statistically in evaluating a language program.

Qualitative Evaluation Studies

As I noted earlier, *qualitative data* consist of information that is more holistic than quantitative data. Such data are often based on observations that do not readily lend themselves to conversion into quantities or numbers. Table 7.1 indicates the qualitative nature of some of the procedures used in needs analysis or evaluation. Notice that 15 of the procedures in the table are labeled as being used for qualitative information gathering: records analysis, systems analysis, literature review, letter writing, case studies, diary studies, behavior observation, interactional analysis, individual interviews, group interviews, delphi technique, advisory meetings, interest group meetings, review meetings, and opinion surveys. This does not constitute an argument that these 15 procedures are exclusively suitable for gathering qualitative information. However, they are typically used for that purpose and are well suited to such tasks.

While qualitative data may seem to lack credibility for those of us steeped in the Western "scientific" tradition, in the end, these types of data may turn out to be crucial to the actual decisions made in a program—more so than many of us would be willing to admit. Therefore, to belittle these sorts of data gathering and analyses would be to condemn a potentially valuable source of information. For that reason alone, I advocate the use of qualitative data.

However, like all research, qualitative analyses must be systematically performed so that the information gained will be as complete and useful as possible.

A full description of qualitative data collection and analysis is beyond the scope of this book. (For more on the qualitative research in the language field, see Watson-Gegeo 1988; Johnson & Saville-Troike 1992; Davis 1992. For details on qualitative research in the general social sciences, see Agar 1986; Bogdan & Biklen 1982; Fetterman 1989; Fielding & Fielding 1986; Kirk & Miller 1986; Marshall & Rossman 1989; Miles & Huberman 1984; Patton 1980; Punch 1986; Yin 1984.) In general, the goal of qualitative research is ultimately very similar to that for quantitative research: to collect data in order to analyze them in such a way that patterns emerge so that sense can be made of the results and the quality of the program can be evaluated.

Using Both Quantitative and Qualitative Methods

The distinction between quantitative and qualitative data may not be as clear-cut as some evaluators would like it to be. Quantitative data, as provided by test scores, seem quite different from the qualitative data provided by, for example, studying the journals kept by students for a semester in a writing class. Yet an evaluator could examine the test scores from a more qualitative perspective. Consider, for instance, an oral test administered in groups and scored by a single observer who assigns separate scores for content, fluency, and pronunciation. The test would result in number scores and therefore could logically be considered quantitative, but the judgments made by the observer and the categories in which those judgments are being made could be logically classified as at least partially qualitative. Or the results of the oral tests could be further evaluated in a purely qualitative manner to determine what the students were thinking while it was being conducted. Conversely, a journal study might move closer to what would generally be recognized as quantitative data if the observations being made were counts, or tallies, of certain vocabulary items, grammatical structures, functions, and so forth. In short, either the test or the journals could be analyzed from quantitative or qualitative points of view, or some combination of the two.

Clearly, both types of data can yield valuable information in any evaluation, and therefore ignoring either type of information would be pointless and self-defeating. Sound evaluation practices will be based on all available perspectives so that many types of information can be gathered to strengthen the evaluation process and ensure that the resulting decisions will be as informed, accurate, and useful as possible.

□ PROGRAM COMPONENTS AS DATA SOURCES

Evaluation, then, has many different dimensions that must be considered. Will it be formative or summative? Will the focus be on product or process? Will the data gathered be quantitative or qualitative? Or will the evaluation include balanced positions on all of these dimensions, as I advocate in this book? Once evaluators have answered these basic questions, they must consider how all of this might fit with the components of their curriculum.

Inevitably, each component should be considered as a potential source of information that can be fed into the evaluation procedures. The purpose of gathering all this information is, of course, to determine the effectiveness of the program, so as to improve each of the components and the ways that they work together. Here I will propose one system for looking at the components as data sources and selecting the information that is included for each. The question I will address is: How can less useful information be eliminated so that all of the remaining information serves a useful purpose within the evaluation?

The overall purpose of evaluation is to determine the general effectiveness of the program, usually for purposes of improving it or defending its utility to out-side administrators or agencies. Clearly, evaluation is not a simple issue but rather a complex of interrelated issues. In fact, evaluation should be viewed very much like needs analysis. In Chapter Two I indicated that needs analysis involved draw-ing together many sources of information and examining all of this information from different points of view with the goal of forming a cogent and useful picture of what the students' needs were. The same steps are involved in evaluation. In fact, it is best to view evaluation as a never-ending needs analysis, the goal of which is to constantly refine the ideas gathered in the initial needs analysis such that the program can do an even better job of meeting those needs. However, all the components of the curriculum are necessarily involved as sources of informa-tion, and each of these must be considered from different points of view.

Naturally, the curriculum components under discussion are needs analysis, objectives, testing, materials, teaching and the evaluation itself. As Brown (1989a) pointed out, within an evaluation, each of these components can then be viewed from three viewpoints: Were they effective? Were they efficient? What were participants' attitudes toward them? Thus the process of extracting and synthesizing evaluation information can be viewed as a two-dimensional model, as shown in Figure 7.2. The next three sections will explore the three viewpoints as they relate to each of the program components.

Effective?

One overall question of interest in most program evaluations is the degree to which the program was effective. At first glance, this would seem to be a rela-tively simple determination. Using quantitative methods, an experiment can be designed to discover whether or not the students have learned anything, and, if so, how much of that thing. However, in addition to the difficulties I pointed out earlier that are associated with this type of research, Lynch (1986) has noted that a quantitative study that demonstrates that students (who received a language learning treatment) significantly outperformed a control group (who did not receive the treatment) is really only showing that the treatment in question *is bet-ter than nothing*. Of course, the degree to which the treatment is better than

Figure 7.2: Evaluation Components and Viewpoints (adapted from Brown 1989a)

| | | VIEWPOINTS | | |
		EFFECTIVE	EFFICIENT	ATTITUDES
C U R R I C U L U M	NEEDS			
	OBJECTIVES			
	TESTING			
C O M P O N E N T S	MATERIALS			
	TEACHING			
	EVALUATION			

nothing may be of interest. It is nevertheless best to view such information as just one piece in a puzzle that must include more pieces—pieces that can provide more detail about what is going on in the learning process. Other smaller questions may be very useful in this regard.

As a start in deciding what types of questions to investigate in the evaluation process and the sources that should be considered for gathering information to address those questions, Table 7.2 may be helpful. For example, the first curriculum element displayed in table 7.2 is needs analysis. In evaluating that component of the curriculum, the evaluator's central concern with regard to effectiveness would be the degree to which the original perceptions of students' needs were accurate. Hence, that is the focus of the question in the left portion of the table. In order to address this central concern, it would be necessary to determine, based on the original needs assessment documents (see "Primary Data Sources" in the right portion of Table 7.2), whether there have been any

Table 7.2 Program Effectiveness

		QUESTIONS	PRIMARY DATA SOURCES
N E E D S	A N A L Y S I S	Which of the needs that were originally identified turned out to be accurate (now that the program has more experience with students and their relationship to the program) in terms of what has been learned in testing, developing materials, teaching, and evaluation?	All original needs analysis documents
O B J E C T I V E S		Which of the original objectives reflect real student needs in view of the changing perceptions of those needs and all of the other information gathered in testing, materials development, teaching, and evaluation?	Criterion–referenced tests (diagnostic)
T E S T I N G		To what degree are the students achieving the objectives of the courses? Were the norm–referenced and criterion–referenced tests valid?	Criterion–referenced tests (achievement) Test evaluation procedures (Tables 4.3 & 4.4)
M A T E R I A L S		How effective are the materials (whether adopted, developed, or adapted) at meeting the needs of the students as expressed in the objectives?	Materials evaluation procedures (Tables 5.6, 5.7, & 5.8)
T E A C H I N G		To what degree is instruction effective?	Classroom observations and student evaluations (Figures 6.1, 6.2 & 6.3)

changes in the program's views of what the students need since the original needs analysis was conducted. The next step would be to investigate what can be done to better understand and serve the students' needs.

Thus the overall issue could be broken down into more detailed questions as follows:

1. What were the original perceptions of the students' needs?
2. How accurate was this initial thinking (now that we have more experience with the students and their relationship to the present program)?
3. Which of the original needs, especially as reflected in the goals and objectives, are useful and which are not useful?
4. What newly perceived needs must be addressed? How do these relate to those perceptions that were found to be accurate? How must the goals and objectives be adjusted accordingly?

Such analysis of the overall questions asked for each of the components would be equally useful.

Efficient?

A second general question of interest in most language program evaluations is the degree to which the program is efficient. At first glance, this would seem to be a relatively simple determination. Using one of the quantitative designs I discussed above, evaluators could set up a study to investigate the degree to which the amount of time can be compressed to make the learning process more efficient. Of course, time is an important aspect of efficiency, but it is just one aspect. Hence, it would probably be a good idea to use such information as one part of an investigation that gives more detail about the efficiency with which all of the components are operating, individually and collectively.

To begin this process, the questions presented on the left side of Table 7.3 may prove useful. Again, suggested sources of information are listed to the right for the general question in each component. Note that this table is meant only as a starting point from which to depart in more fully addressing each of the central concerns of a language program. To do so, first analyze the overall question as it applies to the program, then break the general issue down into more detailed questions (as shown in the previous section for needs analysis).

Attitudes

The third general area of concern in language program evaluation will usually center on the attitudes of the teachers, students, and administrators regarding the various components of the curriculum as they were implemented in the program. To get at these issues, various combinations of the procedures listed in Table 2.2 can be applied. Evaluators should remember that different procedures are more suitable for answering different types of questions, as Table 2.3 demonstrates. Typically,

Table 7.3   Program Efficiency

	QUESTIONS	PRIMARY DATA SOURCES
NEEDS ANALYSIS	Which of the original student needs turned out to be most efficiently learned? Which were superfluous?	Original needs analysis documents and criterion–referenced tests (both diagnostic and achievement)
OBJECTIVES	Which objectives turned out to be needed by the students and which did they already know?	Criterion–referenced tests (diagnostic)
TESTING	Were the norm–referenced and criterion–referenced tests efficient and reliable?	Test evaluation procedures (Tables 4.3 & 4.4)
MATERIALS	How can materials resources be reorganized for more efficient use by teachers and students?	Materials blueprint and scope-and-sequence charts (see Tables 5.2, 5.3, & 5.4)
TEACHING	What types of support are provided to help teachers? Are they efficient?	Orientation documents (see Table 6.2) and administrative support structure (as in Figure 6.4)

questions about attitudes (see the left portion of Table 7.4) are addressed by using evaluation interviews, various types of meetings, and questionaires.

Notice that the general questions in Table 7.4 are all followed by "Before Program? After?" These subsidiary questions are meant to suggest that, while attitudes are important, it is useful to remember that they are just opinions and that opinions can change. In order to investigate the degree to which they have changed during the program, opinions can be solicited from students before, during, or directly after a program. In addition, opinions can be elicited much later from students who have finished the program and gone on with their lives (see the discussion below of the importance of this factor in the GELC program). Once again, this table and the related discussion are only meant to serve as a starting point for determining more detailed questions that apply to a particular program and for deciding on which sources of information might profitably be used to address those more detailed questions.

EXAMPLE PROGRAM EVALUATION PROJECTS

□ GUANGZHOU ENGLISH LANGUAGE CENTER, ZHONGSHAN UNIVERSITY

Three aspects of the GELC program evaluation procedures may prove interesting to readers. First, formative evaluation occurred at all times during the program. Second, summative evaluation was carried out on a yearly basis. Third, we found it particularly useful to survey students who had finished the program.

Perhaps because we were in the throes of early curriculum development, we were constantly reviewing and evaluating the effectiveness of the various components of our curriculum, which meant that they were always viewed as tentative and under development. Therefore, we necessarily focused on process because we wanted to leave a set of curriculum processes in place that would serve the program well long after the American contingent had been systematically withdrawn. We also realized that concentrating on processes would help us to keep the curriculum development alive and ongoing. As a result, we used every qualitative and quantitative tool available to us to revise and improve our curriculum. Nevertheless, we were forced to recognize that the purpose of these processes, indeed the overall goal of our program, was ultimately to produce products in the form of tests, materials, and teaching procedures that would foster language learning.

This recognition was due in large measure to the fact that we had, in effect, contracted with the Chinese government to admit students at about a 400 level on the TOEFL and bring their overall proficiency level up to 550. From the government's perspective, this level of proficiency was necessary because most American universities required 500 to 550 on the TOEFL for foreign student admissions. Though we wanted to improve our students' TOEFL scores, we did

	Table 7.4 Program Attitudes	
	QUESTIONS	**PRIMARY DATA SOURCES**
N E E D S A N A L Y S I S	What are the students', teachers', and administrators' attitudes and feelings about the situational and language needs of students? Before program? After?	Needs analysis questionnaires and any resulting documents (see Tables 2.4–2.9)
O B J E C T I V E S	What are the students', teachers', and administrators' attitudes and feelings about the usefulness of the objectives as originally formulated? Before program? After?	Evaluation interviews and questionnaires (see Figure 6.3)
T E S T I N G	What are the students', and administrators' attitudes and feelings about the usefulness of the tests as originally developed? Before program? After?	Evaluation interviews, meetings, and questionnaires
M A T E R I A L S	What are the students', teachers', and administrators' attitudes and feelings about the usefulness of the materials as originally adopted, developed, and/or adapted? Before program? After?	Evaluation interviews, meetings, and questionnaires
T E A C H I N G	What are the students', teachers', and administrators' attitudes and feelings about the usefulness of the teaching as originally delivered? Before program? After?	Evaluation interviews, meetings, and questionnaires

not want to simply present a TOEFL preparation course. Plenty of those were already springing up all over the PRC. Instead, we took the position that, if we taught the students English for science and technology (EST) (based on a communicative approach), their TOEFL scores would naturally rise. As a result of this stance, we had to monitor the students' progress on a regular basis—not only their progress in EST (using CRTs), but also their progress in terms of TOEFL (using NRTs to predict TOEFL performance). Thus we set up a testing system to track both aspects of our program, and this led to regular consideration of the degree to which our products were effective from two perspectives. It turned out, in general terms, that students who learn English for science and technology appear to gain systematically in their overall proficiency as measured by tests like the TOEFL. Now, this may seem like a common sense result, but it was far from a given when we were in the middle of developing our program. In short, we were forced to monitor and evaluate our product as well as our processes by both political and contractual exigencies. Much of this activity could be termed "formative evaluation."

Our results were marshalled on a yearly basis because the administration in the UCLA/China Exchange Program was justifiably anxious about our progress. Essentially, we imposed this yearly report requirement on ourselves, which forced us to do summative evaluation on a yearly cycle. Because of our process orientation in general, few of us viewed the summative evaluation as unnecessary busy work. It just became another step in our ongoing curriculum development.

The report that resulted from the first-year review included some general introductory comments and a description of the learning resource center. Then each of the remaining 15 pages contained information about each of the 15 courses. Each team of skill/course teachers was required to pull together the information about their course using a standard form. The format of this standard form was worked out in advance by all the teachers collectively so that the report would be consistent across courses. Such consistency helped to organize the report and probably assisted readers in examining and comparing courses. The form also helped each team to produce a complete description of the course in question. An example of this form is shown in Figure 7.3. Notice that the example is for the Speaking B course discussed in previous chapters. Naturally, some issues touched on in the form would not apply to all language programs, just as other issues that would be of concern in another program are not mentioned in this form. It is the idea of using a form, rather than the shape of this particular one, that is important.

This yearly summative evaluation document was distributed to the UCLA/China Exchange Program as well as to the Ministry of Education in Beijing. Interested parties at Zhongshan University and elsewhere were also given copies. In truth, once produced, such a document is nothing to be ashamed of. It served as good advertising for our program. It helped us to organize our thinking about the courses, individually and collectively. It clearly described our program. And it answered a number of questions that outsiders might have

Figure 7.3: Description of Speaking B in GELC First-Year Report (GELC 1982)

Level _B_

Instructional Module _Speaking*_

1. Course Goals _Presupposing fluency and structural accuracy in short, communicative acts in dyads and small groups, to develop proficiency in more extended discourse in small groups and with professional colleagues; expansion of interactional inventory to include additional conversational strategies leading to the formal discussion framework, with emphasis on precision in the use of discourse markers._

2. Texts/Materials
a. TAKE A STAND, b. READ ON, SPEAK OUT, & c. GAMBITS

3. Staff Members Likely to Teach This Component
Candy Mocko, Celeste Scholz, & Jim Brown

4. Audiovisual Aids (Software and Hardware)

Title/Type	**Utilization hrs per week**
Potential collaboration with listening component.	0

5. Instruction hrs/wk _____5_____ **6. Homework hrs/wk** ___2___

7. Anticipated Number of Students _____100_____

8. Anticipated hrs/wk of Learning Resources Center Use _____0_____

9. Pre- and Posttesting (statement) _Levels of students' proficiency in role-played extended discourse will be assessed (pre/post)._

10. Defined Research Questions Regarding this Component:
Do the students make significant gains in speaking ESL using these materials and teaching techniques? Do the students make significant progress in overall speaking under the same conditions? If the students do not make adequate gains, how do we improve materials/ teaching techniques? What are the Chinese communicative strategies that correspond to those being taught for English (in U.S. setting)? How do they differ? Can communicative competence tests be developed for these students?

11. Special Notes: _* Course content is complementary to LISTEN IN, SPEAK OUT segment of Listening B._

about the program. Perhaps most importantly, the production of this document made us step back and consider the program as a whole, when normally we were focused (in our skill/course teams) on fairly narrow day-to-day issues.

In preparing for the second-year review, we hit upon a particularly useful idea. Since at this point our program had produced graduates who had gone on to study at various institutions overseas, we decided to survey them as part of our program evaluation. This idea was useful for two reasons. First, we decided to involve a number of groups in the preparation of this questionnaire, including the current student representatives, who contributed a number of useful ideas. The Chinese teachers were also heavily involved. They provided interlinear translations on the questionnaire and a number of insights into the ways that Chinese students were likely to interpret our questions—sometimes quite differently from our original intentions.

Second, once the survey was sent out, we were surprised and pleased to discover that the results were so positive. The survey convinced us that students might have certain negative attitudes toward the program while they were in it, but that their attitudes would change once they went overseas to study. In essence, many of our students had belatedly recognized the utility of topics, strategies, and activities that we had put them through. Many of our graduates understood that we had provided them with English for science and technology which had been well planned and executed and had served them well in their overseas university experiences. We began to use this survey information to convince our current students that some day they would see the utility of what we were doing in class.

This brief window on the evaluation processes at GELC is natually a simplification of what was actually a fairly complex and large-scale endeavor. Remember, we were in a position to draw on the energy and talent of seven Chinese teachers, hundreds of Chinese students, and nine American teachers trained in the field of ESL.

□   ENGLISH LANGUAGE INSTITUTE, UNIVERSITY OF HAWAII AT MANOA

As indicated in the systematic approach model (shown in Figure 1.2), the crucial curriculum activities are conducting a needs analysis, setting objectives, testing, developing materials, and teaching. The process of reviewing, revising, and improving all of these curriculum elements is what I call formative evaluation. In the ELI, such renewal activities included examination of each of the components themselves along with the processes that related to interactions among people involved in the curriculum.

To those ends, formative evaluation was set up on a cyclical basis such that each fall the curriculum committee in cooperation with the various skill/level groups of teachers worked on updating the needs analyses, objectives, and criterion-referenced tests. In the spring, our attention turned to the norm-referenced tests, materials, and teacher support issues. Thus each component was the focus of our efforts on a cyclical basis at least once per year.

In addition, beginning in the fall of 1989, the ELI initiated preparation for a summative evaluation motivated by outside forces in the form of the normal five-year review process that takes place in all departments at the UHM. As a subunit of the Department of English as a Second Language, the ELI was required to marshall its evaluation resources in a number of ways. Our first task was to organize and present an evaluation document, which did all of the following:

1. Defined the role of the ELI
2. Listed its goals and objectives
3. Presented evidence for the reliability, validity, and utility of all its tests (criterion-referenced and norm-referenced)
4. Listed the materials and described the materials evaluation process
5. Described the ELI instructors while summarizing the observation and student evaluation procedures
6. Explained the formative evaluation procedures that are conducted on a regular basis.

Because of the formative evaluation procedures that had been going on for three years, it was not very difficult to pull together the material needed to produce this document. In fact, this task (which initially caused a certain amount of dread within the ELI) turned out to be a very useful exercise that forced us to look at the ELI as a whole and to consider issues that might have otherwise been ignored because of our typical focus on more fragmented details and day-to-day survival in the formative evaluations of the individual curriculum components. Nevertheless, I think everyone involved agreed that it is fortunate that such evaluations only occur every five years.

SUMMARY

This chapter has considered a number of different aspects of program evaluation as an ongoing part of curriculum development. The chapter began by considering various definitions of program evaluation, then turned to a review of the various approaches that have been used to accomplish evaluation. Thus the product-oriented, static-characteristic, process-oriented, and decision-facilitation approaches were all discussed. Next, three dimensions were covered that help to shape points of view on evaluation. They included dimensions that are related to: (1) the purpose for gathering the evaluation information (formative-summative), (2) the types of information (process-product), and (3) the types of data and analyses (quantitative-qualitative). There was also some discussion of the ways that these three dimensions interact within an evaluation.

The next major section of the chapter turned to issues related to actually gathering program evaluation information. This section began with a discussion of quantitative methods for conducting evaluation studies. Qualitative methods were also addressed. However, the main thrust of the argument was that both quantitative and qualitative methods should be used in any evaluation study.

The discussion then turned to the importance of program components (needs, goals, tests, materials, teaching, and evaluation) as data sources. This section outlined three ways that these data sources can be viewed: in terms of effectiveness, efficiency, and attitudes. General questions were suggested for each curriculum component within this framework of three views.

As usual, the chapter ended with discussion of example evaluation projects drawn from the GELC program in China and the ELI at the University of Hawaii at Manoa.

■■■ CHECKLIST

The following checklist is provided to help remind you of the various elements that should be considered in performing program evaluations.

☐ Have you considered various approaches to program evaluation?
  ☐ Product-oriented approaches?
  ☐ Static-characteristic approaches?
  ☐ Process-oriented approaches?
  ☐ Decision-facilitation approaches?

☐ Have you considered all three dimensions?
  ☐ Purpose of the information?
  ☐ Types of information?
  ☐ Types of data and analyses?
  ☐ Interactions among dimensions?

☐ Have you considered options in performing evaluation?
  ☐ Gathering evaluation data?
    ☐ Quantitative?
    ☐ Qualitative?
    ☐ Quantitative and qualitative?
  ☐ Program components as data sources?
    ☐ Effective?
    ☐ Efficient?
    ☐ Attitudes?

■■■ TERMS

accreditation
control group
decision-facilitation approaches
discrepancy model
efficient
experimental group
goal-free evaluation
observations
process-oriented approaches
product-oriented approaches
quantitative data
summative evaluation
treatment

attitudes
countenance model
dimensions
effective
evaluation
formative evaluation
measurement
process evaluation
product evaluation
qualitative data
static-characteristic approaches
testing

■■■ REVIEW QUESTIONS

1. How would you characterize the product-oriented approaches to curriculum evaluation? The static-characteristic approaches? The process-oriented approaches? The decision-facilitation approaches?

2. What are the important differences among the terms testing, measurement, and evaluation as used in this chapter?

3. What is the fundamental difference between a formative and a summative evaluation? Is summative evaluation necessarily crisis-oriented?

4. What are the differences between the process and product types of information? How is this process-product dimension related to the formative-summative dimension? How is it different?

5. What are the relative advantages and disadvantages of using quantitative and qualitative studies in a language program evaluation?

6. How do the formative-summative, process-product, and quantitative-qualitative dimensions interact?

7. What are some data sources that could be tapped to evaluate each of the program components (needs, objectives, tests, materials, and teaching) as well as the success of the program with regard to the students' learning and in relation to other programs around the world?

8. How will you know that each of the components listed in question seven is effective and efficient?

9. What kinds of questions would you ask during an evaluation to find out what the attitudes of the teachers, administrators, and students are toward each of the curriculum components?

■■■ *APPLICATIONS*

A1. Consider the descriptions provided in this chapter for the GELC program and the ELI at UHM (in the "Example Program Evaluation Process" section). Briefly describe the overall approach taken in one of these programs. Would it best be described as a product-oriented, a static-characteristic, a process-oriented, or a decision-facilitation approach, or some combination of the above?

A2. Next, list the positions taken with regard to the formative-summative, process-product, and quantitative-qualitative dimensions presented in the chapter. Do you think that these positions are justified within the context of the particular program involved?

A3. Like other curriculum activities, evaluation is a political act. What strategies were used to smooth out potential difficulties and avoid the crisis orientation that arises in some summative evaluations?

B1. Consider some language program that you are now involved in or know about. Take out a piece of paper and jot down ways that you see formative evaluation going on. What strategies are used?

B2. What types of questions would you advise addressing in any evaluation of the program, whether formative or summative? Be sure to focus on ideas that would improve the curriculum in one way or another so that the evaluation becomes more than just unnecessary busy work.

SOME OF THE MAJOR PUBLISHERS OF ESL MATERIALS

(WITH ADDRESSES IN THE UNITED STATES)

Addison-Wesley/Longman
Order Department
1 Jacob Way
Reading, MA 01867

Cambridge University Press
ESL Marketing Department
40 West 20th Street
New York, NY 10011-4211

Harcourt Brace & Company
6277 Sea Harbor Drive
Orlando, FL 32887

Heinle, Cengage Learning
Newbury House
20 Park Plaza
Boston, MA 02116

Longman Publishing
Department of ESL
10 Bank Street
White Plains, NY 10606-1951

McGraw-Hill, Inc.
1221 Avenue of the Americas
New York, NY 10020

Oxford University Press
ESL Department
200 Madison Avenue
New York, NY 10016

Prentice Hall Regents
Order Department
200 Old Tappan Road
Old Tappan, NJ 07675

Scott Foresman
International Markets
1900 East Lake Avenue
Glenview, IL 60025-9881

The University of Michigan Press
P.O. Box 1104
Ann Arbor, MI 48106-1104

REFERENCES

Agar, M. H. (1986). *Speaking of ethnography.* Beverly Hills, CA: Sage.

Alderson, J. C., Krahnke, K. J., & Stansfield, C. W. (1987). *Reviews of English language proficiency tests.* Washington, DC: TESOL.

Alkin, M. C. (1969). Evaluation theory development. *Evaluation Comment,* 2(1).

Allwright, R. L. (1983). Classroom-centered research on language teaching and learning: A brief historical overview. *TESOL Quarterly,* 17(2) 191–204.

American Council on the Teaching of Foreign Languages. (1986). *ACTFL proficiency guidelines.* Hastings-on-Hudson, NY: American Council on the Teaching of Foreign Languages.

Anthony, E. M. (1965). Approach, method, and technique. In H. B. Allen (Ed.), *Teaching English as a second language: A book of readings.* New York: McGraw-Hill.

Asahina, R., & Okuda, J. M. (1987). Lecture skills for foreign teaching assistants: goals, microskills and objectives. Honolulu: Department of English as a Second Language, University of Hawaii at Manoa.

Asahina, R., Bergman, M., Conklin, G., Guth, J., & Lockhart, C. (1988). ELI 82 curriculum development project. Honolulu: Department of English as a Second Language, University of Hawaii at Manoa.

Asher, J. J. (1983). *Learning another language through actions: The complete teacher's guidebook.* Los Gatos, CA: Sky Oaks.

Azar, B. S. (1989). *Understanding and using English grammar* (2d ed.). Englewood Cliffs, NJ: Prentice-Hall Regents.

Babbie, E. R. (1973). *Survey research methods.* Belmont, CA: Wadsworth.

Bachman, L. F. (1989). The development and use of criterion-referenced tests of language proficiency in language program evaluation. In K. Johnson (Ed.), *The second language curriculum.* Cambridge: Cambridge University Press.

———— (1990). *Fundamental considerations in language testing.* Oxford: Oxford University.

Bailey, K. D. (1982). *Methods of social research* (2d ed.). New York: Free Press.

Bailey, K. M. (1980). An introspective analysis of an individual's language learning experience. In R. C. Scarcella and S. D. Krashen (Eds.), *Research in second language acquisition.* Cambridge, MA: Newbury House.

Barr, P., Clegg, J., & Wallace, C. (1983). *Advanced reading skills.* Harlow, England: Longman.

Bates, M., & Dudley-Evans, T. (1976). *Nucleus English for science and technology: General science.* London: Longman.

Bennett, G. K. (1972). Review of the Remote Associates Test. In O. K. Buros (Ed.), *The seventh mental measurements yearbook.* Highland Park, NJ: Gryphon.

Blair, R. W. (Ed.). (1982). *Innovative approaches to language teaching.* Cambridge, MA: Newbury House.

Bloom, B.S. (Ed.). (1956). *Taxonomy of educational objectives, Book 1: Cognitive domain.* London: Longman.

Bobbitt, F. (1924). *How to make a curriculum.* Boston: Houghton Mifflin.

Bogdan, R.C., & Biklen, S. K. (1982). *Qualitative research methods for education: An introduction to theory and methods.* Boston: Allyn and Bacon.

Brindley, G. (1984). *Needs analysis and objective setting in the Adult Migrant Education Program.* Sydney, Australia: Adult Migrant Education Service.

Brinton, D. & Neuman, R. (1982). *Getting along: English grammar and writing, Book 1.* Englewood Cliffs, NJ: Prentice-Hall.

Brinton, D. M., Snow, M. A., & Wesche, M. B. (1989). *Content- based second language instruction.* New York: Newbury House.

Brown, G. (1977). *Listening to spoken English.* London: Longman.

Brown, H. D. (1988). *Principles of language learning and teaching* (2d ed.). Englewood Cliffs, NJ: Prentice-Hall.

Brown, J. D. (1981). Newly placed versus continuing students: Comparing proficiency. In J. C. Fisher, M. A. Clarke, & J. Schachter (Eds.), *On TESOL '80 building bridges: Research and practice in teaching English as a second language.* Washington, DC: Teachers of English to Speakers of Other Languages.

_____ (1984). Criterion-referenced language tests: what, how and why? *Gulf Area TESOL Biannual,* 1, 32–34.

_____ (1988). *Understanding research in second language learning: A teacher's guide to statistics and research design.* Cambridge: Cambridge University Press.

_____ (1989a). Language program evaluation: A synthesis of existing possibilities. In K. Johnson (Ed.), *The second language curriculum.* Cambridge: Cambridge University Press.

_____ (1989b). Improving ESL placement tests using two perspectives. *TESOL Quarterly,* 23(1), 65–83.

_____ (1990a). Short-cut estimates of criterion-referenced test consistency. *Language Testing,* 7(1), 77–97.

_____ (1990b). Where do tests fit into language programs? *JALT Journal,* 12(1), 121–140.

_____ (1992a). Classroom-centered language testing. *TESOL Journal,* 1(4), 12–15.

_____ (1992b). The biggest problems facing ESL/EFL teachers today. *TESOL Matters,* 2(2), 1, 5.

_____ (1992c). What roles do members want TESOL to play? *TESOL Matters,* 2(5), 16.

_____ (1993a). A comprehensive criterion-referenced language testing project. In D. Douglas & C. Chapelle (Eds.), *A new decade of language testing research.* Washington, DC: Teachers of English to Speakers of Other Languages.

_____ (1993b). Social meaning *in* language curriculum, *of* language curriculum, and *through* language curriculum. In J. Alatis (Ed.), *Proceedings of the 1992 Georgetown University Round Table. Washington, DC: Georgetown University Press.*

_____ *(unpublished ms) Guidelines for Class Observations.* Honolulu: Department of English as a Second Language, University of Hawaii at Manoa.

_____ *(forthcoming). Language testing: A practical guide to proficiency, placement, diagnostic and achievement testing.* New York: Regents/Prentice-Hall.

Brown, J. D., Chaudron, C., & Pennington, M. (1988). Foreign teaching assistant training and orientation pilot project. In *Report on the Educational Improvement Fund 1987/1988.* Office of Faculty Development and Academic Support, University of Hawaii at Manoa, Honolulu, HI.

Brown, J. D., Guth, J., Lindsay, C., Lockhart, C., Murdoch, W., Rickard, D., Stanley, J. (1989). *Teacher's handbook for graduate assistants and lecturers.* Honolulu: Department of English as a Second Language, University of Hawaii at Manoa.

Brown, J. D., & Hilferty, A. (1986). Listening for reduced forms. *TESOL Quarterly,* 20(4), 759–763.

_____ (1987). The effectiveness of teaching reduced forms for listening comprehension. *RELC Journal,* 17(2), 59–70.

Brown, J. D., & Pennington, M. C. (1991). Developing effective evaluation systems for language programs. In M. C. Pennington (Ed.), *Building better English language programs: Perspectives on evaluation in ESL.* Washington, DC: NAFSA.

Butler, C. (1985). *Statistics in linguistics.* Oxford: Blackwell.

Campbell, D. T., & Stanley, J. C. (1963). Experimental and quasi-experimental designs for research on teaching. In N. L. Gage (Ed.), *Handbook of research on teaching.* Chicago: Rand-McNally.

Candlin, C. N., Kirkwood, J. M., & Moore, H. M. (1978). Study skills in English. In R. Mackay & A. Mountford (Eds.), *English for specific purposes.* London: Longman.

Carroll, B. J. & Hall, P. J. (1985). *Make your own language tests: A practical guide to writing language performance tests.* Oxford: Pergamon.

Cartier, F. A. (1968). Criterion-referenced testing of language skills. *TESOL Quarterly,* 2(1), 27–32.

Center for Applied Linguistics (CAL). (1981). *Program design considerations for English as a second language.* Washington, DC: Center for Applied Linguistics.

Chaudron, C. (1988). *Second language classrooms: Research on teaching and learning.* Cambridge: Cambridge University Press.

Chomsky, N. (1957). *Syntactic structures.* The Hague, The Netherlands: Mouton.

Clark, J. L. (1987). *Curriculum renewal in school foreign language learning.* Oxford: Oxford University Press.

Cook, G. (1989). *Discourse.* Oxford: Oxford University Press.

Corder, S. P. (1973). *Introducing applied linguistics.* Middlesex, England: Penguin Educational.

Coulthard, M. (1979). *An introduction to discourse analysis.* London: Longman.

_____ (Ed.). (1992). *Advances in spoken discourse analysis.* London: Routledge.

Crombie, W. (1985). *Discourse and language learning: A relational approach to syllabus.* Oxford: Oxford University Press.

Curran, C.A. (1972). *Counseling-learning: A whole-person model for education.* New York: Grune and Stratton.

_____ (1976). *Counseling-learning in second languages.* Apple River, IL: Apple River Press.

Cziko, G.A. (1982). Improving the psychometric, criterion-referenced and practical qualities of integrative language tests. *TESOL Quarterly,* 16(3), 367–379.

_____ (1983). Psychometric and edumetric approaches to language testing. In J. W. Oller, Jr. (Ed.), *Issues in language testing research.* Cambridge, MA: Newbury House.

Davis, K. A. (1992). Validity and reliability in qualitative research on second language acquisition and teaching: Another researcher comments. *TESOL Quarterly,* 26(3), 605–608.

de Beaugrande, R. & Dressler, W. (1981). *Introduction to text linguistics.* London: Longman.

Dick, W., & Carey, L. (1985). *The systematic design of instruction* (2d ed.). Glenview, IL: Scott, Foresman.

Dubin, F., & Olshtain, E. (1986). *Course design.* Cambridge: Cambridge University Press.

Dunkel, P. (1985). Listening and notetaking: What is the effect of pretraining in note taking? *TESOL Newsletter,* 19(6), 30–31.

Edmondson, W. (1981). *Spoken discourse: A model for analysis.* London: Longman.

ELI. (1991). Materials developed at the English Language Institute, University of Hawaii at Manoa, Honolulu, HI.

Fetterman, D. M. (1989). *Ethnography: Step by step.* Newbury Park, CA: Sage.

Fielding, N. G., & Fielding, J. L. (1986). *Linking data.* Beverly Hills, CA: Sage.

Findley, C. A., & Nathan, L. A. (1980). Functional language objectives. *TESOL Quarterly,* 14(2), 221–231.

Finocchiaro, M., & Brumfit, C. (1983). *The functional-notional approach: From theory to practice.* Oxford: Oxford University Press.

Florida State Department of Education. (1983) Teacher Observation Form. Tallahassee, FL: Florida State Department of Education.

Gattegno, C. (1972). *Teaching foreign languages in schools: The silent way* (2d ed.). New York: Educational Solutions.

GELC. (1982). Materials developed at the Guangzhou English Language Center, Zhongshan University, Guangzhou, Guangdong, People's Republic of China.

Graham, C. (1978). *Jazz Chants: Rhythms of American English for students of English as a second langauge.* New York: Oxford University Press.

Grasse, C. (1982). Burnout in teachers of second languages. *TESOL Newsletter,* 16(1), 4–5.

Gronlund, N. E. (1985). *Stating objectives for classroom instruction* (3d ed.). New York: Macmillan.

Guilford, J. P., & Fruchter, B. (1973). *Fundamental statistics in psychology and education* (5th ed.). New York: McGraw-Hill.

Hall, D., & Bowyer, T. (1980). *Nucleus English for science and technology: Mathematics.* London: Longman.

Halliday, M. A. K., McIntosh, A., & Strevens, P. (1964). *The linguistic sciences and language teaching.* Bloomington: Indiana University.

Harper, A., Gleason, A., & Ogama, A. (1983). A needs assessment and program design for an academic listening comprehension course. Honolulu: Department of English as a Second Language, University of Hawaii at Manoa.

Hatch, E., & Farhady, H. (1982). *Research design and statistics for applied linguistics.* Cambridge, MA: Newbury House.

Hatch, E., & Lazaraton, A. (1991). *The research manual: Design and statistics for applied linguistics.* New York: Newbury House.

Hatch, E., & Long, M. H. (1980). Discourse analysis, what's that? In D. Larsen-Freeman (Ed.), *Discourse analysis in second language research.* Cambridge, MA: Newbury House.

Henerson, M. E., Morris, L. L., & Fitz-Gibbon, C. T. (1987). *How to measure attitudes.* Newbury Park, CA: Sage.

Henning, G. (1987). *A guide to language testing: Development, evaluation, research.* Cambridge, MA: Newbury House.

Hoey, M. (1983). *On the surface of discourse.* London: George Allen and Unwin.

Howatt, A. (1974). The background to course design. In J. P. B. Allen & S. P. Corder (Eds.), *Techniques in applied linguistics.* Oxford: Oxford University Press.

Hudson, T., & Lynch, B. (1984). A criterion-referenced approach to ESL achievement testing. *Language Testing,* 1, 171–201.

Johnson, D. M., & Saville-Troike, M. (1992). Validity and reliability in qualitative research on second language acquisition and teaching: Two researchers comment. *TESOL Quarterly,* 26(3), 602–605.

Johnson, K. (1982). *Communicative syllabus design and methodology.* Oxford: Pergamon.

Johnson, R. K. (1978). Syllabus design and the adult beginner. *Modern English Teacher,* 6(2), 19–22.

_____ (1981). On syllabuses and on being communicative. *The English Bulletin* (Hong Kong), 7(4), 39–51.

_____ (Ed.). (1989) *The second language curriculum.* Cambridge: Cambridge University Press.

Jolly, D. (1984). Writing tasks: *An authentic-task approach to individual writing needs.* Cambridge: Cambridge University Press.

Jones, L., & von Baeyer, C. (1983). *Functions of American English: Communication activities for the classroom.* Cambridge: Cambridge University Press.

Keller, E., & Warner, S. (1979a). *Gambits 1 conversational tools: Openers —the first of three modules.* Hull, Quebec, Canada: Canadian Government Printing Office.

_____ (1979b). *Gambits 2 conversational tools: Links—the second of three modules.* Hull, Quebec, Canada: Canadian Government Printing Office.

_____ (1979c). *Gambits 3 conversational tools: Responders, Closers and Inventory - the third of three modules.* Hull, Quebec, Canada: Canadian Government Printing Office.

Kimzin, G. & Proctor, S. (1986). An ELI academic listening comprehension needs assessment: Establishing goals, objectives, and microskills. Honolulu: Department of English as a Second Language, University of Hawaii at Manoa.

Kirk, J., & Miller, M. L. (1986). *Reliability and validity in qualitative research.* Beverly Hills, CA: Sage.

Kramer, J. J., & Conoley, J. C. (1992). *The eleventh mental measurements yearbook.* Lincoln, NE: Buros Institute of Mental Measurements.

Krashen, S. D., & Terrell, T. D. (1983). *The natural approach: Language acquisition in the classroom.* Hayward, CA: Alemany.

Krathwohl, D.R., Bloom, B. S., & Masia, B. B. (1956). *Taxonomy of educational objectives, Handbook 2: Affective domain.*

Lanier, A. R. (1973). *Visiting the USA.* Tokyo: Yohan.

Larsen-Freeman, D. (1986). *Techniques and principles in language teaching.* Oxford: Oxford University Press.

Levine, D. R., & Adelman, M. B. (1982). *Beyond language.* Englewood Cliffs, NJ: Prentice-Hall.

Long, M. H. (1984). Process and product in ESL program evaluation. *TESOL Quarterly,* 18(3), 409–425.

Long, M.H., Allen, W., Cyr, A., Pomeroy, C., Ricard, E., Spada, N., & Vogel, P. (1980). *Reading English for academic study.* Cambridge, MA: Newbury House.

Loschky, L., Stanley, J., Cunha, C., & Singh, S. (1987). Evaluation of the University of Hawaii English Language Institute Reading Program. Honolulu: Department of English as a Second Language, University of Hawaii at Manoa.

Lozanov, G. (1978). *Suggestology and outlines of suggestology.* New York: Gordon and Breach.

Lynch, B. (1986). Evaluating a program inside and out. Paper presented at the 20th annual TESOL Convention. Anaheim, CA. March, 1986.

Mackay, R. (1981). Developing a reading curriculum for ESP. In L. Selinker, E. Tarone, & V. Hanzeli (Eds.), *English for academic and technical purposes: Studies in honor of Louis Trimble.* Cambridge, MA: Newbury House.

Mager, R. F. (1962). *Preparing objectives for programmed instruction.* Belmont, CA: Fearon-Pitman.

_____ (1975). *Preparing instructional objectives.* Belmont, CA: Fearon-Pitman.

Marshall, C., & Rossman, G. B. (1989). *Designing qualitative research.* Newbury Park, CA: Sage.

Mason, C. (1985). ELI curriculum needs. Honolulu: Department of English as a Second Language, University of Hawaii at Manoa.

McCarthy, M. (1991). *Discourse analysis for language teachers.* Cambridge: Cambridge University Press.

McKay, S. (1978). Syllabuses: Structural, situational, notional. *TESOL Newsletter,* 12(5), 11.

Metfessel, N. S., & Michael, W. B. (1967). A paradigm involving multiple criterion measures for the evaluation of the effectiveness of school programs. *Educational and Psychological Measurement,* 27, 931–943.

Miles, M. B., & Huberman, A. M. (1984). *Qualitative data analysis: A sourcebook of new methods.* Beverly Hills, CA: Sage.

Mohan, B. A. (1986). *Language and content.* Menlo Park, CA: Addison-Wesley.

Munby, J. (1978). *Communicative syllabus design.* Cambridge: Cambridge University Press.

Murphy, J. M. (1985). Examining ESL listening as an interpretive language process. *TESOL Newsletter,* 19(6), 23–24.

NICE. (1990) A needs analysis done at the New Intensive Course of English, University of Hawaii, Honolulu, HI.

Nunan, D. (1985). *Language teaching course design: Trends and issues.* Adelaide, Australia: National Curriculum Resource Centre.

_____ (1986). Communicative language teaching: The learner's view. Paper presented at the RELC Regional Seminar, Singapore. April 1986.

_____ (1987). *The teacher as curriculum developer.* Adelaide, Australia: National Curriculum Resource Centre.

_____ (1988). *The learner centered curriculum.* Cambridge: Cambridge University Press.

_____ (1991). *Syllabus design.* Oxford: Oxford University.

Oller, J. W., Jr. (1979). *Language tests at school.* London: Longman.

Oller, J. W., Jr., & Richard-Amato, P. A. (Eds). (1983). *Methods that work: A smorgasbord of ideas for language teachers.* Cambridge, MA: Newbury.

Oppenheim, A. N. (1966). *Questionnaire design and attitude measurement.* New York: Basic Books.

Patton, M. Q. (1980). *Qualitative evaluation methods.* Beverly Hills, CA: Sage.

Pennington, M. C. (1983). ESL administrators and teachers: Getting together on curriculum. *TESOL Newsletter,* 17, 30–31.

Pennington, M. C., & Brown, J. D. (1991). Excellence in language education: A function of curriculum process. In M.C. Pennington (Ed.) *Building better English programs: Perspectives on evaluation in ESL.* Washington, DC: National Association of Foreign Student Advisors.

Perry, F. A. (1976). The systems approach to basic English language training in the Canadian armed forces. System, 4, 80.

Pifer, G., & Mutoh, N. W. (1977). *Points of view.* Cambridge, MA: Newbury House.

Popham, W. J. (1975). *Educational evaluation.* Englewood Cliffs, NJ: Prentice-Hall.

Power, K. M. (1986). Needs analysis for ESL 100. Honolulu: Department of English as a Second Language, University of Hawaii at Manoa.

Pratt, D. (1980). *Curriculum design and development.* New York: Harcourt Brace Jovanovich.

Provus, M. M. (1971). *Discrepancy evaluation.* Berkley, CA: McCutchan.

Punch, M. (1986). *The politics and ethics of fieldwork.* Beverly Hills, CA: Sage.

Rassias, J. (1968). A philosophy of language instruction. Hanover, NH: Department of French, Dartmouth College.

_____ (1972). Why we must change. *ADFL Bulletin,* March, 1972.

Richards, J. C. (1983) Listening comprehension: Approach, design, procedure. *TESOL Quarterly,* 17(2), 219–240.

_____ (1984). Language curriculum development. *RELC Journal,* 15, 1–29.

Richards, J. C., Platt, J. & Weber, H. (1985). *Longman dictionary of applied linguistics.* London: Longman.

Richards, J. C., & Rodgers, T. (1982). Method: Approach, design, and procedure. *TESOL Quarterly,* 16(1), 153–168.

Rivers, W. M., & Temperley, M. S. (1981). *A practical guide to the teaching of English as a second or foreign language.* Oxford: Oxford University Press.

Robin, A., Fox, R. M., Martello, J., & Archable, C. (1977). Teaching note-taking skills to underachieving college students. *Journal of Educational Research,* 71, 81–85.

Robinson, P. (1980). *ESP (English for specific purposes).* Oxford: Pergamon.

Rossett, A. (1982). A typology for generating needs assessments. *Journal of Instructional Development,* 6(1), 28–33.

Rothkopf, E. Z. (1970). The concept of mathemagenic activities. *Review of Educational Research,* 40, 325–336.

Schmidt, M. F. (1981). Needs assessment in English for specific purposes: The case study. In L. Selinker, E. Tarone, & V. Hanseli (Eds.), *English for academic and technical purposes.* Cambridge, MA: Newbury House.

Schumann, F.M., & Schumann, J. H. (1977). Diary of a language learner: An introspective study of second langauge learning. In H. D. Brown, C. A. Yorio, & R. H. Crymes (Eds.), On *TESOL '77.* Washington, DC: Teachers of English to Speakers of Other Languages.

Scriven, M. (1967). The methodology of evaluation. In R. E. Stake (Ed.), *Curriculum evaluation.* Chicago: Rand-McNally.

Seliger, H. W., & Shohamy, E. (1989). *Second language research methods.* Oxford: Oxford University Press.

Shavelson, R. J. (1981). *Statistical reasoning for the behavioral sciences.* Boston: Allyn and Bacon.

Sinclair, J. McH., & Coulthard, R. M. (1975). *An introduction to discourse analysis.* London: Longman.

Smith, L. C., & Mare, N. N. (1990). *Issues for today: An effective reading skills text.* Rowley, MA: Newbury House.

Smith, P. D., Jr. (1970). *A comparison of the cognitive and audiolingual approaches to foreign language instruction: The Pennsylvania Foreign Language Project.* Philadelphia: Center for Curriculum Development.

Stake, R. E. (1967). The countenance of educational evaluation. *Teachers College Record,* 68(7), 523–540.

Steiner, F. (1975). *Performing with objectives.* Cambridge, MA: Newbury House.

Stevick, E. W. (1971). *Adapting and writing language lessons.* Washington, DC: U.S. Government Printing Office.

Strevens, P. (1977). *New orientations in the teaching of English.* Oxford: Oxford University Press.

Stufflebeam, D. L. (1974). Alternative approaches to educational evaluation. In W. J. Popham (Ed.), *Evaluation in education: Current applications.* Berkley, CA: McCutchan.

Stufflebeam, D. L., Foley, W. J., Gephart, W. J., Guba, E. G., Hammond, R. L., Merriman, H. O., & Provus, M. M. (1971). *Educational evaluation and decision making in education.* Itasca, IL: Peacock.

Stufflebeam, D. L., McCormick, C. H., Brinkerhoff, R. O., & Nelson, C. O. (1985). *Conducting educational needs assessments.* Boston: Kluwer-Nijhoff.

Tickoo, M. L. (Ed.). (1987). *Language syllabuses: State of the art.* Singapore: SEAMEO Regional Language Centre.

Tucker, G. R., & Cziko, G. (1978). The role of evaluation in education. In J.E. Alatis (Ed.), *International dimensions of bilingual education.* Washington, D.C.: Georgetown University Press.

Tuckman, B. W. (1978). *Conducting educational research* (2d ed.). New York: Harcourt Brace Jovanovich.

Tumposky, N. R. (1984). Behavioral objectives, the cult of efficiency and foreign language learning: Are they compatible? *TESOL Quarterly,* 18(2), 295–310.

Turk, L. H., & Espinosa, A. M., Jr. (1970). *Foundation course in Spanish* (2d ed.). Lexington, MA: D. C. Heath.

Tyler, R. W. (1942). General statement on evaluation. *Journal of Educational Research,* 35, 492–501.

——— (1949). Achievement testing and curriculum construction. In E. G. Williamson (Ed.), *Trends in student personnel work.* Minneapolis: University of Minnesota Press.

——— (1951). The functions of measurement in improving instruction. In E. F. Lindquist (Ed.), *Educational measurement.* Washington, DC: American Council on Education.

Uhl, N. P. (1990). Delphi technique. In H. J. Walberg & G. D. Haertel (Eds.), *The international encyclopedia of educational evaluation.* Oxford: Pergamon.

University of Hawaii at Manoa (UHM). (1987). *General information bulletin: University of Hawaii at Manoa 1987–1989.* Honolulu: University of Hawaii at Manoa.

Ur, P. (1984). *Teaching listening comprehension*. Cambridge: Cambridge University Press.

Valette, R. M. (1980). Evaluating the second-language learning program. In F. M. Grittner (Ed.), *Learning a second language*. Chicago: University of Chicago Press.
van Dijk, T. A. (1977). *Text and context: Explorations in the semantics and pragmatics of discourse*. London: Longman.
van Ek, J.A., & Alexander, L. G. (1980). *Threshold level English*. Oxford: Pergamon.
Vincent, M., Foll, D., & Cripwell, K. (1985). *Time for English*. London: Collins.

Watson-Gegeo, K. A. (1988). Ethnography in ESL: Defining the essentials. *TESOL Quarterly, 22*(4), 575–592.
Weaver, J., Pickett, A., Kiu, L., & Cook, J. (1987). Foreign TA training project needs analysis. Honolulu: Department of English as a Second Language, University of Hawaii at Manoa.
White, R. V. (1988). *The ELT curriculum*. Oxford: Blackwell.
Whitten, M. E. (1975). *Creative pattern practice* (2d ed.). New York: Harcourt Brace Jovanovich.
Widdowson, H. G. (Ed.). (1980). *Reading and thinking in English: Exploring functions*. Oxford: Oxford University Press.
_____ (1981). English for specific purposes: Criteria for course design. In L. Selinker, E. Tarone, & V. Hanzeli (Eds.), *English for academic and technical purposes: Studies in honor of Louis Trimble*. Cambridge, MA: Newbury House.
Wilkins, D. (1976). *Notional syllabuses*. Oxford: Oxford University Press
Willing, D. (1985). *Learning styles in adult migrant education*. Sydney, Australia: NSW Adult Migrant Education Service.
Wilson, G. H. (Ed.). (1976). *Curriculum development and syllabus design for English teaching*. Singapore: SEAMEO Regional Language Centre.
Winitz, H. (Ed.). (1981). *The comprehension approach to foreign language instruction*. Cambridge, MA: Newbury House.
Woods, A., Fletcher, P., & Hughes, A. (1986). *Statistics in language studies*. Cambridge: Cambridge University Press.
Works, N. M. (1985). Materials used for the teaching of listening comprehension: A survey. *TESOL Newsletter, 19*(6), 27–29.
Worthen, B. R., & Sanders, J. R. (1973). *Educational evaluation: Theory and practice*. Worthington, OH: Charles A. Jones.

Yalden, J. (1983). *The communicative syllabus: Evolution, design and implementation*. Oxford: Pergamon.
_____ (1985). *Principles of course design for language teaching*. Cambridge: Cambridge University Press.
_____ (1988). *The communicative syllabus*. Cambridge: Cambridge University Press.
Yin, R. K. (1984). *Case study research: Design and methods*. Beverly Hills, CA: Sage.
Yorkey, R. C. (1970). *Study skills for students of English as a second language*. New York: McGraw-Hill.

INDEX

Desk Copy Information

To place your desk copy request or for more information, please call
1-877-633-3375 or write to:
> Heinle
> 20 Channel Center Street
> Boston, MA 02210

To place a purchase order, please call 1-800-354-9706 or write to:
> CL Distribution Center
> Attn: Order Fulfillment
> 10650 Toebben Drive
> Indepdendence, KY 41051

Canada
Nelson, Cengage Learning
1120 Birchmount Road
Toronto, Ontario M1K 5G4
Tel: 800-668-0671

Asia
Cengage Learning
5 Shenton Way
#01-01 UIC Building
Singapore 068808
Tel: 65-6410-1200
Fax: 65-06410-1208

Latin America
Cengage Learning
Corporativo Santa Fe 505
Av. Santa Fe No. 505 piso 12
Col. Cruz Manca
C.P. 05349 Mexico D.F.
Mexico
Tel: (52 55) 1500-6000
Fax: (52 55) 5281-2656

Japan
Cengage Learning
Brooks Bldg 3-F
1-4-1, Kudankita
Ciyoda-Ku
Tokyo 102-0073
Japan
Tel: 81-3-3511-4390
Fax: 81-3-3511-4391

CPSIA information can be obtained
at www.ICGtesting.com
Printed in the USA
FFOW04n2150090415
12534FF